American Citizenship and Constitutionalism in Principle and Practice

Studies in American Constitutional Heritage

Justin Wert and Kyle Harper, Series Editors

American Citizenship and Constitutionalism in Principle and Practice

Edited by
Steven F. Pittz and Joseph Postell

University of Oklahoma Press : Norman

Publication of this book is made possible through the generosity of Edith Kinney Gaylord.

Library of Congress Cataloging-in-Publication Data

Names: Postell, Joseph, 1979– editor. | Pittz, Steven F., 1981– editor.
Title: American citizenship and constitutionalism in principle and practice/ edited by Steven F. Pittz and Joseph Wesley Postell.
Description: Norman : University of Oklahoma Press, [2022] | Series: Studies in American constitutional heritage ; volume 6 | Summary: "From the founding, Americans' contests over the Constitution and what it should mean for their actions have profoundly shaped the country's political direction. With a cast of characters ranging from Montesquieu, Adams, and Henry Clay, to the transcendentalists, Cherokee freedmen, and modern identitarians, American Citizenship and Constitutionalism in Principle and Practice brings an interdisciplinary and comparative group of scholars to the task of forwarding discussion on American political thought and American political development. The result is an original volume raising as many interesting questions as it answers, especially about the themes of membership and civic virtue"—Provided by publisher.
Identifiers: LCCN 2021021863 | ISBN 978-0-8061-7539-3 (hardcover) | ISBN 978-0-8061-7538-6 (paperback)
Subjects: LCSH: Constitutional law—United States—Philosophy. | Constitutional history—United States. | Citizenship—United States— Philosophy.
Classification: LCC KF4552 .A44 2022 | DDC 342.7308/3—dc23
LC record available at https://lccn.loc.gov/2021021863

American Citizenship and Constitutionalism in Principle and Practice is Volume 6 in the Studies in American Constitutional Heritage series.

The paper in this book meets the guidelines for permanence and durability of the Committee on Production Guidelines for Book Longevity of the Council on Library Resources, Inc. ∞

Contents

Preface

Perhaps the decisive questions about nationhood—what the nation is and who its people are—are never answered determinately. Questions surrounding citizenship and debates over the U.S. Constitution are ever-present and evergreen. Nevertheless, the early twenty-first-century United States has been marked by particularly powerful pressure to come to terms with itself over these perennial issues. It its most extreme form, this pressure has pushed on the most fundamental aspects of American citizenship and constitutionalism: interrogating the initial justice and wisdom of our constitution; reconsidering who really belongs and flourishes here (and, more practically, who can vote); and challenging the merits and justice of our political founding.

As unsettling as some of these questions may be, we must not shy away from the task of addressing them. The motivating impulse behind this volume is to make sure that the level at which we address these questions is equal to the gravity of the task itself. A critical, nonpartisan, and intellectually honest approach holds the most promise if we wish to foster meaningful, and ultimately successful, public debate. Our belief is that the authors in this volume work in that spirit, and their contributions to our understanding of the issues they bring to light are a model of how we should engage with questions about citizenship and constitutionalism going forward.

—

Many people contributed to the creation of this volume, and the editors would like to show our gratitude to a few in particular here. Our thanks to Kent Calder, our editor at the University of Oklahoma Press, for shepherding the project to completion. We also thank two anonymous reviewers for helpful comments and encouragement. This project received generous support from the Kinder Institute on Constitutional Democracy at the University of Missouri and the Center for the Study of Government and the Individual at the University of Colorado–Colorado Springs. The initial collaboration of scholars in this volume emerged from the Shawnee Trail Regional Conference on American Politics and Constitutionalism, sponsored annually by the Kinder Institute.

Introduction

Finding Common Ground as Citizens in the Practice of American Constitutionalism

Steven F. Pittz and Joseph Postell

The twenty-first century in American politics has been defined by the erosion (and indeed breakdown) of civility, social cohesion, and constitutional norms. Political discourse has become increasingly partisan and divisive. The ideological sorting of citizens into homogeneous communities has exacerbated these partisan divides and led to a breakdown in courtesy and common sympathy. Partially as a consequence of these developments, political and constitutional norms are increasingly placed under stress or abandoned altogether as both sides play "constitutional hardball."[1] In short, Americans are increasingly divided, and increasingly hostile to one another.

Many scholars and commentators have looked upon these developments with dismay. But they are typically unable to offer a guide for moving in a different direction. Instead, the commentaries carry an air of resignation.[2] A few scholars, however, have called for a return to social capital and communitarianism in response to the problems plaguing American democracy.[3] In their telling, the American experiment—and perhaps even the experiment in liberal democracy in general—has failed, and this failure necessitates a return to the values of an older order centered around virtue, community, and social cohesion.

In light of the challenges facing America in the twenty-first century, is such a radical departure necessary, as these authors suggest? The chapters in this book, in various ways and from a variety of perspectives, point toward a less radical conclusion. Americans do need to return to some conception of shared principles that serve as a basis for citizenship and a foundation for orderly governance. We can, however, find those principles in the American practice of citizenship and constitutionalism.

The first five chapters of the book raise various questions about the nature of American citizenship. Although they relate to different topics and adopt a variety of perspectives, they all suggest the need to rethink traditional notions of citizenship in light of the new challenges facing the country. Chapters 6–11 make the case that American constitutionalism, as it has been shaped to adapt to several centuries of experience, can serve as the basis for a shared notion of American citizenship. Such a notion of citizenship will admittedly be grounded in "thin" political principles that serve as procedural grounds for shared identity and provide a viable platform for widespread agreement. It may be the case that a more robust, substantive account of the common good that all American citizens will strongly adopt is unachievable in this century. Yet this does not rule out the possibility of political community, and the course that this volume begins to chart moves us toward the grounding of a genuinely shared political future. The goals are notions of citizenship and constitutionalism—that is, of shared political community—which are both achievable and capable of fostering genuine solidarity and a sense of shared purpose that is lacking in our current politics and culture.

AMERICAN CITIZENSHIP: MEMBERSHIP AND CIVIC VIRTUE

What it means to be an American citizen is a question garnering much recent interest, both within the academy and without. The notion of American citizenship has become increasingly contested, instigating a deeper and more self-conscious search for its roots and meaning. This soul searching, as it were, seems to be occurring on both sides of the political aisle. Those on the left and right seek to conceptualize citizenship in ways that appeal to their traditional base; the former focus on openness and inclusivity, the latter on the practice of citizenship and what it means to be an American. Both sides emphasize essential components of citizenship, and we may conclude that American citizenship revolves around two themes: membership (who gets to be a citizen) and civic virtue (what it means to act as a citizen, and what reasonable obligations may be placed on citizens). Like all political societies, America has needed to address these themes, and this volume aims to reveal the particularly American tradition of citizenship. The traditional American motto, "*E pluribus unum*," is a lodestar for thinking about this tradition. In the end, it may also be the key to bridging the gap between the political left and right. The unique historical circumstances of the American founding provided an opportunity for multiple and diverse groups to join a unified political community voluntarily. The allegiance was to American principles first and foremost, rather than to tribe, race, creed, or the historical nations of Europe from which most of the first American settlers escaped. Whether or not this is still true today, or can continue to hold true into the future, is an open question. The chapters on citizenship in this volume cannot claim to answer this question but, together, they do sharpen our interrogation and lead us toward a greater appreciation of what is at stake in the joint effort to conceptualize American citizenship.

The chapters all address the two themes mentioned above: membership and civic practice or virtue. Paul Carrese begins by introducing a conundrum: in a moderate, constitutional republic, how should citizens be educated in a way that enables them to live together harmoniously? Montesquieu, Carrese argues, points the way toward a solution. The standard modes of civic education in republics and monarchies tend toward extremes, but moderate citizens can be produced by mixing these more extreme elements. Carrese writes that, although this moderate education cannot be expressed in abstract principles and requires prudence to be translated into specific circumstances, the American founders' recommendations and practices about civic education exemplify the moderation Montesquieu would have endorsed. In other words, Carrese argues for civic education as a core component of producing a moderate republic where people engage in peaceful deliberation with each other on how to live together, as members of a shared community.

Carrying this theme forward, Rebecca Burgess also examines America's founding period to show how civic education was used to communicate shared political values throughout a diverse population. According to Burgess, the founders were well aware that the passions, opinions, and interests of American citizens were bound to be as diverse as the citizens themselves. Part of the educator's mission was to communicate the common purpose of self-government among this diversity—to "transmit," rather than transform, the original message of liberty and self-government to all American citizens. A successful system of education must be able to teach democratic principles and the habits of self-government—put simply, civic virtue—in order to preserve the regime over time and to nourish the "cords of affection" that hold the union together. Drawing from writings of Washington, Madison, Adams, and Jefferson, Burgess finds widespread agreement on the need for public education that addresses basic knowledge of the American constitutional regime. In addition to this, she notes that the founders also saw education as instruction in citizenship itself, guiding citizens toward the exercise of their rights, privileges, and obligations as active democrats.

Steven Pittz likewise focuses on what it means to be an American citizen in practice. Once one has become a citizen, what role is she expected to play? What obligations are placed on citizens as they carry out this role? Not all American philosophical traditions agree on the answers to these questions, and Pittz illuminates the disagreements by presenting two extremes. Two practices of citizenship emerge—a politics of detachment preferred by transcendentalists, and a politics of recognition preferred by identitarians. The former practice seeks to place minimal burdens on individual citizens, leaving the realm of identity formation and character development in the private sphere. The latter practice urges us to recognize that identity formation is ineluctably a political matter. Therefore, what is at stake in political debates is enlarged to include many issues formerly considered private. This reality is summed up in the slogan "The personal is political." Pittz interrogates these practices and lays out the implications of each. He argues that when discussing citizenship we must not remain abstract but consider carefully the practical implications of the decisions about identity made at the theoretical level.

Pittz's chapter acknowledges some of the contemporary challenges that stand in the way of constructing a conception of American citizenship that will appeal to all. Aaron Kushner's chapter reveals additional challenges surrounding the notion of membership in a multicultural society. Here Kushner adroitly traces the historical development of the membership status of the Cherokee freedmen, a group of African American former slaves of the Cherokee tribe, as they seek their own tribal citizenship. Although the federal government chose to grant the freedmen Cherokee citizenship, the Cherokee tribe considered this as a perversion of their own idea of citizenship and a violation of their tribal sovereignty. In this chapter we are brought to see, in vivid historical detail, the inherent tensions between cultural identity and political citizenship. This case study serves to test the notion of *E pluribus unum*, questioning the right of a larger political body (America) to impose its own understanding of citizenship on a minority cultural group (Cherokee). It brings to life one of the most vexing issues facing multicultural societies—who is a member and how membership is defined.

In light of the challenges raised by Pittz and Kushner, it becomes imperative to look for a solid foundation on which to ground political membership in a multicultural society. Nick Drummond brings us back to the American founding to investigate how the framers of the Constitution thought about cultural diversity and political membership. Drummond analyzes the writings of Hamilton, Madison, and Jay. Significant and important differences notwithstanding, these framers were all concerned about the effect that too much cultural heterogeneity might have on the workings of the constitutional regime. Of particular concern was the prevalence and resilience of religious differences, which remained active in America—part of a European residue—despite the attempt to enter into a political society unified by common liberal principles. Religious differences rendered parts of the early republic vulnerable to a strategy of "divide and rule." In response, these framers advocated cultural homogeneity in order to bind the union together and to foster the spirit of republicanism and a shared defense of liberty. Drummond's warning is that our current political tendency to divide Americans up into cultural groups poses the same threat. Without shared political principles as an umbrella over diverse cultural identities, American politics is increasingly vulnerable to a sort of despotism facilitated by a cynical political strategy of *Divide et impera*.

AMERICAN CONSTITUTIONALISM: AN ADAPTABLE STRUCTURE GUIDED BY FIXED PRINCIPLES

Some of the chapters in the first section of the book suggest that American constitutionalism can and should serve as the basis for a shared conception of American citizenship. Typically, when this claim is offered, it usually refers to a notion of American constitutionalism as fixed, and as exceptional among all of the world's modern democracies. However, as those chapters indicate, the reality of American constitutionalism is more complex. America's founders, and subsequent generations, have borrowed much of their political practice from Europe, adjusting it in light of experience. They knew that the political system they designed was not perfect and would have to adapt in light of the lessons of experience. And that experience revealed the importance of institutional innovations to make the American Constitution function effectively for all citizens in practice.

Leading off the second section, which focuses on constitutionalism, James Stoner argues that the authors of *The Federalist* were wrong about several important points regarding how the Constitution would function in practice. They predicted that the legislative branch would predominate in our system, that the Electoral College would guard against demagoguery, and that the state governments would effectively resist encroachment by the federal government. In addition, there is no systematic treatment of political parties in *The Federalist*, yet those institutions have profoundly affected the way the Constitution functions in practice. Stoner explores all of these limits of *The Federalist* and shows how they demonstrate the need for the constitutional system to adapt to the lessons of experience.

Following Stoner, Timothy Burns and Kevin Burns reveal a fascinating twist in the story of the ratification debates in their chapter. They show that correspondence between John Adams and French political economist Anne Robert Jacques Turgot shifted the terms of debate surrounding the separation of powers at the time of ratification. Turgot, a classical liberal, argued against American adoption of three government branches, claiming that it preserved the system of classes that the new democratic, capitalist modern world was determined to overthrow and replace with an egalitarian commercial society. Adams, writing to Turgot, defended the three branches on the basis of enduring and natural classes, casting the American regime as a modern version of Aristotle's mixed regime. This disagreement unintentionally played into the Federalist–Anti-federalist debates over the Constitution. The Anti-Federalists mistakenly accepted Adams's position as that of the Federalists, when in reality the Federalist position was closer to that of Turgot.

In so doing, the Anti-Federalists aimed their rhetorical attack at the apparent aristocratic tone of the Federalists (through Adams) rather than focusing their debate on the true position of the Federalists, which aligned more with the egalitarian commercial ethos of the classically liberal Turgot. Burns and Burns provocatively suggest that this case of misplaced strategy fatefully changed the shape of the ratification debate and may even have reversed the outcome.

Burns and Burns demonstrate, in short, that the American founders were highly indebted to European thought when constructing the American political system. Sung-Wook Paik elaborates on this theme through a case study that occurred nearly two centuries after the ratification of the Constitution. Paik argues that the notion of judicial review for fundamental rights protections is not an aspect of America's "exceptional" Constitution. Rather, this notion of judicial protection of fundamental rights was strongly influenced by European thought and emerged in America well after the nation was founded. Rather than something America exported to the world, as is commonly argued, judicial review for fundamental rights protections is an innovation on the constitutional design that was borrowed from European thought.

The notion of constitutional innovation continues through the next two chapters. Samuel Postell describes Henry Clay's contribution to American constitutionalism as a twofold project: first, the development of legislative leadership to prevent executive encroachment and to promote deliberation and choice, and second, the building of a national political party to promote union and compromise. Clay's example, in Samuel Postell's view, shows that political parties and legislative leadership—two institutional reforms that are not addressed in the original Constitution—were necessary to promote harmony among various interests in a diverse republic and to preserve the primacy of Congress in the American republic. Contrary to many scholars who point to Martin Van Buren as the first great positive theorist of political parties in America, he argues that Henry Clay deserves to share in that honor.

Whereas Samuel Postell points to Henry Clay, at the beginning of the golden age of America's political parties, to show the importance of parties to American constitutionalism, Joseph Postell examines the defenders of parties a century later, when political parties came under attack during the Progressive Era. Focusing systematically on the defenders of political parties during the early twentieth century, such as William Howard Taft, Elihu Root, and Calvin Coolidge, Joseph Postell argues that many of the problems plaguing American democracy today can be attributed to the collapse of parties beginning in the previous century. Taft, Root, Coolidge, and others correctly predicted the effects of the decline of political parties as mediating institutions in American democracy, according to Postell. Understanding their arguments would help return a sense of moderation, compromise, and decency into American politics, building a stronger foundation for political consensus.

Completing the second group of chapters, Connor Ewing focuses on the notion of sovereignty in American politics. Ewing explains that American politics transformed the idea of sovereignty "from predicate to object." Prior to the American founding, sovereignty was typically understood as a predicate of political order. It was the precondition for the exercise of political power. In the American context, sovereignty is both a precondition for and a product of politics. Consequently, sovereignty must be understood dynamically, and disputes about the location of legitimate political authority are never fully resolved. Under the Constitution, the scope and location of political power depend on public opinion, which influences the distribution of authority within the constitutional order. Just as the other chapters in this section emphasize how the constitutional system has adapted in light of experience and historical development, so Ewing also emphasizes that the scope and locus of political power are not fixed but dynamic.

Finally, Colleen Sheehan reflects on the role of public opinion, and civic virtue, in maintaining the "public trust." Republican citizenship requires some contribution to maintaining legitimate sovereignty of the Constitution over time. As Madison taught, the role of the majority in maintaining the public trust is crucial, and we should not consider the majority only something to be wary of, guarding against its potential tyranny. Although Madison ensured that the Constitution protected minority rights, he also endeavored to teach that the majority—through reasonable and civic-minded public opinion—was essential to the maintenance of the republic.

The chapters in this volume attempt to grapple with a serious challenge presented by the conditions of American politics in the twenty-first century. They present a variety of perspectives and use a variety of case studies, most of which are underexplored in the current literature. From systematic treatments of identity politics, to case studies about Cherokee constitutionalism, to explorations of political parties and the emergence of judicial review, the chapters attempt to move beyond traditional topics associated with American citizenship and constitutionalism. Although they point toward the need for a shared conception of American citizenship through participation in the constitutional order, they do not rely upon formulaic repetition of traditional arguments. Instead, they suggest that conceptions of American citizenship and constitutionalism are shaped by experience and adapt to historical development. Nevertheless, they still serve as a sufficient foundation for civil politics in an increasingly pluralistic and diverse republic.

NOTES

1. Mark V. Tushnet, "Constitutional Hardball," *John Marshall Law Review* 37 (2004): 523–53.

2. See, for an illustrative example, Steven Levitsky and Daniel Ziblatt, *How Democracies Die* (New York: Crown, 2018).

3. The best-known effort along these lines is Patrick Deneen's *Why Liberalism Failed* (New Haven, CT: Yale University Press, 2018).

1

Montesquieu's Call to Civic Education

Roots of and Remedies for America's Civic Crisis

Paul Carrese

In the aftermath of America's 2016 election—a seismic surprise bringing an avowed populist and nationalist to the presidency—one of the few points of consensus in American public life has been concern that our civic fabric is deteriorating. The contentious 2020 national election, then the refusal by President Trump and many supporters to accept the results, has shifted the concern from civic decay to civic disintegration. Signs include a destructive polarization of negative partisanship that impedes governing through consensus policies on major public issues; low legitimacy of or confidence in most national institutions and professions; and episodes of political violence—still occasional but no longer rare. Another widely held concern in recent decades is substantial civic illiteracy about our founding political principles, institutions, and history.[1] Ironically, our academic elites, including most political scientists, are concerned about polarization and violence from certain sources or causes but not so worried about a citizenry marked by civic ignorance. It is the conjunction of these two debilitating conditions, however, that should spur thoughtful Americans to consider whether declining civic literacy merely correlates with or in fact causes our declining attachment to both the idea and effective practice of democratic-republican government itself (which we sacrifice as we indulge our righteous demonizing of political opponents) and also causes the declining legitimacy for all national institutions and professions save the military.

Elsewhere I have criticized my own discipline and profession, political science and higher education, for undermining both liberal education and civic education through their predominant commitments to ever-new projects of intellectual, political, and societal progress. Here I more leniently suggest that a paradox in America's founding is a more legitimate cause of our civic education failings, thus at least partially of our civic dysfunction.[2] Although leading Enlightenment philosophers provided clear principles and guidelines on formation of a new species of constitutional republic, they offered no similarly clear guidance on the companion civic education needed to perpetuate and operate such a polity. Hints and suggestions are scattered across several important philosophers; Montesquieu provides better guidance for founding statesmen and leading civic thinkers than any other source, since he emphasizes the necessity of civic education right amid his main work on a politics of moderation and liberty, *The Spirit of Laws* (1748)—rather than addressing it separately from his main constitutional work, as did the other leading influences on America. This is good news for Americans concerned with civic education, since Montesquieu is the single greatest influence on the formation of our constitutional order. Yet *Spirit of Laws* ultimately provides no clear guidance on citizenship education for the complex constitutional polity it recommends as best providing for liberty, the very model our framers most consulted. We might admit that American political scientists, other civic thinkers, and civic-minded political leaders inherit a paradox. We are at liberty to ignore or bungle the civic education needed to sustain our intellectual and political liberty in part because the chapter on civic education in the owner's manual of our constitutionalism was demarcated as essential yet was left unfinished by our architectonic guide.

This hypothesis does not absolve American political scientists, past and present, of their errors of omission and commission, since this arguably is the indispensable discipline for citizenship education. The predominant approach in recent American political science is to recast civic education as engagement, activism, or agency that displaces civic literacy and reflective patriotism about our exceptional constitutional order. Instead, this discipline should be leading collaborative efforts with history and other needful disciplines to make civic education, with civic literacy at its core, a

scholarly and educational priority in higher learning. Political scientists also should lead in building collaborations with and support for schools, but here the historians put us to shame, even if it
is fair to argue that the predominant spirit in their discipline has
overcorrected for earlier omissions of comprehensiveness and fair-
ness in its studies of America. With the two most important disciplines largely following the zeitgeist of academic progressivism,
thus neglecting or repudiating American constitutionalism in
favor of democracy and transformation, we have lost awareness of
the necessity of civic education to perpetuate a constitutional
order, and culture, of moderate liberty. American intellectual culture once identified this as a high priority, indeed a civic duty.
Great intellectual and civic figures in our founding era and far
beyond saw the unfinished chapter in our manual of constitutionalism and took it on themselves to finish the text. Most of our
leading scholars, civic thinkers, and political figures no longer do
so, at least not to perpetuate the core principles of our constitutionalism. For well over a century our leading intellectuals have
been deficit spending the principles and culture that sustain our
peculiar constitutional order, taking for granted the liberty and
prosperity that allow them to undertake projects of transformation for progress and equality so assiduously.

For those of us who perceive that the bill long since has come
due, we might use our liberty by repairing to Montesquieu for his
helpful indications about what civic education is, and why it is an
integral, indispensable category of constitutional thinking—rather
than merely worthy of discrete or occasional efforts. We then could
mine his suggestions, including his basic call to thoughtful citizens
that we have an intellectual and civic duty to formulate the right
civic education for our particular polity. For American scholars and
educators, the call to civic education tasks us with discerning what
content and modes of education would best perpetuate our constitutional order and culture of liberty and complete or refine them
as needed.

Recent discourse on civic education and the American founding occasionally refers to the affirmation, early in *Spirit of Laws*, of
the fundamental importance of this topic for our kind of politics:
"It is in republican government that the full power of education is
needed."[3] This emphatic recommendation makes it all the more
puzzling that, when Montesquieu later recommends the English

constitution as devoted to liberty but also has identified it as a unique blend of republic and monarchy, he provides no further comment there on what kind of civic education would be needed for this peculiar constitutionalism.[4] Deeper study of his full discussion of civic education, and of clues in his later discussions in *Spirit of Laws* about the constitution of liberty he praises, can provide Americans with ideas for how we might address this paradox from our founding and take up the call to civic education in Montesquieu's philosophy.

MONTESQUIEU, MODERATION, AND AMERICA

The Spirit of Laws was the most influential work of political science for Adams, Madison, Hamilton, the early Jefferson, and other framers of the new state constitutions, the 1787 Constitution, and the Bill of Rights. The constitutional debates of the founding era invoked Montesquieu more than any philosophers of radical Enlightenment such as Hobbes, Locke, or Rousseau. The relative scholarly neglect of Montesquieu in our day thus is an unfortunate characteristic of recent American political theory and political science that impedes our capacity to understand our constitutionalism, whether to criticize or endorse.[5] Our intellectual preferences no longer favor the complexity, coupled with concern for governing in particular regimes, that defines his political philosophy; we tend to prefer clear doctrines or bold theoretical provocations.[6] A perennial challenge of Montesquieu's philosophy is that understanding him on any given topic requires understanding him on several others, because, as he argues, human and political reality is irreducibly complex; thus his aim is to discern the "spirit" of laws, their comprehensive, multifarious meaning. It is hard today to believe that this embrace of complexity once was thought an attractive feature of his thought, as making it suitable for both philosophers and statesmen. Contemporary concerns that *Spirit of Laws* achieved not profundity but confusion were in the minority, but the tables long since have turned. For Montesquieu and his admirers this approach of complexity reflects the principle of philosophical moderation or equilibrium he sought to embody in the work, but modernity has shifted its intellectual currents strongly against this view. Thus today only a few scholars adequately address his declaration that the key to his philosophy is moderation—defined as avoiding extremes and finding the political good in the middle (29.1). It therefore is an even greater challenge today first to understand that architectonic principle and then to explore a given topic within his philosophy.[7]

Moderation encapsulates the philosophical complexity Montesquieu thought necessary to comprehend human and political reality, as well as his disposition to avoid extremes in politics. The few pieces of *Spirit of Laws* still widely known in America today, including a complex constitutionalism of separated powers and the principle of federalism as forging a republic of republics, are instances of moderation. The political good is not achieved through singular ideas or powers but by blending, reconciling, and balancing, in just the right way, several ideas or elements in particular circumstances—whether of human nature, or political reality, or legal forms. *The Spirit of Laws* as a whole propounds both a philosophical method and view of justice defined by this balancing and reconciliation of seemingly rival principles. In the wake of the more radically modern and single-minded philosophies of Hobbes, Spinoza, and Locke, it seeks to improve modern liberalism by restoring elements of classical and medieval philosophy that appreciate the multifarious reality, and higher dimensions, of humanity and politics. Near the end of his massive work he finally announces this guiding principle: "I say it, and it seems to me I have brought forth this work only to prove it: the spirit of moderation ought to be that of the legislator; the political good, like the moral good, is always found between two limits" (29.1, 602). His Preface had announced the ideal of the philosopher-legislator who watches over humankind by inculcating prudence about how to moderate a given political order to make it more humane, and he recapitulates this theme in the work (Preface; 1.1; 24.10; 29.19). Indeed, though philosophical moderation required that Montesquieu delay enunciating a single principle until he had "proven" it by investigating the world's complexity—through books on natural law and human laws, forms of government, war, liberty, climate, culture, commerce, religion, history, and more—*Spirit of Laws* inculcates moderation from its opening. The Preface warns that only those with the "genius" to understand a particular regime fully can reasonably propose reforms, since theoretically attractive changes might make matters worse. This blend of philosophical sobriety and humility was offered four decades before the French Revolution and its ultimately radical stances on philosophy, human nature, politics, religion, and violence (Preface, xlv).

There are strong grounds to argue that it is the philosophically moderate Montesquieu and his disciple Blackstone—not the social-contractarian, analytic philosopher Locke nor any other such radical or rationalist minds—who were the foremost philosophical influences upon the framers of the Declaration, 1787 Constitution, and Bill of Rights as a whole. The obviously Lockean dimensions to American constitutionalism and the thinking of leading founders, most evident in parts of the Declaration and in arguments about separating church and state, should not eclipse the larger complexity of principles that characterizes America's founding. America simultaneously draws upon tenets of not only liberalism and modern republicanism but also classical philosophy, Christianity, and classic common law.[8] Such moderation among or balancing of diverse principles pervades American constitutionalism and extends beyond institutions to shape the complexity of American life and thought, evident in our perpetual blending of pluralism and principle, individual rights and public purposes. *The Spirit of Laws* informs this American complexity more than any other book save the Bible; its other philosophical rival for this distinction, Blackstone's *Commentaries on the Laws of England*, in fact draws heavily upon Montesquieu.[9] Moreover, although Montesquieu is best known in our era for his liberal constitutionalism, which utilizes a model of liberty in the English constitution, it is rarely noted that in closing his first portrait of England he warns against its "extreme" liberty as well as extremes "even of reason" that accompany modern political thinking (11.4, 155; 11.6, 166).

Our era will hardly understand America if so few of us study this complex philosophy, given that America still is governed largely by the Constitution and amendments inspired by Montesquieu—arguably encompassing not only the 1787 Constitution and Bill of Rights but the Civil War amendments informed by Lincoln's effort to restore the original spirit of that constitutionalism. Ignorance of Montesquieu and his philosophy of moderation in turn cuts us off from one element of it that is particularly needful given our current civic and civic education crises. His philosophical consideration of civic education points to ideas valuable for assessing what kind of American civic literacy and forms of civic moderation now are needed, and why this topic matters so fundamentally.

MONTESQUIEU'S MODERATELY MODERN CONCEPTION OF CIVIC EDUCATION

The philosophy of moderation explains why, unlike Locke, Montesquieu thematically analyzes civic education as a constituent element of a comprehensive political philosophy, amid the early books of *Spirit of Laws*. In the middle of Part 1 of the work's six parts we find Book 4, "That the laws of education should be relative to the principles of the government." It is a perplexing book, with seemingly contradictory elements along with striking statements that almost beg to be plucked from context and featured in isolation. We first should develop, therefore, a broad perspective on why Montesquieu places his analysis of civic education in this spot, and why this matters for modern political philosophy and constitutionalism. In Books 2 and 3, Montesquieu had in effect adapted Aristotle's concept of regime analysis by investigating the structure or "nature" of four main types of government—democratic republic, aristocratic republic, monarchy, and despotism—then analyzing the animating passion or "principle" that moves any given structure to function. It thus is telling that education is such an early, formative topic in his long analysis of the multifarious spirit of human affairs, ultimately requiring thirty-one books and, in recent translation, over seven hundred pages. In the Preface and Book 1 he delineates the fundamental aims and premises of his political philosophy, including his conception of divine, natural, and human laws and the main constituent elements of the "spirit" of any government or set of laws. Books 2 and 3 then introduce his novel political science of three main types of government—republic (in two modes), monarchy, despotism—and the further novel concepts of the *nature* (structure) and *principle* (animating passion) for each. The very next topic, quite significantly, is education: that there "should be" an alignment between the education and the principle in each type of government. From the perspective of classical political philosophy, an important place for education is hardly striking; Plato's *Republic* places education at or near the center of philosophy and political philosophy, and Aristotle devotes two books of the *Politics* to education and the regime. What is so striking in modernity is that Montesquieu agrees with this classical tenet even as a modern and liberal philosopher who thus is not concerned, as are classical philosophers, with the search for the best political regime as the home for human virtue—understood as the excellence of the soul and of a community of souls.

Yet as a proto–social scientist Montesquieu aims to describe the kind of government—democratic republic, he calls it—that in historical reality does have something like this aim of human excellence; thus he defines its principle as "virtue" but gives it a new meaning, as a kind of patriotic fervor. He also describes a somewhat elevated aim and character of monarchy, deeming its principle "honor," which is neither the classical conception of human virtue nor his new concept of the democratic citizen's "love of the laws and of the homeland" (4.3, 36; see also 2.3). His monarchical principle of honor, as the passion animating that politics and government, is the commitment of the nobility and royalty to the self-regard required to embody a peculiar code of conduct (2.5–7). Neither Hobbes nor Locke has any time for this historical and theoretical messiness. Hobbes's *Leviathan* does address education, to set forward the new philosopher's authority to guide the one rational mode of government in perpetuating a new politics of human, bodily security, with the right education as a prophylactic against recurrence of dangerous metaphysical notions of virtue, a best regime, and religion. Hobbes thus inverts the classical conception of the positive, constitutive role for education in political philosophy and the proper modes of politics. Locke does publish *Some Thoughts Concerning Education* a few years after publishing his *Two Treatises of Government*, but he leaves readers to discern why he separates education from his main statement of political philosophy, and what this says about both education and his new, seemingly materialist philosophy. Locke's *Second Treatise* defines the sole legitimate focus of government as security of the radically individual rights to life, liberty, and property, coupling this with a theory that human natural asociability requires the mechanism of the social contract to construct a fundamentally artificial thing called political society. Just as it takes no education in the state of nature to feel bodily insecurity and be pulled toward a mutual pact for reducing one's insecurity, so, Locke implies, it should take no education for the new citizens of the contracted society to feel whether the government is securing their material life, liberty, and property. One might infer from this that Locke saw no need for education to be a positive, integral (or explicitly integral) element of political philosophy. If Hobbes inverts the classical conception, Locke seems to ignore it as only indirectly relevant, at best, for the new objectives of politics, the new philosophy propounding them, and the perpetuation of both.

Montesquieu's reintegration of education as a positive, constitutive element of political philosophy, to ensure the proper functioning of any government, thus reintegrates elements of classical philosophy to correct the extreme materialism and negativity of his radical predecessors. His account of education is an important step, then, toward ultimately achieving a properly moderate liberal philosophy. The positive role of education he sees in both republics (mostly in the democratic mode) and monarchy is evident from the brevity, and pure negativity, of his analysis of education in a despotism (4.3). Whereas "education in monarchies works to elevate the heart," and the education to virtue in democracies inspires citizens to strive for the "greatness and glory" of their republic, in despotism the principle is fear—which the singular ruler needs in all subjects to sustain his absolutism. For despotism "education is, in a way, null there" and really is the "ignorance" needed to maintain the "servility" and "obedience" of cowering subjects (4.3, 34–35; 4.6, 37; see 2.9). The negative role for education in radical Enlightenment political philosophy—prophylactic in Hobbes, absent in Locke—is closer to the sheer materialism and soul-crushing obedience of Montesquieu's despotism than to the latter's account of education in honor or in virtue in the nondespotic, potentially moderate governments. The emphasis on the extremism and inhumanity of despotism in Book 4, with no real education permitted, reinforces a crucial point Montesquieu makes near the end of Book 3—that although it is important to grasp the distinctions in natures and principles between the three (effectively four) types of government, there really are only two kinds of government: moderate and despotic. He introduces into his political science a correction toward complexity, and this approach to unfolding one's philosophical argument gradually is another instance of moderation—offering the reader a journey through argument and evidence to steadily reveal deeper, more comprehensive understandings of the multifarious spirit of human affairs. Thus at the close of Book 3, Montesquieu indicates that although in one sense there are four distinct kinds of government, having delineated the principles that animate them (democratic virtue, aristocratic moderation, monarchical honor, and despotic fear), he declares in the title of chapter 10 that the fundamental distinction is "between moderate governments and despotic governments" (3.10, 29). Moderation, as rising above the politics of despotic fear, means rising above materialism or mere animality and passions, such that reason can educate and elevate the passions toward a more humane politics. Of course, for Montesquieu as a modern, too high an elevation would mean a return to the unrealistic aspirations, possibly semidespotic or fully despotic, of classical political philosophy: to find the one true account about excellence of the soul and the one true regime of strongly harmonized souls. A moderate kind of elevation is required.

Indeed, as several scholars have noted, a theme running through Part 1 of *Spirit of Laws* is that the purest mode of classical republicanism is despotic in its demand for virtue as the individual's categorical commitment to the greatness and glory of the democratic republic.[10] The first characterization of democratic-republican education in Book 4 is that "in republican government the full power of education is needed"—because "political virtue is a renunciation of oneself, which is always a very painful thing" (4.5, 35). Montesquieu deepens this depiction in the next book, defining democratic-republican political virtue as "a very simple thing: it is love of the republic" and "a feeling" rather than "a result of knowledge." The total love for the political community means demotion or repudiation of one's own passions, a characterization that invites comparison to a religious fervor or total commitment. Like despotism, knowledge is not needed, or at least not primarily. He abstractly describes the psychology of absolute commitment in ancient republican citizens—"The less we can satisfy our particular passions, the more we give ourselves up to passions for the general order"—then reinforces his point with modern readers by turning to a Christian, thus medieval and modern, analogy: "Why do monks so love their order?" The clinical, social-scientific answer is that the rule (of, say, the Benedictines) is loveable precisely because "intolerable," for as a rule "deprives" the monks of all ordinary passions it leaves them only "the passion for the very rule that afflicts them" (5.2, 42–43). Like all analogical reasoning this obscures the differences between the cases, but even brief consideration of these two cases suggests that the political mode of complete devotion is, in that peculiar context, a kind of extremism or fanaticism, in a way it would not be for religious contexts. True, a family might push a young man into monastic life in violation of the process of prayerful discernment about a vocation to religious life properly grounded, per Christian theology, in awareness of God's love and a loving commitment in return. A certain kind of skepticism about religion—not to mention Freudianism—of course views all such commitments as basically coerced either by internal psychology or externally imposed conditioning. Nonetheless we cannot simply presume that Montesquieu is such a skeptic, whether of the Machiavellian or Spinozist variety, even if many serious scholars press that argument.[11] It is just as plausible here to think that, if the comfortable analogical case for explaining the degree of devotion felt by ancient republican citizens is a monk's personal commitment to Christian religious life, then Montesquieu also implies that what may be admirable personal devotion in the religious setting is a species of collective fanaticism or extremism in a political setting.

The moderation of Montesquieu's political philosophy points to a complex constitutionalism it ultimately will endorse—both English and, as we will see, Gothic; and a crucial step in this larger argument is restoring civic education to an important place in political philosophy. The test of civic education is crucial for discerning the relative moderation of a government by way of discerning what kinds of education would correspond with or cultivate more moderate, and less despotic, modes of politics.

EXTREMISM AND MODERATION IN CIVIC EDUCATION— ANCIENT, MEDIEVAL, MODERN

This larger understanding of the placement and significance of the book on education in *Spirit of Laws*, within Montesquieu's unfolding argument for a balanced philosophy blending classical, medieval, and modern elements of political philosophy, prepares us for a close analysis of the opening moves in Book 4 itself. He immediately elevates the status of monarchy within modern liberal philosophy by indicating that "the laws of education," which "prepare us to be citizens," apply not only to republics but to monarchies. In a monarchy one is a citizen, not a subject (4.1, 31). He had gestured toward affirming liberty in monarchy when stating in Book 3 that "in well-regulated monarchies everyone will be almost a good citizen," but the qualified phrasing left it unclear whether monarchy, alike with republic, regards the people as citizens per se (3.6, 26).

The second chapter of Book 4 confirms the parity by discussing monarchy before republic, which breaks the predominant pattern in Part 1 of the work. The typology of the three (effectively four) governments frames the analysis of politics from Books 2 to 8, the bulk of Part 1; and the predominant pattern for these seven books is analysis of republic, monarchy, and despotism in turn. In two of these books Montesquieu changes the sequence for some reason—in Book 4 on education and in Book 6 on civil and criminal laws, courts, and penal law. Perhaps in the unfolding of his philosophy of moderation, which seeks to understand extremism and despotism in their various forms while also fostering amelioration toward moderation in any given government, the predominant sequence (republic, monarchy, despotism) signals a descent from moderate to immoderate governments. The break of pattern in the book on civic education, and the book on judicial proceedings affecting the security and tranquility of individuals summoned to court, indicates that a different ranking of moderate to despotic applies to these topics. Montesquieu seems to judge the civic education in monarchies, and this government's judicial protection for individual security, as relatively more moderate (thus just in his sense), whereas these dimensions of politics are more immoderate or despotic in republics—democratic republics especially.[12]

Having introduced the book on education and its importance, the second chapter turns to "education in monarchies" and focuses on its principle, honor. Montesquieu affirms that people are "fellow citizens" there, which elevates monarchy for the modern liberal mind, yet he also extends the candid analysis from Book 2 about what honor really is (4.2, 31). As a nobleman in a monarchy he knows the topic well, and the censors of both the monarchy and the church took issue with his primary affiliation of virtue with the democratic republic. This implied, they protested, that virtue is not a primary concern for monarchies and was a political rather than ethical and Christian principle; they also protested his frank, even unsparing description of monarchical honor.[13] Book 3 stated that "speaking philosophically" it is "a false honor," because adherence to the code is not directly concerned with affirming the nobility or greatness of the kingdom, nor with serving one's community. The essence of honor, rather, "is to demand preferences and distinctions," such that a nobleman undertaking a great deed for the kingdom or adhering to the code in effect "works for the common good" even though his primary motivation is "believing he works for his individual interest" (3.7, 27).[14] Montesquieu implies that this medieval or feudal principle of honor really is quite modern in its focus on the individual's concerns. Indeed, Book 4 deepens an important theme of *Spirit of Laws*, the distinction between ancient and modern, which is signaled in the Preface to the work and mentioned in the early books, then in Book 4 is elevated to a chapter title: "The difference in the effect of education among the ancients and ourselves" (4.4, 35). He further signals that Book 4 is a particularly fitting moment for larger philosophical comment by employing the term "modern" for the first time in the work, contrasting the "extraordinary" character of the ancient democratic republic—their institutions and the deeds of their citizens—with "the dregs and corruptions of our modern times" (4.6, 37). These two chapters seem to portray modernity as lesser than antiquity, by which Montesquieu means the ancient democratic republics, because chapter 4 declares that the "effect" of the ancient education in virtue was deeds the likes of which "we no longer see" and which "astonish our small souls" (4.4, 35). The dregs and corruption of our modern times (chapter 6) seem hardly to rate.

Understanding Montesquieu's counsel on civic education requires, however, a search for the larger meaning conveyed by the complexity of these first six chapters of Book 4. These chapters praise monarchy for educating citizens, not subjects, and for elevating the heart, while further implying that the real meaning of monarchy is modern or European and not ancient; yet at the same time they seem to praise the grandeur of ancient republics in contrast with the pettiness and decay of modern monarchies. Finding the key to this apparent labyrinth involves recourse to later passages in the work—but it also requires us to recall that Montesquieu notifies readers early in *Spirit of Laws* that one will need to find the meaning of any one part by clarifying the meaning of another, then discerning a larger meaning, perhaps of the whole work. Readers should assess "the whole book," not this or that passage. Those seeking the "design of the author" will discern it in "the design of the work"; further, "Many of the truths of the work will not make themselves felt until after one sees the chain which links them to the others" (Preface, xliii–xliv). Philosophical moderation means seeking the truth about parts to find the meaning of larger wholes or a whole, while also accepting the messiness or complexity of discerned wholes instead of distorting the parts by reducing them, in Procrustean fashion, to fit a single idea or principle in a tidy doctrine or system.

Many commentaries interpret Montesquieu's use of the terms "ancient" and "modern," including his identification as a modern, as indicating his affirmation of Machiavelli's stark binary between them. This would mean that for Montesquieu there is no intermediary philosophical or historical period, the medieval, to consider seriously. It is true that *Spirit of Laws* never uses the term "medieval" and introduces feudal law or the feudal era only quite late, in Book 28. That said, the feudal law and its inherent moderation become the main theme of Part 6, in Books 30 and 31 as well. Moreover, Montesquieu makes clear in the middle of the work that one sense of "we" for him is the French or Gothic tradition of politics and culture, and he declares this immediately after his great—but not unqualified—praise for England's constitution of liberty. Scholars often overlook two of the closing pronouncements on England's politics of liberty in Book 11, and how these prepare for a striking affirmation in the sequel that medieval monarchy is the best form of government yet devised. The first pronouncement is that the English idea for a constitution of liberty is not the work of philosophers but rather is Gothic: "The English have taken their idea of political government from the Germans. This fine system was found in the forests." Radical Enlightenment philosophers with their singular stances and rationalism are put in their place. The sequel declares that the English have taken this idea to an extreme: "I do not claim hereby to disparage other governments or to say that this extreme political liberty should humiliate those who have only a moderate one" (11.6, 166). He cites Tacitus on the Germanic origin of such a politics—descending from the people whom the ancient Roman republic-turned-empire could not permanently defeat and who ultimately extinguish the Western empire. The Gothic has, so to speak, ancient roots, but it is not ancient per se. Further, he reinforces his contrast between extreme and moderate liberty by adding here his first statement that a larger principle of moderation guides his philosophy: he never would disparage governments of moderate liberty because he believes that "the excess even of reason is not always desirable, and that men almost always accommodate themselves better to middles than to extremes" (11.6, 166).

The next two chapters deepen this affirmation of moderation by stating that the complex, moderate monarchies are modern and indeed are a fine model for humane, decent government. Chapter 7 of Book 11, "The monarchies that we know," clarifies that the first-person plural of "our modern times" in Book 4 means modern monarchies. Montesquieu also declares here that though the European monarchies do not take liberty for their direct object, as do the English, nonetheless their politics of honorably seeking "the glory of the citizens, the State, and the prince" in fact generates "a spirit of liberty" that "can" produce "equally great things" and "perhaps contribute as much to happiness as liberty itself" (11.7, 166). The title of chapter 8, "Why the ancients had no clear idea of monarchy," affirms that "ancients" predominantly means ancient republics, and that monarchy in its true sense is modern, European, and Christian. Moreover, this chapter contains the clearest statement in *Spirit of Laws* regarding which government Montesquieu thinks is the best in human history. The monarchies we moderns know stem from "the Germanic nations"—again citing Tacitus, *On the Mores of the Germans*—but they retain more moderation about liberty than the English have done, a distinction signaled by calling the modern European monarchies "Gothic." The "origin of Gothic government among us" was a blend of aristocracy and monarchy that "was a good government" yet "had within itself the capacity to become better." By emancipating serfs, the Europeans eventually balanced "the civil liberty of the people" with the status of the nobility, "the clergy," and the "power" of a monarch. These constituent elements then came into "such concert" that "I believe there has never been a government on earth as well tempered as that of each part of Europe during the time that this government continued to exist, and it is remarkable that the corruption of the government of a conquering people should have formed the best kind of government men have been able to contrive" (11.8, 167–68).

As noted, this judgment does not endorse the aim of classical political philosophy to find the best regime per se, nor does it delineate the one core model for various instantiations of that best government. Moderation requires affirming natural right, natural law, and the natural rights of individuals, as *Spirit of Laws* does in the Preface and fairly obviously in Books 1, 3, 6, 10, 12, 26, and 29, while also affirming, as he does in Book 1, that it is only reasonable that "the political and civil laws of each nation" would be different. "Laws should be so appropriate to the people for whom they are made that it is a very great chance if the laws of one nation can suit another" (Preface, 8). This is not relativism but the recognition that one can clearly discern that despotism in various forms violates natural right, and also that moderate governments protect natural right by protecting individuals against despotic acts (3.10, 29–30).[15] These moderate governments are more likely to be modern, thus shaped by Christianity, than to be ancient and democratic-republican.

RELIGION AND A MODERATING SPIRIT IN MODERN CIVIC EDUCATION

This larger context for the analysis of civic education sheds light on further complexities in Book 4 itself, as they arise from its opening to its close, including several striking, almost aphoristic statements that seem self-explanatory but arguably have a more subtle aim. We learn in the first substantive chapter that education in monarchies requires "a certain nobility" in one's practice of "virtues," "a certain frankness" in mores or an internal code of conduct, and "a certain politeness" in manners or external actions toward others (4.2, 31; see 19.16, 317). The effects of education in honor include that one seeks to "distinguish" oneself from "fellow citizens"; there is much sophistry and hypocrisy; the mores are frank but impure; and the commitment to speaking the truth stems not from "the love of truth" but because it is seen as "daring and free." Yet Montesquieu also portrays monarchical honor as educating citizens to produce grand, elevated, virtuous actions. The consideration of politeness in manners induces an observation echoing the definition in Book 1 that humans are naturally sociable, contra Hobbes and Locke: "Men, born to live together, are also born to please each other" (4.2, 32; see 1.2, 7). Moreover, honor educates one to check the potential despotism of "the prince" if he should "prescribe an action that dishonors us." Thus a nobleman, Crillon, was ordered "to assassinate the Duke of Guise" but refused. Montesquieu then recounts an episode of religious intolerance extending to mass murder, when after Saint Bartholomew's Day King Charles IX revoked the toleration of some Protestants in the Edict of Nantes and "sent orders to all the governors to have the Huguenots massacred." This touches two despotic practices targeted throughout *Spirit of Laws*: excessive and arbitrary use of capital punishment, and religious intolerance—especially when enforced through criminal laws (see especially Books 6, 12, 24, 25, 26). The episode evokes one of the most remarkable passages in the work: "The Viscount of Orte, who was in command at Bayonne, wrote to the king, 'Sire, I have found among the inhabitants and the warriors only good citizens, brave soldiers, and not one executioner; thus, they and I together beg Your Majesty to use our arms and our lives for things that can be done.' This great and generous courage regarded a cowardly action as an impossible thing" (4.2, 33).[16]

The next chapter, briefly analyzing education in despotism, affirms the relatively humane and elevated character of monarchy; it also defines despotism as forbidding real education, and ironically this portends criticism of republicanism's extreme emphasis on education. The despot cannot tolerate citizens, only subjects who really are "slaves," thereby permitting no role for "reason" or "knowledge"; this "brings down" the heart (in contrast to monarchy) by demanding "extreme obedience" (4.3, 34–35). In Book 3 political virtue was described not only as a passion (as for all of Montesquieu's principles of governments) but more particularly as a "force." In the next chapter of Book 4, which transitions to the republic, Montesquieu seems to leave behind despotism and completely focus on the striking distinctiveness of republicanism. Yet chapter 4, emphasizing the differing "effect" of "education among the ancients" and "among ourselves," echoes the depiction of republican virtue as a force, irrational: "Most of the ancient peoples lived in governments that had virtue for their principle," and when it was "in full force" these republics did things "that astonish our small souls" (3.3, 22; 4.4, 35). Many scholars take the sequel as only a criticism of modernity and monarchies, and as only praise of ancient republicanism, since he describes the single-mindedness of ancient education as "another advantage over ours"—beyond, that is, the forcefulness of political virtue. Montesquieu then seems to lament the complexity, multiple authorities, or mixed messaging of modern monarchical education: "Today we receive three different or opposing educations: that of our fathers, that of our schoolmasters, and that of the world. What we are told by the last upsets all the ideas of the first two. This comes partly from the opposition there is for us between the ties of religion and those of the world, a thing unknown among the ancients" (4.4, 35).

Our families (fathers) and schoolmasters offer a predominantly religious education that, because Christian, is in tension with the ways of the world. The immediate sequel, however, in chapter 5—the first chapter dedicated solely to "education in republican government"—opens by indicating that this contrast of single-mindedness versus complexity in education might well be intended as a praise of the relative moderation and pluralism of modern, monarchical, Christian education. It now becomes evident that it is because ancient civic education is all about force—making it extreme and inhumane by Montesquieu's standards—that it is solely "in republican government that the full power of education is needed" (4.5, 35). We get a reminder that honor is a species of self-interest, thus accords with the passions, with the result that education there does not need the degree of imposition or discipline required for education in virtue. It is at this point that Montesquieu declares that such powerful education is needed in republics because "political virtue is a renunciation of oneself," which is "always a painful thing"—the point he will reinforce in Book 5 by comparing pagan political virtue to the deep personal devotion of Christian monks, who love the "suffering" their rule imposes because it is the only passion allowed (4.5, 35; 5.2, 42–43). Book 4 then delivers a more complete definition of virtue than in its introduction in Book 3 as the democratic-republican principle: virtue is "the love of the laws and the homeland," and this requires "a continuous preference of the public interest over one's own" (4.36). Thus by the close of chapter 5 we have a mixed assessment of republicanism, noting extraordinary but also shocking and even extreme qualities, at least to moderns—who are characterized as Christians. This reminds us that in chapter 2 of this book Montesquieu had added a note on religion, after criticism by Christian theologians, clarifying that monarchical honor is "supreme" in monarchy only from the political perspective Montesquieu necessarily takes for a work on politics; although his intent is to describe "what is" in that sense, description does not entail that this is as it "should be" in a larger theological sense. He will elaborate this view in Books 24 and 25 on religion; here, he states awareness of the larger perspective: he knows that "religion sometimes works to destroy" the "prejudice" that honor represents toward one's self-distinction and the greatness of one's kingdom, and also that religion works "sometimes to regulate" or moderate such honor.

Montesquieu need not be deemed a believer in order to consider that he appreciates how Christianity can be a moderating, ameliorating influence in modern life. This may be a utilitarian approach, but it could be so in a higher, respectful sense such as Tocqueville held as a philosopher while personally not believing the Christian faith. It therefore could be that Montesquieu focuses upon the ancient republican "advantage" of single-mindedness in education for its greater power of "effect" largely so that he can define this effect as rightly "astonishing" to modern, Christian, monarchical, moderate souls. In a work committed to moderation and avoiding extremes, this allows him to portray political single-mindedness as fanaticism and extremism, in contrast to a complex, balanced, pluralistic civic education that would reduce political fanaticism and extremism. Indeed, the next book contrasts the simplicity and power of despotism—one absolute will governing all, lacking internal balance or resistance—with the complexity and balancing of distributed powers in "a moderate government" (5.14, 63). This theme sets up one of the emphatic moments of the work, showcased in its longest chapter yet—analyzing and praising the blend of monarchy and republic in England. Soon thereafter comes praise for the complex balance of orders in Gothic monarchies, as the best mode of government humanity has yet devised. Both the English and Gothic modes also are praised as "moderate" forms of government (11.5–8).

Montesquieu's subtle characterization in Book 4 of modern Christian monarchies as moderate in contrast to the fanaticism of ancient republics then deepens in chapter 6, one of the most arresting and widely discussed chapters of the entire work. The innocuous title "On some Greek institutions" hardly prepares the reader for the experience, which includes travel to the modern Spanish colony of Paraguay and also to Penn's Colony in British North America to understand just how "singular" are the ancient Greek institutions invented "to inspire virtue." The focus in the first third of the chapter is great lawgivers such as Lycurgus of Sparta and the claim that their laws are the models for Plato (citing *The Laws*) and for the modern utopian writer Denis Varaisse, who modeled his *History of Sevarambes* more immediately on More's *Utopia* (4.6, 36). The laws of Lycurgus were a completely unprecedented and unimaginable concatenation of contradictions. The education of the elite Spartiates included encouragement to steal yet devotion to strict "justice"; this education was coupled with a political order promising extraordinary collective "liberty" for the unconquerable Spartans yet was premised upon "the harshest slavery" for the Helots supplying their physical needs. The effect of this singular civic education was "greatness and glory" for Sparta. Montesquieu then devotes the middle third of the chapter to showing how "extraordinary" these Greek institutions were by contrasting them, as noted, with "the dregs and corruption of our modern times." It is here that he introduces William Penn in North America, and then the seventeenth- and eighteenth-century Jesuit missionaries in Paraguay: "That extraordinariness which we saw in the Greek institutions, we have seen that amid the dregs and corruption of our modern times."[17] "A legislator, a true gentleman, has formed a people in whom integrity seems as natural as bravery was among the Spartans. Mr. Penn is a true Lycurgus; and, though he has had peace for his object as Lycurgus had war, they are alike in the unique path on which they have set their people, in their ascendency over free men, in the prejudices they have vanquished, and in the passions they have subdued" (4.6, 37).

It is perplexing, amid a discussion of ancient warlike republics, to find this seemingly unqualified praise of the Quaker founder of Pennsylvania, for successfully establishing what Montesquieu presumably knew was both a Protestant and commercial republic, further defined by religious toleration. This is more of a contrast to Lycurgus than an imitation, for it rests not upon indoctrination in passion, sans knowledge, but upon education in a civic ethic of peace and self-government, and without slaves. The consent of the governed is freer because grounded in Protestant Christian ethics of mutual regard, freely chosen by each individual rather than through tradition or ecclesial authority. As a commentary on civic education broadly, the praise for Penn foreshadows principles emphasized later in the work. Taken by itself, the passage is commonsensical to Americans—all the more so if we note that in the second long analysis of England, focusing upon the changes in political culture and character affected by the complex monarchy-republic of their constitution, Montesquieu particularly praises the success of the English colonies in North America given their adaptations of the complex constitutionalism of the mother country: "As this government would carry prosperity with it, one would see the formation of great peoples even in the forests to which it had sent inhabitants" (19.27, 329).[18]

Thus for Americans or advocates of complex constitutional liberal democracies this interjection of Penn perhaps is less perplexing upon reflection, as a further if subtle casting of ancient political virtue as despotic and a preview of the moderate alternatives Montesquieu identifies. Yet perplexity returns given the chapter's immediate turn to praise another modern example of Christian lawgiving, the Jesuits in Paraguay. This Catholic example does not fit so easily with the Protestant blending of the spirits of Christianity, egalitarian liberty, and commerce emphasized later in the work and familiar to Americans (and Max Weber); moreover, the Jesuits are more ambitious because new laws are given not to fellow Europeans (as with Penn) but to indigenous Americans. The thread seems to be praise for modern lawgivers who successfully, and nondespotically, educate people into some kind of moderated republican virtue, in a unique, transformative, all-encompassing way—albeit with the Jesuits in a domineering way as well.

If this entire interlude on modern lawgivers in the Americas can be interpreted as sly criticism of Christian fanaticism, it is the deprecations of the Jesuits, including their attitude that "the pleasure of commanding is the only good in life," which provide the best traction.[19] These criticisms, however, pale next to great praise for the Jesuits as embodying for the new world "the idea of religion joined with that of humanity"—the virtue of gentleness and respect for human dignity so central to Montesquieu's moderate modern philosophy and political science. This hardly seems a depiction of fanaticism alone, especially since the proper Christian presence of the Jesuits is "repairing the pillages of the Spaniards," thus healing "one of the greatest wounds mankind has yet received" (4.6, 37; see 10.4, 142). He lists the many improvements the Jesuits supply to the living conditions of native peoples, but his summary judgments sweep away all details and any criticism: they have been "successful" in undertaking "great things," and they confirm that "governing men by making them happier will always be a fine thing" (37).

Montesquieu seems to offer these provocative or jarring passages as a way for the reader to rediscover, in the middle of chapter 6, the earlier thread in Book 4 that Christianity can temper both honor and political virtue. These premodern political qualities might be acceptably adapted to modern republics and monarchies—or governments that blend these—if the proper elements of Christian charity and humaneness also are present to temper the ends, ways, and means of politics. Nonetheless, Montesquieu signals that these portraits of supposed Christian successors to Lycurgus must be handled with care given the context he provides them; they are rare instances of how the fanaticism or single-mindedness of ancient civic education could be salvaged for moderate and humane ends. They would seem to be exceptions that prove the rule about the fanaticism of republican political virtue, for the final third of this extraordinary chapter together with the final two chapters of the book restore and deepen the critique of Platonic utopianism signaled earlier in chapter 6. Plato's *Republic* is depicted only as if intended as a practical blueprint for a polity rather than an excursion in political philosophy and its fraught relationship with political realities. Scholars criticize the opening and closing references to classical political philosophy in chapter 6 as a caricature, since Montesquieu offers not a word about the ultimate role of philosophy, only a focus on the political and economic mechanics of the *Republic*'s preliminary proposals for reform—especially communism of property and repudiation of commerce for the new guardians, and their severe moral discipline in selflessness (4.6, 38; compare the critique of philosophers as "legislators" in 29.19, 618). Fairly or not, Montesquieu intends that this final section of chapter 6, and the reinforcing points in chapters 7 and 8, together conclude Book 4 by emphasizing the weird, despotic character of ancient political virtue, thus pointing to the need for finding moderate modern alternatives. The final dismissal of the despotic political virtue of the ancients, and perhaps unfairly of those elements of classical political philosophy that support such a virtue, is that "one must regard the Greeks as a society of athletes and fighters" (4.8, 40). Modern and potentially moderate peoples, with larger scales of society and government, need not know of the bizarre commercial or economic views required to sustain such single-minded, small-republic cults (chapter 7); nor need they understand the peculiar ideas about music soothing the savage beast of the citizen-warrior cult, let alone the practices of male homosexuality used to reinforce the civic and martial bonds of the few who enjoyed this odd liberty built on the slavery or noncitizenship of those providing the needs of life (chapter 8). If moderate,

Christian modernity looks petty, as mere dregs and corruption against the glorious Spartan and Roman models of warlike republics turned empires, then Montesquieu ultimately is praising a moderate modernity with such faint damnation.[20]

If Penn and the Jesuits are exceptions proving the rule, then philosophers or founding statesmen might be cautious about adopting those extraordinary efforts of the Americas as models for export. As Book 19 clearly articulates, the English political culture is a kind of modern Athens, a commercial republic with a powerful navy protecting the merchant marine; yet the English political culture is deeply moderated by a greater interest in commerce for its own sake, by Christianity, and by a Protestant Christian aversion to military empire per se (19.27). Nonetheless, England's naval capacity for war and deterrence is salient, and Montesquieu devotes two books (9 and 10) to these topics apart from other comments in *Spirit of Laws* on war and peace. Surely the Montesquieuan questions would be these: Can Quaker pacifism survive in the forests of the New World if not for Britain's naval-commercial empire protecting it? Would all such genuinely good-intentioned experiments like the Jesuit mission in Paraguay yield such humane results? Montesquieu's moderation, which includes the sobriety of his political philosophy, cautions against enthusiasm even for admirable instances of modern Christian humanism.

RENEWING A MONTESQUIEUAN SPIRIT IN AMERICAN CIVIC EDUCATION

Montesquieu's analysis of civic education leaves thinkers and legislators in particular polities the task of discerning how his general lessons and approach might guide formation of a particular civic education for their regime. America, to borrow Tocqueville's view of our initial founding (that would be 1620, not 1619) and of our political-constitutional founding from 1776 onward, is the kind of blended, complex constitutional order and political culture recommended later in *Spirit of Laws* as more moderate and humane. Awareness of that lineage, descending from a republic with monarchical elements, can guide American civic educators. Yet Montesquieu also criticizes English liberty in Book 11 as extreme and repeats this in his second study of the English in Book 19, adding new criticisms; he also notes that the Gothic constitutionalism of a mixed monarchy might be a better fit for some peoples. Thus we must accept that to expect further direct guidance on the civic education he recommends for England's blended constitutionalism, or any other particular polity not a pure echo of classical republicanism or early modern monarchy, would violate a philosophy of moderation that balances discernment of universal natural principles of justice with the rational requirement for judgment in particular circumstances about how to actually live up to them. We should recognize that Montesquieu has done his part by restoring civic education to an early, important place in his masterwork of political philosophy and moderate constitutionalism. His call to philosophical readers and thoughtful statesmen is to take up their own work, in their particular places and governments, of assessing, building, or renewing the appropriate constitutionalism and civic education to achieve a moderate, humane life. To have attempted a sequel in *Spirit of Laws* to Book 4, as if providing the one manual on civic education for all moderate governments across diverse places and civilizations, would be both self-contradictory and futile. A people, through their leading thinkers and statesmen, must devise or revise their constitution, and even more particularly the civic education for such governments—including blends of earlier types of governments. America might be fortunate to inherit a larger manual for our complex constitutionalism needing only adaptation, but certainly we must write the civic education chapter ourselves.

As noted, *Spirit of Laws* first provides the call to civic education and broad guidelines in Book 4, then illustrates moderating elements in politics to stimulate thinking about a more balanced political order and civic education. Broadly surveyed, these include judicial and legal reforms (Books 6 and 12), complex constitutional orders (Books 11 and 12), federalism (Book 9), careful critiques of slavery and polygamy (Books 15–17), commerce (Books 20–22), and the appropriate place for religion in supporting a moderate political order (Books 24–25). By the middle of Part 3 of the philosophical journey, amid careful but clear denunciations of slavery, he can coin a general maxim for a moderate politics and civic education: "Knowledge makes men gentle, and reason inclines toward humanity; only prejudices cause these to be renounced" (15.3, 249). This echoes striking declarations in the Preface, that Montesquieu would be the happiest of mortals if readers became less prejudiced and more civil, whatever their particular regime. A later episode of interest to Americans in particular is his analysis of the English political and civic culture produced by their complex constitutional forms and extreme liberty; here he warns of other extremes, including English tendencies to individualism and materialism. Given America's current crises, a further episode in that study of the English is salient, warning that all thinking can tend toward mere partisanship in such a freewheeling modern republic; perhaps it takes a foreign visitor to discern the single-mindedness or philosophical extremism that can afflict any school of thought in a liberal republic. The paradox is that, although English liberty promotes both free discourse and free party conflict, these phenomena also produce intellectual insularity or narrowness. The example Montesquieu gives is English historians, but since his own works (including both *Considerations on the Romans* and *Spirit of Laws*) weave together history and philosophy, his warning can be read to address all intellectual disciplines or schools about human affairs: "In extremely absolute monarchies" or despotisms, "historians betray the truth because they do not have the liberty to tell it"; yet "in extremely free states, historians betray the truth because of their very liberty, for, as [liberty] always produces divisions, every one becomes as much the slave of the prejudices of his faction as he would be of a despot" (19.27, 333).

His message that we must think for ourselves about constitutionalism and civic education is mostly implicit, but the closing passage of his extraordinary book on liberty in constitutions approaches an explicit call to do our intellectual and civic duty. He might "like to seek in all the moderate governments we know" the distribution of power and the liberty provided, but "one must not always so exhaust a subject that one leaves nothing for the reader to do. The question is not that of making him read, but of making him think" (11.20, 186). Nonetheless we are fortunate that his heirs, such as Tocqueville, took up that call to think about both constitutionalism and civic education. The complex political science of Montesquieu and Tocqueville thus can be a general guide for discerning America's needed civic education, and Tocqueville can offer more particular guidance given that *Democracy in America* also devotes chapters and sections to education as part of his complex analysis of modern democracy and America particularly.

Tocqueville's very Montesquieuan effort asks us to consider not only institutional forms and first principles of constitutional liberal democracy but also the new kind of civic education and "reflective patriotism" fitting for our commercial and very egalitarian polity. This includes the challenge of preserving study of classic works and ideas of Western civilization amid the constant press for democratic progress.[21] His comprehensive political science pushes us to consider how to balance and integrate these complex elements. Tocqueville's assessments of and recommendations for civic education are so valuable because he had studied both Montesquieu and several writings of the American founders, themselves influenced by Montesquieu—then he observes the new American constitutionalism not only through its theory but its half-century of practice since its political founding.

A closing example of the twenty-first-century salience of both philosophers for discerning what civic education is needed for our America is that both would grasp why a kind of democratic license, among other factors, has weakened our understanding and appreciation of our founding constitutionalism—but they also would grasp why some of the complexity of our original political culture survives nonetheless. They would understand how a political culture that could draft the Declaration of Independence could still admire, after centuries and both triumphs and travails, the peculiarly honorable profession of the volunteer military above all other institutions and professions—this amid an era otherwise dominated as much or more by cynicism and apathy as by the fanatical political devotion of a few, left or right. Montesquieu and Tocqueville take seriously the aristocratic legacy of honor and how it might adapt and survive in changed circumstances. They would take some hope from the fact that the polarized, demoralized, and inadequately educated citizenry of our era still could honor the honorable, in accord with the spirit of the closing pledge made in 1776—even if the Declaration itself is not so widely or deeply studied today as it should be. A legacy from the signers persists, that individual natural rights to life, liberty, and the pursuit of happiness not only are compatible with but require their closing statement on their support for these declared truths: "With a firm reliance on the protection of Divine Providence, we mutually pledge to each other our Lives, our Fortunes and our sacred Honor."

NOTES

1. I cite the recent sources on these conditions, and the competing argu-ments about their causes, in "America's Civic Crisis and the Failure of Politi-cal Science: Reconnecting Civic Education and Liberal Education," forthcoming in *The Politics of Liberal Education: Academic Inquiry and Civic Responsibility*, ed. Steven McGuire and John-Paul Spiro (Lexington Books, anticipated 2022).

2. The indictment is in "America's Civic Crisis," which in turn develops the argument in Paul Carrese, "Constitutionalist Political Science: Rediscover-ing Storing's Philosophical Moderation," *American Political Thought* 4 (Spring 2015): 259–88.

3. Charles de Montesquieu, *The Spirit of the Laws*, ed. Anne M. Cohler, Basia Miller, and Harold Stone (Cambridge University Press, 1989 [1748]), Book 4, chapter 5, 35. Subsequent references are parenthetical, citing book and chapter of *Spirit* and page in this edition. I occasionally revise the Cohler trans-lation. See Lorraine S. Pangle and Thomas L. Pangle, *The Learning of Liberty: The Educational Ideals of the American Founders* (Lawrence: University Press of Kansas, 1992), 132; Walter Berns, *Making Patriots* (Chicago: University of Chicago Press, 2001), 66; and George Thomas, *The Founders and the Idea of a National University: Constituting the American Mind* (Cambridge: Cambridge University Press, 2014), 2.

4. Montesquieu implicitly describes England in Book 5 as "a nation where the republic hides under the form of monarchy" and confirms this in his sec-ond long chapter devoted to England—that one often sees there "the form of an absolute government over the foundation of a free government" (5.19, 70; 29.27, 330). His famous study of "The Constitution of England" as unique in its direct devotion to liberty is in 11.6 (156–66).

5. See, for example, Donald Lutz, "The Relative Influence of European Writers on Late Eighteenth-Century American Political Thought," *American Political Science Review* 78 (1984): 189–97. My larger approach to Montes-quieu's political philosophy and why it matters more than ever for America is Carrese, *Democracy in Moderation: Montesquieu, Tocqueville, and Sustain-able Liberalism* (Cambridge: Cambridge University Press, 2016).

6. Two recent books on Montesquieu's philosophy of complexity, as bal-ancing adherence to universal principles of right with necessary attention to the particulars of diverse polities and peoples, are Joshua Bandoch: *The Politics of Place: Montesquieu, Particularism, and the Pursuit of Liberty* (Rochester, NY: University of Rochester Press, 2017); and Keegan Callanan, *Montesquieu's Lib-eralism and the Problem of Universal Politics* (Cambridge: Cambridge Univer-sity Press, 2018).

7. This argument is elaborated in Carrese, *Democracy in Moderation*. I indicate there my debts to, and some differences with, several Montesquieu

scholars. This chapter cites only some of these scholars, focusing on particular insights about Montesquieu's conception of civic education.

8. Carrese, *Democracy in Moderation*, 118 n. 20, cites a range of scholarly sources on these points. I am indebted to several works by James Stoner for the basic insight.

9. I argue this in Carrese, *The Cloaking of Power: Montesquieu, Blackstone, and the Rise of Judicial Activism* (Chicago: University of Chicago Press, 2003).

10. See, for example, Thomas L. Pangle, *Montesquieu's Philosophy of Liberalism* (Chicago: University of Chicago Press, 1973); Paul Rahe, *Montesquieu and the Logic of Liberty* (New Haven, CT: Yale University Press, 2009); and among several writings by Diana Schaub, most recently "The Regime and Montesquieu's Principles of Education," in *Montesquieu and the Spirit of Modernity*, ed. David W. Carrithers and Patrick Coleman (Oxford: Voltaire Foundation, University of Oxford, 2002), 77–100. A careful study of Montesquieu's complicated analysis of republics is David W. Carrithers, "Democratic and Aristocratic Republics: Ancient and Modern," in *Montesquieu's Science of Politics: Essays on The Spirit of Laws*, ed. David W. Carrithers, Michael Mosher, and Paul Rahe (Lanham, MD: Rowman and Littlefield, 2001), 109–58.

11. See, for example, Thomas L. Pangle, *The Theological Basis of Liberal Modernity in Montesquieu's Spirit of the Laws* (Chicago: University of Chicago Press, 2010); and Diana Schaub, "Of Believers and Barbarians: Montesquieu's Enlightened Toleration," in *Early Modern Skepticism and the Origins of Toleration*, ed. Alan Levine (Lanham, MD: Lexington Books, 1999); as well as several subsequent articles. I discuss these and my contrary view in a chapter on religion in Carrese, *Democracy in Moderation* that discusses both Montesquieu and Tocqueville, and in Carrese, "Montesquieu and Christianity in the American Project: The Moderate Spirit of Religious Liberty," in *Civil Religion in Modern Political Philosophy*, ed. Steven Frankel and Martin Yaffe (University Park: Penn State University Press, 2020).

12. Diana Schaub notes, but does not develop, the change in sequence in "Regime."

13. Montesquieu added an "Author's notice" to the second edition of *Spirit of Laws*, published posthumously in 1757 (in Cohler, "Author's foreword," xli–xlii) mostly to address these criticisms; he clarified his meanings for virtue and honor, and for designating only one quality as the principle of a government; as well, he noted revisions that "further specify" these ideas (sometimes in the text, often in new notes). The notice adds this philosophical declaration: "I have had new ideas, new words have had to be found or new meanings given to old ones" (xli).

14. Adam Smith, his thinking deeply shaped by *The Spirit of Laws*, arguably takes his idea of "the invisible hand" in free economies from this analysis of honor.

15. This is the theme of the recent books by Callanan and Bandoch noted above.

16. The implication that Books 4 and 6 reinforce each other through their out-of-sequence analysis is supported by Montesquieu's parallel invocation in Book 6 of a senior judge (*président a mortier*) of a regional French court (*parlement*) protesting judicial interference by a king in a case against a nobleman; the "president of Bélievre" openly criticized Louis XIII acting as judge to "condemn a gentleman to death" (6.5, 79). Montesquieu once held this same office of president in the Parlement of Bordeaux; moreover, 6.5 opens by praising Machiavelli as "a great man" in order to condemn categorically his advocacy of popular judgments that strip access to professional judges and courts, endangering "the security of individuals" (77).

17. This revises the Cohler edition translation, 37, in important ways, emphasizing clarity of meaning in translating Montesquieu's stylish belles-lettres sentence at the cost of gracefulness in modern English.

18. Montesquieu, a Latinist, would know that "Pennsylvania" basically translates as "Penn's woods" or "Penn's forests." Moreover, shortly after this comes a passage early in Book 20 praising the English blend of religious toleration, moderate modern republicanism, and commerce, which is just what Penn achieved in his 1682 *Pennsylvania Frame of Government:* "This is the people in the world who have best known how to take advantage of each of these three great things at the same time: religion, commerce, and liberty" (20.7, 343).

19. Schaub, "Regime," notes the reference to Penn and the Jesuits (92, 99) but only as a commentary on theocracy.

20. This point is reinforced if his *Considerations on the Causes of the Greatness of the Romans and Their Decline* is understood not as neo-Machiavellian but as warning those fascinated by Rome's triumphs and sway that more careful study reveals the ultimate horror, inhumanity, and butchery the Romans inflicted on others, and themselves, across centuries.

21. Tocqueville, *Democracy in America*, ed. Harvey Mansfield and Delba Winthrop (Chicago: University of Chicago, 2000 [1835, 1840]); in vol. 1, pt. 2, chap. 6, the section "On Public Spirit in the United States" discusses the new "reflective patriotism" needed (225–27); all of vol. 2, pt. 1, is devoted to "intellectual movements" in American democracy, including chap. 9 on why the Americans do have some aptitude and taste for sciences, literature, and the arts (428–33), and chap. 15, "Why the Study of Greek and Latin Literature Particularly Useful in Democratic Centuries" (450–52).

2

Crafting the "Cords of [Constitutional] Affection"

What Ties to Bind Civic Education to a Democratic Citizenry?

Rebecca Burgess

In response to the glut of surveys, studies, and editorials linking an increased need for and interest in civic education to Donald Trump's 2016 presidential election, a heightened political partisanship and gridlock, and a declining trust in American principles and institutions, *Washington Post* education writer Jay Mathews has a curt rejoinder: Civic education is not the answer for America's contemporary ills. Not only is "ignorance of American government and history [a] part of our culture," but education in and of itself also has proven to be too weak to make Americans more civically enlightened or better voters.[1] Despite long-held public assumptions about civic education, it appears disconnected, if not disparate, from good or active citizenship. Civic education is presented as a matter of formal if opaque coursework; citizenship, as a legal concept, is essentially relegated to electoral activity.

The cause of the disconnect, Mathews implies initially, is much more expansive than that Americans simply find civics classes lacking in intellectual stimulation or unnecessary for professional advancement. Rather, looking backward at a hundred years' worth of unimpressive civic test scores, Mathews suggests that civics has always been "an unpopular course," because Americans have pragmatically understood that the level of formal civic knowledge makes no demonstrable difference to the success or jeopardy of their national democratic experiment and have adjusted their academic behavior accordingly.[2] Democracy at times may truly be in jeopardy, but Americans' behavioral belief reinforces that it is not the lack of "A pluses" in civics classes across the fifty states that poses the threat.

Mathews advances yet another step further, however, when, looking at the public record of civic behavior, he concludes that how one votes is likely "to be more influenced by [one's] fears and ambitions" than by how much one learns in school. Correlating the fact that 22 million college graduates voted for President Trump in 2016 with primal "fight or flight" emotions as the motivation behind their vote choice, he casts in doubt the efficacy of education in general to address political ignorance or transform political behavior. In doing so, he exposes a fundamental skepticism about the feasibility of the American regime. If education is powerless to tame the fear and ambition human beings experience, then having the type of rational deliberations across a diverse body that have traditionally been understood to be vital for self-government appears an impossible dream on the order of John Dewey's "kingdom of mythological social zoology."[3]

OF FOUNDINGS, CIVICS, AND CITIZENSHIP

In citing the influence fears and ambitions can have on political behavior, Jay Mathews invites, at least at one level, a turn to America's founding generation of political theorists and practitioners. Thomas Jefferson, James Madison, George Washington, John Adams, Benjamin Rush, Benjamin Franklin, and Noah Webster (among so many others of that period) were deeply concerned about the role that ignorance and untamed passions—such as fear and ambition—could play in an experimental political project organized around the principle of representative self-government. The dichotomy between "reason and choice" and "accident and force" that Hamilton invokes in the introductory *Federalist* essay is precisely that between an informed or educated intellect and untamed emotions or passions. It sets the stage, then as now, for the arguments about the feasibility of the American project of liberal democracy. And enrooted there is the deceptively straightforward question: if human beings are capable of collectively establishing just government, are they equally capable of maintaining such a government? Through what means?

Hamilton frames the argument for ratifying the newly drafted Constitution with this question and infers for his audience the framework by which we are to measure the response. Establishment of the regime proposed in *The Federalist* implies some amount of sustainability and longevity, which cannot happen through force but through the choice of citizens desiring to perpetuate it. But establishment also implies on the part of the various state legislatures an awareness of the public good and how the proposed constitutional order will nourish it. How does this awareness happen? The problem of establishing this particular liberal democratic regime, Hamilton slyly informs us, is the perpetual problem of education and self-government, fueled by a type of passionate attachment to principles and necessarily encouraged by persuasive speech. Self-government presupposes or implies then a mass enlightenment that moderates the individual's fear and ambition about her rights through a concern for the welfare of the community.[4] But perpetuating self-government also requires a type of passionate attachment on the part of individuals to the principles that undergird its defense of individual rights.[5]

Hamilton's suggestion in *Federalist* 1 is that the American people will prove, through ratifying the Constitution or not, whether such a thing as mass enlightenment is possible. More to the point from the founder's or statesman's perspective is the consideration of whether such enlightenment is probable. His fellow *Federalist* authors and contemporary statesmen join Hamilton in an extended conversation, through their public and private writings and lawmaking throughout the founding era, about this probability or possibility, as well as about the devices of statecraft and innovations of political science they will need to weld together the government architecture of a just, liberal democratic order in which free and equal citizens can thrive. And they are agreed that equally as important as the formal government structures of this order for the success of the union are the more qualitative elements of character and behavior of that citizenry, shaped by public and private education.

Though Jefferson is not alone in his ebullient statement at the close of his life about universal enlightenment—"All eyes are opened, or opening, to the rights of man. The general spread of the light of science has already laid open to every view that the mass of mankind has not been born with saddles on their backs, nor a favored few booted and spurred, ready to ride them legitimately, by the grace of God"—he is also not alone in his less pithy concern that, despite the possibility of universal moral enlightenment, reason alone is not a sufficient guarantee that all will act either well or reasonably as citizens.[6] Jefferson is aware that, for most of humankind most of the time, the workings out of reason are not accessible enough to inform immediate action; something else is needed to inform them, a set of commonly held opinions or beliefs, prominently promulgated in public and through a variety of mediums.

It is not surprising, then, to find such a set of held beliefs ("We hold these truths") articulated in the Declaration of Independence—primarily authored by Jefferson—and heralding in the most public way the intellectual principles of the American experiment of self-government. Nor is it surprising to find that the system of public law ensconced in the "supreme law of the land"—the U.S. Constitution—is the articulation of the legal framework for the Declaration's stated beliefs. Both public articulations express through which formal institutions and arrangements of offices the American people will engage with each other on a daily basis—what the American regime will be. In this sense, the public law sets the tone for the education of citizens in its regime.

Yet the Declaration raises a challenge to the Constitution and the formative role it plays in the life of the nation: are even well-designed institutions and laws enough to bind a people together in the friendly, shared pursuit of individual rights and toward the common good? The founding generation is keenly aware that, on the one hand, even well-designed laws and institutions do not touch all aspects of democratic life; and, on the other hand, neither reason nor commonly held opinions are always enough to ensure good government and a healthy society. The education in citizenship that the public law and institutions can give appears insufficient to form the hearts and minds of its citizens.

What must government, statesmen, and founders do to address this insufficiency? In the ensuing pages, I offer an examination of how the fundamental questions about the limits of mass enlightenment and the need for self-government engaged the most prominent minds of the founding era in questions about the forms and content of civic education, informed attachment or patriotism, and democratic citizenship. Theorists and practitioners of politics alike, Jefferson, Madison, Washington, Adams, Rush, Franklin, and Webster, all wrestled with the fact that, even in a rights-based social compact order informed by "reflection and choice," a robust citizenship involves not only a set of intellectual principles but also emotions or passions that are not readily quantifiable.

Weaving together the various complementary strands of these individuals' unique arguments, the collective argument that appears supports a far richer understanding of citizenship and civic education than is acknowledged by current education writers. In this earlier understanding of citizenship, citizenship is presented as something beyond the realm of merely legalistic formulations or quantitative data to one in which, in the language of the Declaration of Independence, lives, fortunes, and "sacred Honor" are mutually pledged.[7] The content of the civic education that flows from this, in the founders' estimation, thus encompasses the whole "way of life" of a people—not just the government and the culture but the institutions, ideas, values, mores, habits, customs, and traditions. Each of these aspects needs attending to under self-government.[8]

A SOVEREIGN PEOPLE AND THE COMMON GOOD

The concern about democratic citizens and perpetuating the American regime reflects the understanding, on the part of the American statesmen listed above, that despite the "laws of Nature" mandating that just government is narrowed in scope to protecting individual rights, the republican principle of the consent of the governed requires of the individuals making up the community a broad concern with the common good. Whereas in a monarchy the king or single sovereign bears responsibility for the common good, the Constitution assigns that responsibility to the sovereign plurality, "We the People." How do you make "We the People" care about anything other than their individual selves—especially when their sovereignty flows from a theory of natural rights that automatically elevates into importance the private sphere?

Madison famously observed in *Federalist* 55 that republican government presupposes "qualities in human nature which justify a certain position of esteem and confidence," and to a higher degree than does any other form of government.[9] This seems to imply that republican citizens consciously cultivate attitudes and behaviors, or virtues, that harmonize their self-interest with the good of the community. But he layered this observation on his more frequently cited, and somber, observations about an imperfect human nature in *Federalist* 51 and *Federalist* 10 and the corresponding need for institutions and constitutional arrangements to pick up the slack.

Government is necessary precisely because human nature tends not to moderate its internal or external desires—people are not angels. Human beings are "much more disposed to vex and oppress each other than to co-operate for their common good"; they have a "propensity to fall into mutual animosities." Thus, "ambition must be made to counteract ambition" among leaders and competing sectors and factions of society. Government's powers must be separated among different branches, and each branch given the means to check and balance the others; a representative form of government that "refine[s] and enlarge[s] the public views" needs to be instituted, but also over an "extended sphere," so that the greater number of citizens and the "greater sphere of country" can counteract corruption coming from unchecked local prejudices. This prevents tyrannical government, which is the sustained goal of the Constitution.[10]

That "extended sphere" and the diversity of citizens it encompasses pose their own problem to the hope of a coherent union, however. The benefit to the republic they bring of preventing majority faction, by multiplying interests and parties, is offset by the difficulties they erect against that republic effectively communicating to its parts a common purpose and uniting around it. Madison is no Rousseauian; he does not believe that it is possible to give all citizens the same opinions, passions, and interests, especially not in a free society where liberty, especially of conscience and speech, "is essential to political life."[11] He *does* believe that it is crucial to the success of self-government to form "a people" united by common principles and a common purpose.

In order to collect, form, and refine the will of society—the essential backbone of a uniform system of laws that reflects a shared understanding of what it means to "insure domestic Tranquility, provide for the common defence, [and] promote the general Welfare"[12]—a people depend upon the possibility of communication. Communication is the necessary vehicle to give voice to the public will, in order for it to be acted upon. Thus Madison emphasizes the desirability of a "republic of mean extent," where a certain kind of majority can feasibly form without it becoming factious or tyrannical. Key to enabling this type of majority are both political institutions, such as a House of Representatives distinct from a Senate and with different electoral requirements and schedules, and "whatever generates intercourse of sentiments." These include such things as "good roads, domestic commerce, a free press, and particularly a circulation of newspapers though the entire body of the people," Madison writes in his Party Press essay "Public Opinion."[13]

There is of course the intercourse of political sentiments, but there is equally an intercourse of less tangible sentiments and emotions that Madison knows the republic must rely on for there to be a people uniting in it. In *Federalist* 14, Madison takes note of the "mingled blood which [American citizens] have shed in defense of their sacred rights," which "consecrate their Union and excite horror at the idea of their becoming aliens, rivals, enemies." Their blood, commonly shed in defense of their rights, he argues, knits them together in the very fabric of this new form of republican government "by so many cords of affection."[14] Thus at the foundation of the union, perhaps even constituting the vital springs of that union, Madison places a shared (communicated) affection and a shared knowledge about what is sacred to it, its originating principles. Echoing the resounding final paragraph of the Declaration of Independence, Madison's reminder is that the mutual pledge of lives, material support, and honor that enables the union to exist both nourishes and is nourished by a particular set of known, annunciated principles.

These known principles must be repeatedly communicated or shared with new generations of citizens, whether children or immigrating adults. Affection, as a passion or emotion, is vital but inherently tricky because less facile to pass down generationally and to a multitude. It is also less stable than reason, but an appeal to reason can help to spark it. The founding generation as a whole frequently articulated the need for a robust system of public education to inform and undergird the "chords of affection" in order for the people to remain "the mutual guardians of their mutual happiness."[15]

True, the circulating print media have a role in this regard, because "it is the duty . . . of intelligent and faithful citizens to discuss and promulgate [political information and ideas] freely" so as to maintain the "censorship of public opinion" against a potentially tyrannous government.[16] Broadly speaking, all intelligent and faithful citizens are civic educators, with their contributions to the public benefit of the community not less vital than that of the farmer or manufacturer. As "cultivators of the human mind," the literati are "manufacturers of useful knowledge," "the agents of the commerce of ideas—the censors of public manners—the teachers of the arts of life and the means of happiness."[17] They cultivate the cultural framework, the necessary qualities in human nature that sustain and strengthen republican self-government.

But as President Washington maintains in his Farewell Address of 1796, this is not sufficient. The nation, in both its public capacity through Congress and through its private associations of civil society, must "promote then, as an object of primary importance, Institutions for the general diffusion of knowledge."[18] Religion and morality are bulwarks for sustaining republican government, but education, Washington argues, is equally key for a free society. It is no small monument to the enormous importance that the nation as a whole placed on education for their mutual endeavor that, even before the Constitution was enacted, Congress in 1787 passed the Northwest Ordinance establishing policies for the vast territories northwest of the Ohio River. Clearly articulated therein is this dictum: "Religion, Morality, and knowledge, being necessary to good government and the happiness of mankind, Schools and the means of education shall forever be encouraged."[19]

One year prior to Washington's Farewell Address, the American Philosophical Society (founded by Benjamin Franklin in 1743 "to encourage and disseminate useful scientific and philosophical information") sponsored the first national competition for education scholars in the history of the United States.[20] The prompt was to write an essay formulating a liberal education adapted to "the genius of the government and best calculated to promote the general welfare of the United States," one that included a plan for a system of public schools. The APS recognized both Samuel Harrison Smith and the Reverend Samuel Knox as contest winners in 1797.

Both men wrote of the importance of suiting an enlightened education system to produce enlightened citizens who know their rights, understand the rights of others, and "discerning the connection of [their] interest with the preservation of these rights . . . will firmly support those of [their] fellow men as [their] own."[21] Such enlightened citizens would truly be freemen, wrote Smith. But both contestants identified key themes that remain continued sources of contention in debates about education and citizenship. These revolve around the tension between local and centralized control of curriculum, management, and funding of public schools; the tension between intellectual freedom and social cohesion; and the "problem of intense diversity." At heart, both essays wrestle with the question of what the role of formal education in a republic ought to look like when it is in the public sphere.[22]

The immediate challenge to crafting a national system of education has to do with the federal structure of the Union. Since control of education rests with the states and localities, the founding generation understood that a single central authority such as the federal government could not mandate a common curriculum (although it could influence it).[23] America's public schools thus needed to be, and were, local in their origins. As Johann Neem argues, this ensured that America's schools truly were "democracy's schools"; following the revolution, schools were built and administered "by the labor of ordinary citizens who pooled their time and resources to provide a public good." Fueled by the revolution's lively rhetoric of self-rule, American citizens wanted their schools overseen by locally elected trustees and tied to the communities they served. This was a successful dynamic, Neem shows: Americans enrolled more students in public schools, as a percentage of the population, than did most European countries.[24]

Various state constitutions of the era reflected the public importance accorded to more local control of education and the role that the states, rather than the federal government, played in overseeing educational institutions. Out of twelve states that adopted constitutions by 1790, seven had provisions for education: Massachusetts, North Carolina, Georgia, New Hampshire, Vermont, Pennsylvania, and Delaware. By 1802 all northern states except Rhode Island and New Jersey had passed laws for public funding of elementary schools and also provided some taxpayer support to privately owned high schools, called "academies."[25] As the New Hampshire constitution directly stated, "Knowledge, and learning, generally diffused through a community, being essential to the preservation of a free government; . . . the legislators . . . [shall] cherish the interest of literature and the sciences, and all seminaries and public schools."[26]

Political theorist Jean Yarbrough has argued that, in providing in various ways for education, religion, and political participation, "the states took the question of character seriously indeed." Other than embodying democratic order and local control, what are these schools supposed to teach to Americans in order for them to sustain the American constitutional republic as a united nation? The founders are well aware that, despite the faint role of the federal government in the schools, the schools' curricula, especially at the primary level, must be designed to provide a democratic education in the content they deliver. This is in regards to both the civic literacy they need to develop in the people, for them to know their rights and jealously guard them against unjust encroachment by their rulers, and the interior dispositions and habits they need in order to be "fit for a free society."[27]

John Adams is explicit that "children should be educated and instructed in the principles of freedom." The content of American education, he believes, needs to be wholly different from that of a European classical education. It needs to be newly designed to meet the particular challenges of self-government by a free and equal people: "The education here intended is not merely that of the children of the rich and noble, but of every rank and class of people, down to the lowest and the poorest."[28] Thomas Jefferson agrees, because he also believes that history has proved that the people and not the rulers are more often the wronged than the wrongdoers. Elites of politics and organized religion have traditionally conspired to maintain their power at the expense of ordinary people. A mass education that diffuses the knowledge necessary to undertake a meaningful life and to secure liberty for every American, no matter how poor, is the effective counterweight against such elites.

Educating future elites, especially future statesmen, should not be neglected, however. An education in democratic principles and habits is another vital hedge against traditional elitist behavior. The rich and the intellectual elites need to be educated properly just as much as the great bulk of common men and women for the democratic experiment to succeed. Washington, Jefferson, and Madison made a concerted effort to establish a national university in part to answer this need.

"To the security of a free Constitution [knowledge] contributes in various ways," Washington writes to Congress in his first State of the Union, "By convincing those who are entrusted with the publick administration, that every valuable end of government is best answered by the enlightened confidence of the people."[29] He returns to this theme at the sunset of his presidency, emphasizing that a national university's primary objective should be "the education of our Youth in the science of *Government*. In a Republic, what species of knowledge can be equally important? And what duty, more pressing on its Legislature, than to patronize a plan for communicating it to those, who are to be the future guardians of the liberties of the Country?"[30] Though Congress and the public took such admonitions seriously, Washington and his allies ultimately failed in their efforts to have Congress establish a national university. The need to have a more specialized, elite education for a democratic society's future elite rests uneasily with the egalitarian principles such a society espouses.

MAKING CITIZENS

It is no surprise to find Jefferson arguing in favor of his home state of Virginia offering a free education to every Virginian. Although he does not assume that all students are equally gifted, or that better students will become state leaders and require more education, he is firm about the baseline knowledge that every young citizen needs at their fingertips to participate in free government. This leads him to propose a pyramid structure in which elementary schools teach basic skills (reading, writing, arithmetic) and knowledge (history, science, and ethics) necessary for every child's own private pursuits and for effective citizenship—so that he is able to "judge for himself what will secure or endanger his freedom"—but in which advanced education opens up his access to a broad cultural literacy in order to make decisions about the public welfare (botany, chemistry, philosophy, legal ethics, and the law of nature and of nations).[31]

Jefferson's pyramid structure is a helpful counterweight against Progressive Era and later theorists who want especially civic education to function as a fundamental questioning of the regime, at every level of instruction. If, to echo Madison, "a people who mean to be their own Governors must arm themselves with the power which knowledge gives," then a government designed to be of, by, and for the people is only as strong and as durable as its citizens' understanding of the principles, institutions, and habits required to maintain a free and equal society, as articulated in their foundational documents, by statesmen, and at national moments.[32] This presupposes that such a people will familiarize themselves first with these things as they are, before they proceed to question, evaluate, or propose altering them.

The former is civic education properly understood, as scholars William Galston and James Ceaser point out, because it transmits or preserves the regime. The latter is more properly understood as philosophical or political education, because its purpose is to conduct a thread of rational inquiry designed to undermine, to change, or to transform the existing regime toward some new perceived or discovered good.[33] In the spirit of the former, Jefferson sketches out just how a citizen ought to be educated civically and habituated in his rights and duties. Citizenship, he explains, requires a basic civic knowledge (the identification of rights, how to exercise "with order and justice" those rights the citizen retains, and how to choose "with discretion" the officials tasked with employing the citizen's delegated rights), the inculcation of sound civic habits, and an informed attachment to the American regime and the principles of the Constitution. "To instruct the mass of our citizens in these, their rights, interests, and duties, as men and citizens, [is] is the object of education."[34]

Thus, just as the democratic citizen by definition participates in the activities of governing as well as of being governed, so civic education must provide a complex array of knowledge to a wide array of citizens. At a minimum, it includes knowledge for effective participation in public affairs, knowledge needed to elect officials who best demonstrate such an understanding, and an understanding of the rights and obligations we have as citizens. In its deepest sense, civic education thus reaches beyond simply helping individuals have a working familiarity with government structure and citizen rights. It also implies the need to habituate the young and new citizens to the habits of heart and mind on which vigorous democracies rely.

Today, largely because civic education is most commonly perceived through the lens of political education, these core components of its traditional purview seem to have become disassociated from each other, if not placed in competition with each other, even while reflecting aspects of the original understanding. Thus organizations and programs promoting civic literacy exist alongside those promoting "action civics," civic engagement, or civic participation, and also alongside those promoting character development. The confusion of emphasis among these several types of civics organizations arguably feeds our public confusion about the role of civic education in schools and for democratic society, and, as the steady stream of patriotism surveys attests, the anxiety Americans have over the strength of their fellow Americans' patriotism. We do not trust that election turnout and ritual flag-waving are actual proof that we have maintained those habits of heart and mind vital to self-government, because everywhere we see evidence that we no longer share a unity of national sentiments.

Elsewhere, other history, political science, and education scholars in addition to Ceaser and Galston—including John Fonte and Rita Koganzon—have written that this question reveals a fundamental divide in the understanding of civic education. Either civic education is understood in terms of transmission—its purpose being to "preserve, improve, and transmit the American regime to future generations of Americans"—or civic education is understood in terms of transformation—its purpose being quite literally to transform the American regime through transforming society's understanding and expectations of it, away from its supposedly antiquated originating principles and toward "what it can and should be."[35]

Precisely because generations later than the theorists and practitioners of the founding era believed that American government and society needed to be reformulated according to more enlightened, scientific views, and then disseminated by experts such as certified teachers, civic education began to be narrowed to a topic of only formal education occurring at a defined moment in K–12 education. Over time, this narrow focus has devolved civic education into a one- or two-semester course involving listicles of institutional arrangements and memorization of how a bill becomes a law—which is hardly enlightening, or popular, as our earlier *Washington Post* writer Jay Mathews notes. But this is an impoverished view of civic education, and it contributes to the present confusion about civics, citizenship, and patriotism. To emphasize again, it is a view that has forgotten that it is rather the whole "way of life" of a people—the government and the culture, encompassing the institutions, ideas, values, mores, habits, customs, and traditions—that is civics' proper content. Each of these aspects needs attending to under self-government.

EDUCATION, KEEPER OF THE REPUBLIC

In the wake of the revolution, the founding generation was keenly alive to the need to create such habits of heart and mind indirectly through education rather than directly by government, thereby creating a groundswell of national sentiment to unify the new nation. Noah Webster in particular showed how to do this successfully, through his widely used *New England Primer.* Historians and other educators mirrored Webster's sense of responsibility for fostering national unity through the communication or sharing of the history of American independence and the principles undergirding it.

The sharing, communicating, and teaching of a communal citizenship have always set America apart in its civic dynamics. The *civis* to the Romans was the citizen, or the greater group of citizens, who formed the *civitas*, which represented the social body of citizens in a specific location or area, united by the fundamental things they held in common: "forum, temples, colonnades, streets, statutes, laws, courts, rights of suffrage, to say nothing of social and friendly circles and diverse business relations with many," as Cicero explains.[36] In their *Civic Mission of Schools,* contemporary American scholars Cynthia Gibson and Peter Levine mirror this older understanding when they identity the public sphere as encompassing the numerous aspects of voluntary associations, religious institutions, and schools in addition to the organs of government.[37] Their public sphere is Tocqueville's American public sphere, over which he so marveled in the nineteenth century. Despite the seeming deemphasis on community through the constitutional emphasis on individual, natural rights, Tocqueville saw that "the free institutions that the inhabitants of the United States possess and the political rights of which they make so much use recall to each citizen constantly and in a thousand ways that he lives in society."[38]

The reigning element in the American idea of citizenship is social, an emphasis on the community aspect of a people united by law, customs, and institutions rather than on the spatial component of physical, geographic enclosure. The differentiation between these two components of a city are maintained in Latin by two different words—*civitas* and *urbs,* the latter denoting the physical city. This subtle but decisive differentiation between the communal and the physical city informs the role that the American citizen as well as the body of American citizens fulfill and, consequently, how they ought to be educated and habituated in their rights and duties.

NOTES

I thank this volume's editors for their inclusion of this chapter about civics education; my colleague and director of the Program on American Citizenship at the American Enterprise Institute, Gary J. Schmitt, for his helpful comments; and Anthony "Bear" Brown, Christopher Paludi, and most especially Taylor Hetrick, interns with the Program on American Citizenship, for their dedicated research assistance.

Regarding this chapter's title, in *Federalist* 14 James Madison urges his readers:

> Hearken not to the unnatural voice which tells you that the people of America, knit together as they are by so many cords of affection, can no longer live together as members of the same family; can no longer continue the mutual guardians of their mutual happiness; can no longer be fellow-citizens of one great, respectable, and flourishing empire. Hearken not to the voice which petulantly tells you that the form of government recommended for your adoption is a novelty in the political world; that it has never yet had a place in the theories of the wildest projectors; that it rashly attempts what it is impossible to accomplish. No, my countrymen, shut your ears against this unhallowed language. Shut your hearts against the poison which it conveys; the kindred blood which flows in the veins of American citizens, the mingled blood which they have shed in defense of their sacred rights, consecrate their Union and excite horror at the idea of their becoming aliens, rivals, enemies. (Clinton Rossiter, ed., *The Federalist Papers* [New York: Signet Classic, 2003], 99)

1. Jay Mathews, "Will Better Civic Education Lead to a Better America? Don't Count on It," *Washington Post*, March 4, 2018.

2. Mathews looks backward to a 1917 U.S. history test of 1,500 students in Texas that yielded "only 33 percent correct answers in high school and 49 percent in universities" to prove his point that it is nostalgia to think that schools used to teach social studies better than they currently do, or that formal civic knowledge made a demonstrable difference that proves that we are somehow in unique democratic jeopardy today.

3. A phrase John Dewey used to describe his belief that those who hold that human beings have certain natural rights and liberties believe in a myth, not an accurate depiction of reality. John Dewey, *Liberalism and Social Action* (Amherst, NY: Prometheus Books, 2000 [1935]), 27.

4. I would argue that such is the thrust of the entire *Federalist* 1, "General Introduction," authored by Hamilton, though the first few paragraphs alone signal this project. See *Federalist* 1, 27–31 (all citations of *The Federalist* are to the Rossiter edition noted above).

5. See the first two paragraphs of the Declaration of Independence in particular for the notion of the purpose of government being limited to the preservation of individual rights, and the Declaration as a whole for the argument that, despite being freely equal individuals, once they are entered into a political union their individual concern must include a care for the public good of the community at large.

6. Thomas Jefferson, "To Roger C. Weightman," June 24, 1826, in *The Works of Thomas Jefferson*, "Federal Edition," Vol. 10, ed. Paul Leicester Ford (New York: G. P. Putnam's Sons, 1904–5), 390–92.

7. The Declaration of Independence ends on this note: "And for the support of this Declaration, with a firm reliance on the protection of divine Providence, we mutually pledge to each other our Lives, our Fortunes and our sacred Honor."

8. See John Fonte, "Is the Purpose of Civic Education to Transmit or Transform the American Regime?," in *Civic Education and Culture*, ed. Bradley C .S. Watson (Wilmington, DE: ISI Books, 2005), 95–97.

9. James Madison, *Federalist* 55, 343.

10. James Madison, *Federalist* 10, 73, 77.

11. James Madison, *Federalist* 10, 73.

12. Preamble, U.S. Constitution.

13. Robert A. Rutland et al., eds., *The Papers of James Madison* (Chicago: University of Chicago Press, 1962–91), 14:170. See also Colleen A. Sheehan, "The Politics of Public Opinion: James Madison's 'Notes on Government,'" *William and Mary Quarterly* 49, no. 4 (1992): 609–27, www.jstor.org/stable /2947174.

14. James Madison, *Federalist* 14, 99.

15. James Madison, *Federalist* 14, 99.

16. Marvin Meyers, ed., *The Mind of the Founder: Sources of the Political Thought of James Madison* (Indianapolis: Bobbs-Merrill, 1973), 336. See also Colleen A. Sheehan, "The Commerce of Ideas and the Cultivation of Character in Madison's Republic," in Watson, *Civic Education and Culture*, 49–71.

17. As quoted in Sheehan, "Commerce of Ideas," 60.

18. George Washington, "Farewell Address, 1796," in *The Founders' Constitution*, ed. Philip B. Kurland and Ralph Lerner (Chicago: University of Chicago Press, 1987), vol. 1, chap. 18, doc. 29, http://presspubs.uchicago.edu /founders/documents/v1ch18s29.html.

19. "Northwest Ordinance of 1787, Article III," in *Founders' Constitution*, vol. 1, chap. 1, doc. 8, http://press-pubs.uchicago.edu/founders/documents /v1ch1s8.html.

20. Benjamin Justice, "'The Great Contest': The American Philosophical Society Education Prize of 1795 and the Problem of American Education," *American Journal of Education* 114 (February 2008): 191–213.

21. Benjamin Justice, ed., *The Founding Fathers, Education, and "The Great Contest": The American Philosophical Society Prize of 1797* (New York: Palgrave Macmillan, 2013), 216, cf. 232.

22. Justice, "Great Contest."

23. James W. Ceasar, "The Role of Political Science and Political Scientists in Civic Education, *American Enterprise Institute*, August 8, 2013.

24. Johann N. Neem, *Democracy's Schools: The Rise of Public Education in America* (Baltimore: Johns Hopkins University Press, 2017), 1–4.

25. Thomas G. West, *The Political Theory of the American Founding: Natural Rights, Public Policy, and the Moral Conditions of Freedom* (Cambridge: Cambridge University Press, 2017), 192–201.

26. Constitution of New Hampshire, 1789, pt. 2.

27. Jean Yarbrough, "The Constitution and Character: The Missing Critical Principle?," in *To Form a More Perfect Union: The Critical Ideas of the Constitution*, ed. Herman Belz, Ronald Hoffman, and Peter J. Albert (Charlottesville: University Press of Virginia, 1992), 237.

28. Lorraine Smith Pangle and Thomas L. Pangle, *The Learning of Liberty: The Educational Ideas of the American Founders* (Lawrence: University Press of Kansas, 1993), 96.

29. George Washington, State of the Union Address, January 8, 1790. www .mountvernon.org/education/primary-sources/state-of-the-union-address.

30. George Washington, *The Writings of George Washington*, ed. John Fitzpatrick (Washington, DC: Government Printing Office, 1931–44), vol. 35, 316–17.

31. Neem, *Democracy's Schools*, 9–11.

32. "James Madison to W. T. Barry," in *Founders' Constitution*, vol. 1, chap. 18, doc. 35, http://presspubs.uchicago.edu/founders/documents/v1ch18s35.html.

33. See Galston, *Liberal Purposes*; and Ceaser, "Role of Political Science."

34. Thomas Jefferson et al., "Report of the Commissioners Appointed to Fix the Site of the University of Virginia," in *Founders' Constitution*, vol. 1, chap. 18, doc. 33, http://press-pubs.uchicago.edu/founders/documents/v1ch18s33.html.

35. As quoted in Fonte, "Is the Purpose of Civic Education," 96–97.

36. Cicero, *De Officiis*, trans. Walter Miller (Cambridge, MA: Harvard University Press, 1913), bk. I, sec. 53, www.constitution.org/rom/de_officiis.htm.

37. Cynthia Gibson et al., *The Civic Mission of Schools*, Center for Information and Research on Civic Learning and Engagement, 2003, www .civicyouth.org/special-report-the-civic-mission-of-schools.

38. Alexis de Tocqueville, *Democracy in America*, trans., ed. Harvey C. Mansfield and Delba Winthrop (Chicago: University of Chicago Press, 2000), 488.

3

Identity and the Practice of American Citizenship

From Transcendentalists to Identitarians

Steven F. Pittz

The character of citizenship in American politics has long been contested. What it means to be an American citizen is not strict or precise, outside of the liberal rights that we all share. We all have rights, but that tells us little about how we view our role as citizens. Two central questions about citizenship are how it ties into identity, and how far the obligations of political citizenship extend. The juxtaposition of two distinct modes of practical American politics—the politics of detachment of the transcendentalists, and the politics of recognition of contemporary identitarians—sheds some light on these questions. Though it is commonplace to speak about American political citizenship in terms of liberalism, republicanism, communitarianism, and the like, I jettison these "-isms" with a view toward the lived experience of the two modes of politics mentioned above. In a similar vein, I bracket questions of justice and morality surrounding these modes of politics to focus more sharply on the practical effects of their adoption.[1] In other words, how does the practice of these modes of politics affect citizenship? What lessons about practical citizenship can they teach us?

Our two central concerns, about identity and the proper role of citizenship, are addressed by answering the following questions: How much of our lived experience ought to be decided, determined, or discussed in the political arena? What do we owe our fellow citizens politically, and what are the reasonable political demands our fellow citizens can make on us? How might we view the distinction between what is public and what is private? Our two modes of politics help us achieve a more concrete sense of what these questions entail and a better vantage point from which to discuss them. The modes of political detachment and political recognition represent extremes of practical politics. Indeed, the former seeks to minimize politics as much as possible, whereas the latter expands the range of issues dealt with politically to a degree that blurs the line between public and private. Naturally, the majority of citizens practice a mode of politics somewhere within these extremes, but the presentation of these two modes clarifies what is at stake as we think about our practice of politics. The nature of each of these modes of politics becomes clearer as we proceed.

A POLITICS OF RECOGNITION

The first mode of politics under our microscope is the politics of recognition.[2] As we explore this mode, we focus on the political practice itself, without diving too deeply into its theoretical foundations. The politics of recognition is connected to what is more commonly referred to as identity politics. Identity politics refers broadly to the political struggles of various groups. These struggles are over recognition and identity and are becoming more and more prevalent in multicultural societies. They are, for the members of these groups, more central than party politics. Struggles over recognition have replaced struggles over rights as time has passed. The goals of identity groups, from ethnic groups to feminists, have largely been consistent with the goals of the civil rights movement in the mid-twentieth century. The concern was to extend basic liberal rights to all members of society. But the goals of identity groups have begun to change, a change that coincides with what is often called the "second wave" of feminism. The goal is no longer to claim rights but to gain "recognition." It is important to understand what this means, and how it shapes these groups'—and the individual group members'—approach to politics.

The notion of recognition can be traced to Charles Taylor's influential 1992 essay "Multiculturalism and the Politics of Recognition":

The demand for recognition . . . is given urgency by the supposed links between recognition and identity, where this latter term designates something like a person's understanding of who they are, of their fundamental defining characteristics as a human being. The thesis is that our identity is partly shaped by recognition or its absence, often by the *mis*recognition of others, and so a person or group of people can suffer real damage, real distortion, if the people or society around them mirror back to them a confining or demeaning or contemptible picture of themselves. Nonrecognition or misrecognition can inflict harm, can be a form of oppression, imprisoning someone in a false, distorted, and reduced mode of being.[3]

Here we observe both the connection between recognition and identity and the role that others play in shaping identity. Identity and recognition are, to be sure, political matters. Taylor continues to say: "Within these perspectives, misrecognition shows not just a lack of due respect. It can inflict a grievous wound, saddling its victims with a crippling self-hatred. Due recognition is not just a courtesy we owe people. It is a vital human need."[4] Indeed, identity and recognition are *determined* politically; they are not subjective concepts arrived at through introspection but intersubjective concepts developed through interaction with others in society. It follows, therefore, that there is a *political obligation* to recognize others properly, because identity is formed in relation to others; it is the result of intersubjective relations. Speaking of minority identities, Abdul JanMohamed and David Lloyd write that such identities are "not a question of essence . . . but a question of position: a subject-position that in the final analysis can be defined only in political terms."[5] In other words, where a group is positioned in the political hierarchy plays a large role in the identities of the subjects of that group.

Moreover, such political identities are inescapable; they will be determined either by the members of the group or by society at large. As Ramon Saldivar remarks, "We would do well to seek to name those identities. If we do not, others will undoubtedly do it for us."[6] Recognition of identity is not a simple matter of categorizing individuals into groups. Identities are not fixed categories at all but rather social constructions. We are who we are in relation to others; our identity is a result of social interactions. Furthermore, our identity is shaped by recognition, or by a lack of it. If others do not recognize us as we are, or misrecognize us, we can suffer real damage. Ignoring identity, or getting it wrong, is not just disrespect-ful; it can cause real harm to its victims as they develop a negative self-image that is not of their choosing. Nonrecognition or misrecog-nition are forms of oppression, and oppressed groups have a right to *demand* they be recognized properly. Citizenship, then, requires engagement in dialogues, entering into mutual negotiations with others in the hope of achieving reciprocal recognition. These dia-logues are inevitable in a multicultural age, according to James Tully: "When the multicultural and multi-national citizens of con-temporary societies participate in the institutions and practices . . . they have two choices. They can either assimilate to the prevailing unjust relations of mis-recognition imposed on them or they can call them into question and attempt to initiate their renegotiation with whose who support them. The resulting clash is the politics of identity or 'struggles over recognition.'"[7]

Citizenship in the body politic becomes a meeting ground for different groups struggling for proper recognition, and the practice of politics becomes engaging in dialogue and negotiation about rec-ognition. More must be said about what this practice involves, but first we need a sense of who and what drive this mode of politics. As Tully observes:

> The forms of recognition and accommodation sought are as various as the struggles. Feminists, gays, and lesbians demand formal and substantive equality and equal respect for their identity-related differences, in opposition to dominant patriar-chal and heterosexist norms of private and public conduct. Minorities seek different forms of public recognition, represen-tation and protection of their languages, cultures, ethnicities and religions. Immigrants and refugees struggle not only for the rights of citizenship but also for freedom from assimilation to a dominant culture and language; for culturally sensitive modes of integration.[8]

The particular goals of identity groups vary, yet all converge around the general goal of recognition.

Identity groups demand recognition, and these demands can come at different institutional levels. Tully summarizes three com-mon types of demands accordingly: A first type of demand is for "cultural diversity," seeking mutual recognition in the cultural sphere. A second is for multicultural and multiethnic citizenship, which allows individuals to participate in public institutions without fear of misrecognition, that is, to participate in ways that affirm their diverse identities. Finally, there are demands for multinational constitutional associations, which are in effect demands for political autonomy and signify strong resistance to assimilation into the broader society.[9] Clearly, the nature and weight of these demands vary widely, but all share the theme of recognition.

How do these various struggles over recognition affect the role of the citizen? Dialogue and negotiation are the key activities mentioned, hence, the general method is quite simple:

> What are the procedures by which the people, in conjunction with their legal and political institutions, negotiate and reach agreements over disputed identities? The widely proposed answer is through the exchange of reasons *pro* and *contra*. The basic idea is that an identity will be worthy of recognition and respect just insofar as it can be made good to, or find widespread support among, those affected through the fair exchange of reasons.[10]

This sounds fair and simple enough, but unsurprisingly the devil is in the details. Engaging in this "fair exchange of reasons" requires a couple of things of citizens. First, to be citizens they must agree to shun any identities that "are incompatible with respect for others"; no identities that are resistant to the requirements of public reason, that are deemed unreasonable and unacceptable by the majority of citizens, are allowed.[11] Second, and more important for the argument here, all citizens have a political obligation to engage in dialogue, all have "a duty to listen."[12] Citizens can be compelled to engage in dialogue, because if they do not they are likely to cause oppression through misrecognition.

DEMANDING CITIZENSHIP

From a practical perspective, the political obligations placed on citizens by the politics of recognition become quite substantial. Proponents of this mode of politics are not unaware of this, and in fact political mobilization and increased political engagement are major and explicit components of identity politics. Renato Rosaldo claims that the key feature of identity politics is the participation in new social movements. "The proximate origins of the new social movements and their processes of change often have to do with consciousness-raising. Processes of consciousness-raising began with the feminist movement. In consciousness-raising sessions participants told stories from their lives about hurts and wounds they had suffered." The practitioners of identity politics must raise the consciousness of others in society, and those others have a duty to listen to their message. Moreover, the line between public and private is blurred, as personal stories which might be considered by some to be private are used to inform the negotiation over recognition. The personal details of all citizens are now part of the political process of negotiation. As Rosaldo remarks, "In this sense, feminists have come to say that the personal is political." Indeed, the realm of the political expands greatly when questions of identity enter into it.[13]

Not only does the range of political issues expand, the knowledge that each citizen must have of "the other" increases dramatically as well. This increase is due to the requirements of the negotiations or dialogues surrounding recognition, so we would do well to look at such negotiations more closely. We receive some guidance from Charles Taylor, who formulated loose guidelines for successful negotiations. First, negotiations must demonstrate "mutual recognition," which stresses the democratic (bottom-up) nature of the talks. All groups in society must mutually participate in the negotiations. Second, the negotiations must be dialogic, not monologic; the understanding of key issues is shared between groups rather than imposed by one. Moreover, there are a few necessary characteristics of a dialogue: it must be critical, without previous prejudices or comprehensive doctrines;[14] it must be oriented not toward agreement but rather toward mutual understanding; and the identities of the participants in the dialogues change as the dialogues proceed. Third and finally, successful negotiations lead to a "fusion of horizons." A fusion has occurred when we reach a shared language of reconciliation where everyone feels at home to cooperate and contest. As Taylor puts it: "What has to happen is what Gadamer has called a 'fusion of horizons.' We learn to move in a broader horizon, within which what we have formerly taken for granted as the background to valuation can be situated as one possibility

alongside the different background of the formerly unfamiliar culture. The 'fusion of horizons' operates through our developing
new vocabularies of comparison, by means of which we can articulate these contrasts."[15] In other words, we come to understand the
"background to valuation" of other, formerly unfamiliar cultures
and are thereby able to develop a new vocabulary through which
we can articulate and compare our differences.

The possibility of a fusion of horizons requires a great deal of
knowledge about the other, not to mention a great deal of knowledge about oneself. It is not enough to have a superficial awareness
of another culture's foundations; we must understand their "background to valuations." Unfortunately, Taylor has nothing else to say
about a "background to valuations" in this essay on political recognition. He does, however, discuss the "background" often in his 2007
book *A Secular Age.* It is here that we discover the background as
the context or framework for all of our knowledge about the world.
Again, it is best to quote Taylor: "That's the very nature of what
contemporary philosophers have described as the 'background.' It
is in fact that largely unstructured and inarticulate understanding
of our whole situation, within which particular features of our world
show up for us in the sense they have."[16] At first glance, we see that
the "background" of our knowledge is not a narrow or limited concept at all but the broadest possible framework within which we
come to knowledge about the world. This first formulation is also
quite abstract, so another quote from Taylor might help us make
more sense of it:

> This emerges as soon as we take account of the fact that all
> beliefs are held within a context or framework of the taken-for-
> granted, which usually remains tacit, and may even be as yet
> unacknowledged by the agent, because never formulated. This
> is what philosophers, influenced by Wittgenstein, Heidegger or
> Polanyi, have called the 'background.' As Wittgenstein points
> out, my research into rock formations takes as granted that the
> world didn't start five minutes ago, complete with all the fos-
> sils and striations, but it would never occur to me to formulate
> and acknowledge this, until some crazed philosophers, obses-
> sively riding their epistemological hobby-horses, put the prop-
> osition to me. But now perhaps I have caught the bug, and I
> can no longer be naively into my research, but now take account

of what I have been leaning on, perhaps entertain the possibility that it might be wrong. This breach of naivete is often the
path to fuller understanding.[17]

We see in this quote that the background consists of the things we
take for granted and the naivete that results from taking these things
for granted. As we "breach" our naivete and begin to question the
background, we embark on a path to fuller understanding.

How might this idea of the background contribute to our social
or political understanding? In the social or political context, Taylor
refers to the background as the "social imaginary." He defines it
accordingly: "The social imaginary consists of the generally shared
background understandings of society, which make it possible for
it to function as it does. It is 'social' in two ways: in that it is generally shared, and in that it is about society."[18] Hence, there is a background for our social knowledge, and this background is shared by
members of society. We can now begin to address what Taylor is
after when he talks about negotiations over recognition leading to
a fusion of horizons, where we understand the "background to valuation" of other cultures or identity groups. To properly recognize
the other, we must be able truly to walk in their shoes, to experience the background to their knowledge or understanding about
the world. What they take for granted in their worldviews must be
made explicit and then known by us, and vice versa, if we are to
properly recognize each other. This seems a tall order, indeed, as
the amount and depth of knowledge required for recognition is substantial. Patchen Markell comes to just such a conclusion: "Unlike
toleration, which can be grudging, and is consistent with utter ignorance about the people to whom it is extended, recognition involves
respecting people precisely in virtue of, not despite, who they are;
and so proper relations of recognition must be founded on accurate
mutual knowledge among the people and groups involved."[19]

Taylor suggests that we achieve such knowledge through "comparative cultural study." This answer is sensible and predictable but
also highly impractical. Unsurprisingly, Taylor does not address the
practical effects of such an agenda at all, choosing instead to focus
on the moral issue:

There is perhaps after all a moral issue here. We only need a
sense of our own limited part in the whole human story to

accept the presumption [that other cultures have great worth].
It is only arrogance, or some analogous moral failing, that can
deprive us of this. But what the presumption requires of us is
not peremptory and inauthentic judgments of equal value, but
a willingness to be open to comparative cultural study of the
kind that must displace our horizons in the resulting fusions.
What it requires above all is an admission that we are very far
away from that ultimate horizon from which the relative worth
of different cultures might be evident.[20]

Although we may agree with Taylor that there is a moral issue
at play, and that we certainly have both things to learn from other
cultures and good reasons to make an attempt to recognize them,
we may also wish to question the demands that recognition places
on citizens. If we evaluate political recognition from a practical perspective, two related conclusions come to the fore. First, the necessary knowledge of the background—both of oneself and of the
other—required for a fusion of horizons appears implausible, if not
impossible, for the majority of citizens. Second, successful efforts
of recognition appear unlikely for any citizens who are not part of
the cultural elite.

The first conclusion might be illuminated by an example, and
in the spirit of identity politics I use an autobiographical account. I
grew up in Colorado Springs but spent extended periods of time
living in Chicago, Austin, and several other cities in Colorado. I also
had the great fortune to live abroad on two occasions, for nearly a
year in Spain and a few months in Guatemala and Honduras,
becoming proficient in the Spanish language. In addition, I have
spent over a decade studying in universities, as an undergraduate
and graduate student, much of which could be considered "comparative cultural study." What is my framework of knowledge, my
"background to valuation," and do I know enough about the back-
grounds of others? Despite these great privileges, I cannot confidently claim sufficient knowledge on either count. For example,
Spaniards routinely make me aware of my ignorance of regional and
local traditions throughout Spain. I may have an adequate grasp of
the cultural, historical, and political differences between Madrid
and Barcelona, but the numerous differences found between or
within regions (say, for instance, between the Basque country and
Catalonia, or between Bilbao and San Sebastian within the Basque

country) are well outside my understanding. It can take many years to peel away the layers that underlie these important differences, and it requires repeated interactions with locals to engage in this knowledge gathering, as well.

As Taylor himself observes, we are often blind to our own background, merely taking it for granted until someone or something forces open our eyes. My study of other cultures, specifically Spanish, and languages has not prepared me to identify adequately the background of Spaniards either. To be sure, it provides a foundation for learning that could be further built through further study and through listening to others. Nevertheless, I do not believe it constitutes the mutual understanding necessary for a fusion of horizons. Thus, I may not be prepared to engage fruitfully in a dialogue or negotiation over recognition. If I do engage, I suspect the process of familiarization will be lengthy—a process that involves several iterations of intimate interaction. I may or may not be able to engage in this way.

The second conclusion follows from the first. To the extent that anyone has done the necessary comparative cultural study required for a fusion of horizons, it is bound to be someone with great resources for both leisure and, most likely, travel. Moreover, it must be someone with great resources who also sees the value in and chooses comparative cultural study. The inventor who chooses to devote the majority of her time to scientific research, the botanist who studies nature, and the artist who diligently studies the human form do not use their leisure in a way that promotes the politics of recognition. Thus, even the small number of persons with the resources to engage in comparative cultural study is decreased by those who choose other pursuits. Ultimately, the practical effects of a politics of recognition may naturally lead to greater and greater disenfranchisement of the citizenry, with the only true practitioners of this mode being a small elite. It should go without saying that the vast majority of the working class, occupied as they are with economic and material concerns, are unlikely to engage in any serious comparative cultural study, let alone the amount required for a genuine fusion of horizons. Due to these inescapable conditions, more and more responsibility would be given to the elite to engage in negotiations over recognition, leaving the greater part of the body politic on the outside looking in. We may witness the disenfranchisement of a very large number of citizens.

These insights may seem obvious, even banal, but they are important if we are thinking seriously about the role of the citizen in both theory and practice. Recognition may be a noble goal, but it also may be a fool's errand, particularly in the domain of practice. A wide-reaching political program of recognition—one that in effect changes what it means to be a democratic citizen—ought to be practically achievable if we are to consider adopting it.

A POLITICS OF DETACHMENT

A second mode of politics, and alternative conception of citizenship, comes to us through the American transcendentalist movement. We find here what we may call a "politics of detachment," a mode of politics characterized by a deliberately chosen distance from politics. This mode represents the other practical extreme, we might say, in that what drives it is a desire to shrink or minimize the role of politics in one's life. This includes the role of politics in shaping one's identity. Robert Galbreath first presented a politics of detachment, looking at how individuals carved a space for themselves outside of politics while working toward inner freedom.[21] The idea, according to Galbreath, is to improve society by focusing inward. Individual liberation is the goal, and this is not achieved by constructing a political platform aimed at macro-liberation on a societal scale. Instead, as Galbreath explains, it requires *inner* transformation aimed at individual self-realization. Naturally, political detachment assumes that great questions of an individual's life, including those of identity and finding one's place in society, are private matters. Yet they are not private merely in the sense that they are "nobody's business," but rather in the sense that struggling with life's great questions *requires* a well-developed inner life, a life of independence and introspection. The individual separates from the group, in this mode, not because he has lost his way but because he seeks to find his own way through such important issues.

Political detachment is represented in American political thought by Ralph Waldo Emerson and Henry David Thoreau. Emerson brought to us the principles of transcendentalism; the younger Thoreau endeavored as much as possible to live the very same principles. According to Brian Paul Frost:

Emerson and Thoreau merit a place together in American political thought for several reasons. First, while Emerson was the philosophical spokesman for what became known as American transcendentalism, Thoreau most famously attempted to put its principles into practice. Second, both men shared a reverential attitude toward nature; a belief that a divine spirit animated all creation; and that each individual was part of a greater whole or oneness. Third, both men were staunch individualists who saw the individual as the sole source of moral authority and worth, and they encouraged creative self-expression, spontaneous action, and hearkening to one's inner voice or intuition. And finally, fourth, Thoreau is one of the most noted expositors of civil disobedience to unjust government, and many of his views are shared by Emerson.[22]

Emerson and Thoreau were engaged in politics, but their politics were founded on the idea that individuals needed to be free from politics in order to flourish. In fact, individuals need distance from politics in order create their own identities. Both thinkers held one's inner life as paramount; they "kept to the sidelines politically and argued that genuine political regeneration could only come through individual spiritual renewal."[23]

Prima facie, political detachment is paradoxical. How can one be political while deliberately detaching from politics? Galbreath, using German-Swiss author Hermann Hesse as his exemplar, explains that "he is truly unpolitical only from a perspective which insists on defining politics in terms of party organization, voting behavior, and legislative activity." Galbreath shows that, despite avoiding such political activity, Hesse retained an important political philosophy and engaged in larger battles over enduring ideas and values. To do so, Hesse needed to detach from politics, meaning he chose "a distancing effect which is intensely personal, a withdrawal from the frantic pursuit of chimerical external solutions so that a calming of the self may ensue."[24]

By focusing inward and improving oneself, an individual can likewise improve society. In other words, inner transformation can result in societal change over time, little by little, individual by individual. For transcendentalists, the formation of identity is an individual, private affair. Cultivating one's inner life, and thereby forming one's character, is the primary method through which we come to have an identity. Politics is seen as a threat to the formation of identity, not as the means to it, as identitarians believe. But this does not mean that one must simply shun all political practice. Citizens may create distance from politics and widen the separation between public and private life, but this detachment provides political benefits in the long run. As well, politically detached citizens may still engage in the battle over ideas and values, in the activity of determining the foundations of a political society. Starting with Emerson, let us get a sense of how the transcendentalists sought inner transformation and how this affected their view of citizenship.

Naturally, Emerson's notion of self-reliance has many similarities with inner transformation and political detachment. Before we discuss self-reliance, however, let us first briefly address Emerson's moral, epistemological, and spiritual beliefs, which together constitute his inner life. Mary Oliver found that "the greater energies of his life found their sustenance in the richness and steadfastness of his inner life." The inner life determines our perceptions and identities, which vary from individual to individual. In "Self-Reliance," Emerson claims that "no law can be sacred to me but that of my nature. Good and bad are but names very readily transferable to that or this; the only right is what is after my constitution; the only wrong what is against it." This should not be read, however, as a simple endorsement of moral relativism. As Emerson tells us in the essay "Character," "a healthy soul stands united with the Just and the True, as the magnet arranges itself with the pole. . . . he is thus the medium of the highest influence to all who are not on the same level. Thus men of character are the conscience of the society to which they belong."[25]

In "Montaigne; or, the Skeptic" in *Representative Men*, Emerson discusses the good and ill of skepticism and presents a type of skepticism that is positive and healthy. "But though we are natural conservers and causationists, and reject a sour, dumpish unbelief, the skeptical class, which Montaigne represents, have reason, and every man, at some time, belongs to it. Every superior mind will pass through this domain of equilibration." The aim of the healthy skeptic is not to doubt everything ("a sour, dumpish unbelief"). Instead, "this then is the right ground of the skeptic,—this of consideration, of self-containing; not at all of unbelief; not at all of universal denying, nor of universal doubting,—doubting even that he doubts;

least of all of scoffing and profligate jeering at all that is stable and good." The healthy skeptic is experimental; he seeks to discover things for himself: "If there is not ground for a candid thinker to make up his mind, yea or nay,—why not suspend the judgment? I weary of these dogmatizers. I tire of these hacks of routine, who deny the dogmas. I neither affirm nor deny. I stand here to try the case." Emerson's hope is that individuals will probe their own inner world and come to their own knowledge. And this quest includes a look within themselves to discover moral laws, along with consideration of their genuine, individualized identities.[26]

A "transcendental citizen" requires, therefore, distance from others—from society and politics—if she is to cultivate her inner life and begin to understand herself and the moral world. A mode of political detachment provides the space necessary for self-reliance and self-discovery. Emerson intimates this requirement in some pertinent passages from his essay "The Transcendentalist": These individuals "are lonely; the spirit of their writing and conversation is lonely; they repel influences; they shun general society. . . . Society, to be sure, does not like this very well; it saith, Whoso goes to walk alone, accuses the whole world; he declares all to be unfit to be his companions; it is very uncivil, nay, insulting; Society will retaliate." Emerson is not unaware of the challenges that detachment from society will foist on those who choose it. Society will retaliate against such behavior, but Emerson urges us to ignore the resentment or social costs that detachment brings: "These persons are not by nature melancholy, sour, and unsocial—they are not stockish or brute—but joyous, susceptible, affectionate." Transcendentalists have good reasons—namely the protection of their inner life—for separation from society; they do not reject conformity for reasons of insecurity or social anxiety. Put simply, they do not consider themselves *outcasts*; rather, they choose to be *outsiders*. Consider this passage from "The American Scholar": "Is it not the chief disgrace in the world, not to be a unit;—not to be reckoned one character;—not to yield that peculiar fruit which each man was created to bear, but to be reckoned in the gross, in the hundred, or the thousand, of the party, the section, to which we belong." A transcendentalist seeks to avoid this disgrace and shuns society because it cannot provide answers to life's great questions and cannot form one's character or identity; only the self-reliance and self-discovery of a profound inner life can.[27]

Identity is a personal, private matter for the transcendentalists. Not only is one's identity separate from one's role in political society, Emerson suggests the effects of politics and society are pernicious. In "Self-Reliance" he identifies societies' supreme principal virtue: conformity: "Society everywhere is in conspiracy against the manhood of every one of its members. Society is a joint-stock company, in which the members agree, for the better security of his bread to each shareholder, to surrender the liberty and culture of the eater. The virtue in most request is conformity. Self-Reliance is its aversion."[28] For Emerson, the mode of political recognition would not be the arena of identity formation but of turning individuals into members of the herd. This holds true whether the herd is large or small, so to speak, whether we conform to our nation, profession, tribe, or some other group. Alex Zakaras explains Emerson's position accordingly: "People are no less conformist when they adhere unreflectively to the demands of their various subcultures, nor even when their lives are steady rehearsals of conventionalisms drawn haphazardly from families, peer groups, professions, churches, nations, and ethnic norms. . . . Though the pressure to conform may be more intense in highly homogeneous and coherent cultures, conformity as Emerson understands it will exist wherever there are groups."[29] Hence, rather than a "duty to listen," Emerson places a very different sort of requirement on the individual: "Whoso would be a man, must be a nonconformist."[30] Achieving self-reliance—true independence of mind and action—requires nonconformity, or detachment from society.

The mode of detachment does not require solitude. True independence of spirit—self-reliance in Emerson's terms—can be found even in the midst of modern society. Indeed, some scholars maintain that modern mass democracy needs the independence of spirit, or "individuality," that Emerson advocates and develops. Self-reliance is a guard against the docility that comes with the democratic pressures to conform.[31] Yet, although maintaining spiritual freedom while living in society is the real challenge, shunning society is relatively easy: "It is easy in the world to live after the world's opinion; it is easy in solitude to live after our own; but the great man is he who in the midst of the crowd keeps with perfect sweetness the independence of solitude." Political detachment, then, is not isolation but the practice of inner freedom within the structure of society. It is necessary for the positive growth of the individual, which in turn improves society. Emerson avers, "but your isolation must not be mechanical, but spiritual, that is, must be elevation."[32]

Emerson wrote prodigiously on these themes, but Thoreau took them a step further in his attempts to live like a transcendentalist. In a sense, Thoreau was a more practical man than the idealist Emerson, and he therefore represents well the practical mode of detachment. Thoreau's "life experiment" at Walden Pond (on land owned, in fact, by Emerson's family) placed him outside of society and civilization for over two years. Let us return to Frost for a sense of what Thoreau was after: "Thoreau went to Walden Pond in order to live the good life as he understood it—a life of independence, leisure, and personal self-enlightenment."[33] Thoreau was always concerned, first and foremost, with individual independence. He viewed morals, ideas, identity, and practice as endeavors pertaining to individuals alone. Moreover, he saw the encroachment of society on these properly individual endeavors coming from many angles. In 1863 the *Atlantic Monthly* published Thoreau's essay "Life without Principle" posthumously. He begins the essay by observing (or better put, complaining) that a lecturer he went to see had none of his own thoughts—or ideas that were intimate, important, and private—but instead resorted to parroting the conventional wisdom of the time. He further laments how hectic civilized life has become, concluding, "I think there is nothing, not even crime, more opposed to poetry, to philosophy, ay, to life itself, than this incessant business."[34] What Thoreau values, instead, is self-reliance, independence of mind, introspection, and the pursuit of poetry and philosophy. The incessant business of bourgeois society works consistently against such values.

Neither is Thoreau coy about the value, or lack thereof, of constant participation in society and politics: "I often perceive how near I had come to admitting into my mind the details of some trivial affair,—the news of the street; and I am astonished to observe how willing men are to lumber their minds with such rubbish,—to permit idle rumors and incidents of the most insignificant kind to intrude on ground which should be sacred to thought." Public opinion ought to be treated with caution, perhaps even contempt: "Whenever a man separates from the multitude, and goes his own way in this mood, there indeed is a fork in the road. . . . His solitary path across-lots will turn out the *higher way* of the two." Thoreau was keenly aware of the negative effects that political engagement could have on one's inner life. "If I am to be a thoroughfare, I prefer that it be of the mountain-brooks, the Parnassian streams, and not the town-sewers. . . . I believe that the mind can be permanently profaned by the habit of attending to trivial things, so that all our thoughts shall be tinged with triviality." Whatsoever we make of Thoreau's apparent contempt for society, we also discover a very real concern: a strong inner life requires political detachment.[35]

Thoreau recognized that one cannot routinely engage with trivial things and expect simultaneously to achieve inner growth, and for him virtually all the activities of politics are trivial things: "What is called politics is comparatively something so superficial and inhuman, that practically I have never fairly recognized that it concerns me at all."[36] Thoreau was clearly cautious about too much engagement with politics, crowding out opportunities for more properly spiritual pursuits, but he also believed there was something lower—that is, tied closely to the material/sensual body, and to interest/power—that drove politics. Consider his famous 1849 essay "Civil Disobedience." We should be cognizant of the manner in which the state attempts to rule: "The State never intentionally confronts a man's sense, intellectual or moral, but only his body, his senses. It is not armed with superior wit or honesty, but with superior physical strength. I was not born to be forced. I will breathe after my own fashion." Put differently, the state aims its efforts at our corporal needs, not our intellectual virtues or spiritual life.

For Thoreau, however, the inner, spiritual life of the individual is paramount. Unsurprisingly, he places the rights and interests of the individual above those of the group. "There will never be a really free and enlightened State until the State comes to recognize the individual as a higher and independent power, from which all its own power and authority are derived, and treats him accordingly."[37] Here we can see the disagreement between transcendentalists and identitarians delineated clearly. The individual—and her inner life and identity—always comes before her membership in groups or her membership in the state. There is no room for political obligations of the sort required by political recognition in the positions of transcendentalists like Thoreau.

MINIMAL BUT ESSENTIAL CITIZENSHIP

That Emerson and Thoreau sought to form their individual identities apart from politics should now be clear, but we do need to understand how and why they did engage in politics. What did citizenship require, in their view? Both found occasions for entry into public life. As in many of our lives, there are times when public affairs beckon, and it is instructive to see just where Emerson and Thoreau became engaged in politics, even through joining political associations. Of particular interest is why and how they became involved in the abolitionist movement. What is remarkable about this involvement is how it illuminates the ambivalence felt by conscientious persons practicing a mode of detachment. Of interest is not only the political actions they took but the manner in which Emerson and Thoreau reasoned about such actions.

Emerson was only a reluctant participant in the politics of abolition, but he eventually emerged as a vocal and influential abolitionist, delivering several public addresses between 1844 and 1862. He entered into the public discourse with his 1844 address "Emancipation in the British West Indies." Emerson had long thought that England should be praised for the progress made against slavery in its colonies, but increasingly he found himself reflecting on the scope of the injustice of slavery in New England.

> Whilst I have meditated in my solitary walks on the magnanimity of the English Bench and Senate, reaching out the benefit of the law to the most helpless citizens in her world-wide realm, I have found myself oppressed by other thoughts. . . . I could not see the great vision of the patriots and senators who have adopted the slaves' cause—they turned their backs on me. No: I see other pictures—of mean men; I see very poor, very ill-clothed, very ignorant men, not surrounded by happy friends—to be plain—poor black men of obscure employment as mariners, cooks or stewards, in ships, yet citizens of this our Commonwealth of Massachusetts—freeborn as we—whom the slave-laws of the states of South Carolina, Georgia and Louisiana have arrested in the vessels in which they visited those ports. . . . This man, these men, I see, and no law to save them.[38]

Emerson begins to become preoccupied with slavery at this time, but it is not until 1850, with the passage of the Fugitive Slave Law, that he places himself firmly at the center of the abolitionist cause. The crucial change, he argues, is that now his own Massachusetts is morally complicit in the institution of slavery. The time had come to fight it directly. In his address "The Fugitive Slave Law," he writes:

> I said I had never in my life up to this time suffered from the Slave Institution. Slavery in Virginia or Carolina was like Slavery in Africa or the Feejees, for me. There was an old fugitive law, but it had become, or was fast becoming, a dead letter, and, by the genius and laws of Massachusetts, inoperative. The new Bill made it operative, required me to hunt slaves, and it found citizens in Massachusetts willing to act as judges and captors. Moreover, it discloses the secret of the new times, that Slavery was no longer mendicant, but was become aggressive and dangerous.[39]

This shift led Emerson to engage more fully in abolitionist politics, including into a friendship with John Brown and to the latter's public defense after Harper's Ferry in 1862.

Clearly, then, Emerson did not reject the demands of citizenship, in this case fighting for the rights of other would-be citizens. Political detachment is not, therefore, tantamount to relinquishing one's membership in society. Public life might call, and in some cases the call should be heeded. Still, Emerson was always reluctant to participate, and when he did make public speeches they nearly always included paeans to self-reliance. We find a representative example in the very first paragraph of "Fugitive Slave Law." While agitating against pro-slavery forces, he still devotes his first remarks to self-reliance and political detachment:

> I do not often speak to public questions—they are odious and hurtful, and it seems like meddling or leaving your work. I have my own spirits in prison—spirits in deeper prisons, whom no man visits if I do not. . . . The one thing not to be forgiven to intellectual persons is, not to know their own task, or to take their ideas from others. From this want of many rest in their

own and rash acceptance of other people's watchwords come the imbecility and fatigue of their conversation. For they cannot affirm these from any original experience, and of course not with the natural movement and total strength of their nature and talent, but only from their memory, only from their cramped position of standing for their teacher. They say what they would have you believe, but what they do not quite know.[40]

He does not begin by condemning the evils of slavery but by admonishing his audience to rely their own intellectual faculties. As we see below, he believes the eloquence and charisma of Daniel Webster—the Massachusetts senator who helped the slave law to pass, and who garnered public support—was the cause of the evil legislation. Instead of thinking for themselves, the citizens of Massachusetts had allowed another to convince them to leave aside their reason and morality. It was not another politician or great thinker that was needed to prevent such calamities but more self-reliance among citizens. George Kateb summarizes Emerson's experience accordingly:

> With the passage of the Fugitive Slave Law of 1850, Emerson embarks on a lengthy episode of agitation for one reform: the containment or abolition of slavery. This spreading of evil—this evil which is truly evil, not only apparently so—forces him to change his attitude on the subject of associating for reform. . . . That profound change is a deviation from his theory of self-reliance, not its transformation. Or, we can say that Emerson accepts the sacrifices of every sort—including the abandonment of aspirations of free persons to self-reliance—which are needed to give all Americans, not just some, the chance for self-reliance. Perhaps a society has no self-reliance anywhere in it if there are slaves anywhere in it.[41]

Kateb rightly explains that Emerson's foray into abolitionist politics was only in one sense a "deviation" from the idea of self-reliance. It was a difficult action to take, and Emerson was ambivalent about it. Yet, in another sense, the action was taken on behalf of self-reliance. All citizens must enjoy the freedom required to achieve self-reliance, and this becomes a moral standard by which

to judge slavery unjust. Citizenship is largely about public engagement *for the sake* of private life, protecting the space and time that
are necessary for inner growth.

We see a similar phenomenon in the experience of Thoreau. Let
us return to Frost, who limns the tension that we also observe in
Thoreau's public life:

> In the final analysis, it is hard not to see a tension in Thoreau's
> position in respect to slavery. On the one hand, he is both hor-
> rified at the practice of slavery and increasingly indignant at
> those who do little or nothing to stop it; on the other hand, he
> cannot bring himself to admit that one has a positive moral duty
> to eliminate this evil. He seems caught between his passion to
> set the world aright and his desire to pursue activities he feels
> are higher than politics.[42]

In the end, the tension here is basic to the idea of political
detachment. Cases will inevitably arise where public action seems
requisite; indeed the action may be predicated on protecting universal freedom in general. Slavery is an affront to the very idea
of freedom and self-reliance, and perhaps no citizen who values
freedom, transcendental or not, can stand by and observe its practice or progress. We see here that some injustices are so extreme as
to compel confrontation and political involvement, but the mode
of political detachment assumes that, in general, the little one citizen can do to sway public opinion is not worth the risk to one's
inner life.

Earlier, we saw that the goal of political recognition seems
implausible for the majority of citizens, but how might we evaluate the plausibility of detachment? Clearly, most do not go to the
extreme of Thoreau, leaving civilized society to live a self-reliant
life in nature. Likewise, most are not as allergic to socialization as
Emerson, protecting inner, spiritual life at all costs. Expecting the
majority of citizens to practice political detachment is foolish. Nevertheless, this mode does not place political obligations on other
citizens, and in this sense it is not impractical to adopt it. Any liberal democratic citizen can detach without obligating others. Moreover, we can imagine citizens detaching to greater or lesser
degrees—adopting a general practice or goal of detachment yet
without the strict adherence of our transcendentalists. We may also

imagine that, if a greater share of citizens adopted the practice of focusing inward and pursuing self-improvement, society would benefit as well.

CONCLUSION

At the outset, we asked three questions in order to analyze the character of American citizenship. First, how much of our lived experience should be decided, determined, or discussed in the political sphere? We may conclude that there is simply a massive difference between a politics of detachment and a politics of recognition in the nature and extent of the demands of citizenship. The freedom, or political space, to explore important life questions—about identity, morality, tradition, spirituality—is much greater in the mode of political detachment. In contrast, a mode of political recognition drastically curtails individuals' freedom to determine such questions on their own. A politics of recognition at once identifies citizens in ways that constrain their freedom to determine such questions; further, it places a great responsibility on citizens to recognize others properly, replete with all the requisite participation in negotiations, comparative cultural study, and the pursuit of a fusion of horizons. Indeed, the burden of recognition may be too great for individuals and peoples and might likely lead to a competitive situation between rights of self-determination; that is, one individual's or group's demand for recognition (for their right to self-determination to be recognized) might conflict with another individual's or group's right to determine themselves.

The second question was this: What do we owe our fellow citizens politically, and what are the reasonable political demands our fellow citizens can make on us? This question is much thornier than the first, and in an important sense we cannot answer it adequately given the structure of this chapter. I chose to set aside, or bracket, questions about the justice of these two modes of politics. This was a deliberate tactic aimed at simplifying our comparison of these two modes and at focusing on their practical effects. Such bracketing does, however, make it impossible to see the issues in their entirety, because questions of justice are intimately connected to both of these political modes, in particular to the politics of recognition. From the perspective of historically marginalized groups, the mode of political recognition is an attempt to remedy historical misrecognition. In other words, the very mode of political recognition is aimed at least partially, if not largely, at rectifying historical injustice. Fighting injustice requires that the political demands placed on other citizens are greater, and these demands can be simultaneously both greater and reasonable. We might recall Martin Luther King's admonishment of the "white moderate" during the civil rights era in his "Letter from a Birmingham Jail." White moderates did not do enough politically to ensure that the rights of African Americans were protected, which in King's view was a primary reason civil disobedience by African Americans was necessary.[43]

Proponents of the politics of recognition believe that they can rightfully place demands on other citizens to correct the record of misrecognition. It is a matter of justice rather than a merely practical mode of politics. Political change is required, and it is reasonable and justified to demand that others work toward it.[44] A second anticipated objection is that the contrasting mode of political detachment reeks of white privilege. Those who can adopt such a mode of politics, like our mostly white and well-to-do transcendentalists (even Thoreau, though not born into wealth, went to Harvard and ran in elite circles), are simply in the privileged position to do so. A politics of recognition is the mode natural to marginalized identities, hence the juxtaposition of the two modes here tells us very little about which is preferable; such a preference would rest almost entirely on one's social position. Again, however, I chose to bracket off such questions in order to make the simpler point about which is preferable, or even possible, in a practical sense. The conclusions here do not account for where one is now and how one got here, but where one would like to go, in the sense of which mode of politics is choice-worthy moving into the future. I contend, quite humbly, that we would all prefer a mode of political detachment if given a genuine choice. As a practical reality, the sheer amount of time and energy required for negotiations over recognition leaves little time for much else, whether that be one's own pursuit of self-knowledge or the choice simply to be engaged in nonpolitical activities such as gardening, art appreciation, or faithfully following a sports team as a means of identity formation. The burden of a political process of recognition is so great as to preclude these alternatives. Even if such time and energy are found, there is still no guarantee that negotiations will result in a genuine fusion of horizons. Moreover, the inevitable dominance of such negotiations by cultural elites renders the political process of recognition sufficiently dubious. The pitfalls of groupthink and elite oppression are not only possible but probable, and it is far too optimistic to hope that "ignorant" commoners would acquiesce to the results of such negotiations in any case. Thus, the politics of recognition comes with the risk of disenfranchisement of a vast majority of citizens.

Our final question designed to test the boundaries of citizenship was about the distinction between what is public and what is private. Where one draws the line between public and private nearly determines what one thinks about the role and scope of citizenship. For contemporary identitarians, the relationship of public to private is indissoluble. American citizenship ought to consist in active and constant public engagement, primarily through dialogues addressing identity and recognition. The slogan "The personal is political" reflects this meshing or blurring of public and private. Unsurprisingly, the demands of citizenship are much greater for identitarians. Exercise and protection of rights are not enough; recognition of identity is also a key part of the political process. Moreover, an individual's inner, spiritual life is, ipso facto, an illusory concern. Questions about identity and meaning are ineluctably public matters, according to identitarians. We can only know ourselves in relation to others, thus detaching for the sake of personal spiritual fulfillment is to have lost one's way.

For the transcendentalists, the relationship of public to private is turned on its head. For them and many others in the nineteenth century, American citizenship revolved around the idea of rights. Exercising one's own rights and protecting the rights of others were the primary concerns of the enlightened and committed citizen. The stakes of engaged citizenship were high, but the practical obligations of citizenship were low. The private sphere was the locus of life; the duties of public engagement called only infrequently. So much the better for the transcendentalist, whose attention could turn toward the cultivation of one's own inner life, one's own identity.

Political recognition and political detachment illuminate the extremes of citizenship. Either we are essentially public beings, or we engage in public life *for the sake of* protecting private life. Any examination of citizenship must take these extremes as parameters, and we should expect most citizens to see their role operating somewhere in between. We may also ask ourselves whether the citizenship proffered by contemporary identitarians is too far afield of traditional American citizenship. Historically, America has protected private life, made evident by both widespread suspicion of government control and praise for private economic and commercial activity. To be sure, other aspects of identity, both religious and ethnic, have played their role in American history. Nevertheless, the history of American citizenship is also a history of downplaying or deemphasizing those aspects of one's identity. Remembering the transcendentalists brings this history back to life.

NOTES

1. Although no evaluation of a mode of politics is complete without due course given to questions of justice, morality, and political "-isms," we are able to gain a clearer view of the practical effects by temporarily leaving them out.

2. Portions of this section and the next, "Demanding Citizenship," also appear in an online essay: Steven Pittz, "The Politics of Identity Is Undone by the Impracticality of Achieving Recognition," *Law and Liberty*, June 6, 2018, www.lawliberty.org/2018/06/06/the-politics-of-identity-is-undone-by-the -impracticality-of-achieving-recognition.

3. Charles Taylor, *Multiculturalism and "The Politics of Recognition,"* ed. Amy Gutmann (Princeton, NJ: Princeton University Press, 1992), 25.

4. Taylor, *Multiculturalism*, 26.

5. Abdul JanMohamed and David Lloyd, eds., *The Nature and Context of Minority Discourse* (New York: Oxford University Press, 1990), 9.

6. Ramon Saldivar, "Américo Paredes and the Transnational Imaginary," in *Identity Politics Reconsidered*, ed. Linda Martin Alcoff, Michael Hames-Garcia, Satya P. Mohanty, and Paula M. L. Moya (New York: Palgrave Macmillan Press, 2006), 150.

7. James Tully, "Identity Politics," in *The Cambridge History of Twentieth-Century Political Thought*, ed. Terence Ball and Richard Bellamy (Cambridge: Cambridge University Press, 2003), 52.

8. Tully, "Identity Politics," 517.

9. Tully, "Identity Politics," 524–25.

10. Tully, "Identity Politics," 529.

11. Tully, "Identity Politics," 531.

12. Tully remarks: "A member (individual or group) of a political association has the right to present demands to modify the forms of recognition of the association, and the others have a duty to listen to and enter into negotiations

if the demand is well supported by those for whom it is presented and if the reasons for it seem plausible." Tully, "Identity Politics," 529.

13. Renato Rosaldo, "Identity Politics: An Ethnography by a Participant," in Alcoff et al., *Identity Politics Reconsidered*, 119.

14. See John Rawls, *A Theory of Justice* (Cambridge, MA: Belknap Press of Harvard University Press, 1971).

15. Taylor, *Multiculturalism*, 67.

16. Charles Taylor, *A Secular Age* (Cambridge, MA: Belknap Press of Harvard University Press, 2007), 173.

17. Taylor, *Secular Age*, 13.

18. Taylor, *Secular Age*, 323.

19. Patchen Markell, *Bound by Recognition* (Princeton, NJ: Princeton University Press, 2003), 40.

20. Taylor, *Multiculturalism*, 73.

21. Robert Galbreath, "Herman Hesse and the Politics of Detachment," *Political Theory* 2, no. 1 (1974).

22. Bryan Paul Frost, "Religion, Nature, and Disobedience in the Thought of Ralph Waldo Emerson and Henry David Thoreau," in *History of American Political Thought*, ed. Bryan Paul Frost and Jeffrey Sikkenga (Lanhan, MD: Lexington Press, 2003), 355.

23. Frost, "Religion, Nature," 355.

24. Galbreath, "Herman Hesse," 64, 66.

25. Ralph Waldo Emerson, *The Essential Writings of Ralph Waldo Emerson*, ed. Brooks Atkinson (New York: Penguin/Random House, 2000), xii, 135, 331.

26. Ralph Waldo Emerson, *Representative Men* (Boston: Phillips, Sampson, 1850), 8.

27. Emerson, *Essential Writings*, 87–88, 59, 134.

28. Emerson, *Essential Writings*, 134.

29. Alex Zakaras, *Individuality and Mass Democracy: Mill, Emerson, and the Burdens of Citizenship* (New York: Oxford University Press, 2009), 44.

30. Emerson quoted in Zakaras, *Individuality*, 44.

31. Zakaras, *Individuality*, esp. chap. 2.

32. Emerson, *Essential Writings*, 136, 145.

33. Frost, "Religion, Nature," 368.

34. Henry David Thoreau, *Walden and Other Writings*, ed. Brooks Atkinson (New York: Random House, 1950), 711.

35. Thoreau, *Walden*, 725, 719, 726. Some scholars would disagree that Thoreau holds society in contempt. For example, *Walden* editor Atkinson claims that

> Thoreau was no misanthrope. He required, as he said, "a broad margin to my life," so that his thoughts might grow freely. His perceptions were so acute, his understanding of men was so penetrating that he was unhappy

in company that misjudged him. A person who was spiritually coarse wounded him grievously. But he was always civil, courteous and kind in his ordinary relationships around town; he had abundant affection for his family and his friends; he was generous with his talents; and in those last ten years of his life, when his private battle with life was won, he overflowed with good will toward good men.

Here we see Thoreau's concern for spiritual freedom over society, but without total solitude. Speaking for myself, I think we also find a tinge of resentment, a bit of contempt for a society that did not fully embrace him. At least, I sense this in Thoreau in a way I do not in Emerson. Yet nothing in the larger argument here rests on the question of whether or not Thoreau was a misanthrope.

36. Thoreau, *Walden*, 730–31.

37. Thoreau, *Walden*, 650–51, 659.

38. Emerson, *Essential Writings*, 767–68.

39. Emerson, *Essential Writings*, 784.

40. Emerson, *Essential Writings*, 779.

41. George Kateb, "Self-Reliance, Politics, and Society," in *A Political Companion to Ralph Waldo Emerson*, ed. Alan M. Levine and Daniel S. Malachuk (Lexington: University Press of Kentucky, 2011), 73.

42. Frost, "Religion, Nature," 372.

43. Martin Luther King Jr., "Letter from a Birmingham Jail," April 16, 1963, African Studies Center, University of Pennsylvania, www.africa.upenn.edu/Articles_Gen/Letter_Birmingham.html.

44. I do think there is a need to distinguish between political change and cultural change when discussing the aim of achieving recognition. Struggles over basic political rights are not the same as calls for recognition in the cultural arena. There are many cultural movements that deal with recognition but do not require large-scale political change, for example, calls for more recognition of African Americans in film, for more women in leadership positions, or for gays in athletics. Until major public policy decisions are made around such issues, it is not clear that these cultural movements are or should be placing *political* burdens on other citizens. The way forward must include a sharp and clear agenda for recognition and clear focus on what truly lies in the domain of political reform rather than cultural reform.

4

The Imposition of Freedom

Tribal Citizenship and the Case of the Cherokee Freedmen

Aaron Kushner

Tribal citizenship is a difficult concept to understand, especially in the United States. Part of this difficulty lies in the differences between American and indigenous political thought. Recent high-profile cases, such as the Cherokee freedmen's struggle for full tribal citizenship rights and Sen. Elizabeth Warren's (D-MA) claims of Cherokee heritage, are especially confusing when viewed solely through an American lens. These cases and others are made clearer by analyzing the idea of exclusive tribal citizenship and how America has played a role in shaping tribal policies.

Scholarship on tribal citizenship tends to emphasize the racial aspect of the issue but has not paid enough attention to how the United States has influenced tribal governments dedicated to exclusive citizenship, like that of the Cherokees. This interaction is important because it illuminates the tensions between liberal and nonliberal political traditions on the issue of citizenship. I add to this discussion by demonstrating that the idea of tribal citizenship among the Cherokees has been shaped by two dynamic processes—a continual struggle against the United States to define and assert national sovereignty over Cherokee affairs, and broader Cherokee efforts to forge, affirm, and maintain a unique cultural identity.

To reveal how the United States' tradition of liberal citizenship has interacted with tribal citizenship, I analyze the case of the Cherokee freedmen. Since 1866 these formerly enslaved peoples and their descendants have challenged the Cherokee Nation legally for admittance into that tribe as full citizens. The conflict is illustrative of larger tensions between American liberalism—the idea of citizenship as inclusive, or open to anyone—and the Cherokee tradition—the idea that citizenship should be exclusive, open to few (Kushner 2020). The principle of American equality dictates that the freedmen and their posterity be granted tribal citizenship. The pushes by U.S. officials to force the Cherokees to admit the freedmen as citizens appears rational from the American point of view.

The Cherokee political tradition, in contrast, posits that the glue holding society together is not consent-based reason but rather kinship and unique cultural experience. The binding ties of family, clan, and tribe are believed to have a greater influence on the good of the community than the logic of inclusive equality. From this perspective, the exclusion of freedmen, many of whom were not blood relatives of the Cherokees, makes intuitive sense. As the Cherokee Nation and United States have clashed over citizenship, the Cherokees have actively resisted U.S. attempts to liberalize their policies, instead favoring their traditional views of the public good.

Although racial tension has played a role in the Cherokees' reluctance to admit their former enslaved peoples into full tribal citizenship, Cherokee citizenship laws were primarily developed out of struggles against the United States over issues of sovereignty and identity. These battles over sovereignty have removed from Cherokees the ability to self-determine many of their own laws. Their desire to preserve and affirm a distinct identity is related. The loss of sovereignty has made it difficult to adhere to traditional customs. The Cherokees have responded by using tools at their disposal to ensure that uniquely Cherokee practices endure. This has in part manifested in the desire to preserve the exclusivity of tribal citizenship for those who adhere to the Cherokee way of life.

The diversity of the United States is grand in scope; America extends its influence over both unincorporated territories, such as Guam, American Samoa, and Puerto Rico, and indigenous nations, such as those of the Cherokees, Creeks, and Seminoles. These governments and their peoples have long been influenced by nonliberal traditions (Bailey 1972; Littlefield 1978; Erman 2018; Kruse 2018). For a fuller picture of citizenship in America, we need to consider how diverse peoples understand citizenship and how their citizenship laws have evolved because of U.S. influence. Exploring how these governments have developed citizenship laws may help shed light on national and state citizenship practices. As America further expands and diversifies, alternate, nonliberal views of citizenship will increase in political relevance. Understanding why certain laws exist and where they came from is crucial to encouraging political engagement and productive discourse.

CHEROKEE CITIZENSHIP

On February 22, 2021, the Cherokee Supreme Court struck out the words "by blood" from the Cherokee constitution where they described the requirements for citizenship and elected office.[1] There are two main implications of this decision: first, descendants of freedmen can run for tribal office; second, the Cherokee Nation adheres to the wishes of U.S. officials, who have repeatedly threatened the removal of federal funding should the Nation not grant freedmen full citizenship privileges. Justice Shawna Baker penned the final order, stating that "the consequences" of retaining such language "could place our nation in peril," since the United States provides 70 percent of the Nation's general operating fund.

U.S. politicians had threatened to rescind funding before. In 2007, Rep. Diane Watson (D-CA) introduced a bill designed to sever U.S. financial ties with the Cherokee Nation unless it regranted full citizenship to the descendants of freedmen. Watson's proposal outlined the development of Cherokee citizenship over time, how Congress viewed that history, and the struggle of the freedmen and their progeny to partake in tribal citizenship.[2] Yet, though the proposed bill implied that racism had fueled the Cherokees' long resistance to admitting their former slaves into full citizenship, racial enmity reveals only part of the story.

Three crucial issues are embedded within the complex reality of Cherokee citizenship. The Cherokee people are simultaneously concerned with the sovereign control of their own identity, the preservation of their sacred cultural practices, and the protection of their practical and financial benefits. These concerns have grown out of the Cherokee political tradition over time, as it has interacted with the United States. These interactions are manifested in struggles over sovereignty and identity. By sovereignty, I mean the government authority of the Cherokees to pass legislation and make executive decisions affecting their people. By identity, I mean the

Cherokees' unique ancestral traditions as fundamental to their culture.

Defining the Cherokee political tradition is challenging. Not only is teasing out uniquely Cherokee political innovations difficult, because of the constant presence of American influence from the nineteenth century on, but many traditional Cherokee mores also defy concrete English definition (Smithers 2015). A recurring theme within Cherokee culture is the idea of "harmony and balance" that exists between all life on earth (Mankiller and Wallis 1993, ix; Awiakta 1993). Family and clan units possessed specific societal roles intended to harmonize life for the community (Littlefield 1978; Stremlau 2011). Cherokee society, as it fused into a single government over time (Conley 2005), was set up in pursuit of the public good, as occurs in a republican form of government. They believed that the public good was best obtained by following the Cherokee "Old Ways"—patterns of living that led Cherokee society toward a state of harmony (Awiakta 1993).

The Cherokee constitutional government, established in the 1820s and modeled after the government outlined by the U.S. Constitution, with a few key differences, was designed to help Cherokees pursue their understanding of the public good (Kushner 2020). Yet, although the new constitutional government was created to facilitate communications with the United States as equals (Ross 1985a, 1985b; Moulton 1985), it was also a reaction to American treatment of Cherokees. Nationally, official American procedure at the founding was to treat native tribes as sovereign entities (Smith 1997, 106, 131). Treaties signed with the indigenous peoples were, however, often founded upon coercion and native concessions. Leaders at both state and national levels habitually regarded Native Americans as inferior conquered peoples—a view Smith contends was derived from "ascriptive" racial biases. Since most native tribes, especially in early America, possessed the power to resist many U.S. policies, the American government left the potential citizenship status of Indians undefined.

Since many Americans feared the cultural gulf between themselves and their indigenous neighbors (and coveted their lands), indigenous peoples were often mocked as savages to justify American expansion. The United States—reflecting popular fear and envy—thus implemented policies that either distanced Americans from the Indian tribes or forced the tribes to conform to American practices (Littlefield 1978; Smith 1997, 106, 109). This sense of fear and envy is echoed in the treatment of indigenous peoples in *The Federalist*, where Indian nations are alternately described as hostile threats (*Federalist* 3, 7, 24, 25) or as trade partners, peoples from whom Americans could benefit (*Federalist* 24, 40, 42). The U.S. Constitution itself acknowledges American Indians as a separate category of persons; many Indians would be treated as outside of the American political community as a result (Smith 1997, 131).

The Cherokees, in reaction to these received messages, retained a view of their own sovereign authority. The Civil War further galvanized feelings of independence among them. Principal Chief John Ross, in his 1861 annual message, spoke of the Cherokee relationship with the United States that would come to an end after a certain Confederate victory (1985b, 492–95). Ross emphasized the precarious situation of the tribe but also the opportunity to secure for themselves a better deal for preserving their lands. While admitting that the Cherokees had been reduced to an inferior position alongside white civilization, Ross maintained a faith in the sacred bonds and institutions uniting his people, giving them strength to endure.

With the Union victory, Ross assumed an official posture of supplication to the victors, in defense of Cherokee autonomy. In an 1866 letter to Andrew Johnson, he expressed the Cherokee need for continued U.S. financial and material support (1985b, 678–80). Cherokees were now fractured politically. Many in the Nation were disenchanted with their treatment by the U.S. government and angry at fellow Cherokees who had joined the Confederates. The Treaty of 1866, a peace treaty signed at the conclusion of the Civil War that redefined Cherokee politics by forcibly including freedmen as Cherokee citizens, was a rallying point over which Cherokees could unite on the issue of citizenship.[3]

THE UNITED STATES AND THE QUESTION OF CITIZENSHIP

The United States wrestled with citizenship in a way entirely unlike the Cherokees. The orthodox liberal concept of the state is an association of rights-bearing free agents who contract with one another for peace and happiness (Collins 2006, 2). Liberal thought prescribes the political equality of rights, levels hierarchies, and politically elevates the individual. Liberal citizenship is a human creation, rooted in a natural reality resting on the consent of the governed, which offers voting rights and access to the highest political offices (Smith 1997, 3). In short, liberal citizenship stresses equality before the law and presents citizenship as a legal condition rather than one of blood ties or identity.[4]

In his challenge to the idea that American citizenship laws have stemmed solely from liberal or republican doctrines, Smith (1997) argued that inegalitarian traditions have also played a substantial role in shaping the United States. These inegalitarian or prejudicial traditions—such as racism or patriarchal hierarchy—have molded citizenship in the United States into a unique patchwork of constitutional law. In James Kettner's (1978, 287) telling, from the earliest days of the republic Americans harbored a sense of citizenship, based on individual consent, that entitled one to fundamental privileges and immunities as articulated in the law. These beliefs influenced the passage of the first citizenship laws at both national and state levels (West 2017). Though membership in the American republic could be acquired automatically, it was presumed that true Americans would be raised from birth educated in the "fundamental values necessary for self-government"—a love of liberty (Kettner 1978, 287–88). There were, however, several contradictions in the law and in popular thinking when it came to citizenship (Smith 1997).

The primary contradiction in American citizenship was that Americans used it negatively to distinguish whites from minorities at home, and also foreigners from abroad (Kettner 1978; Shklar 1991). The valued principle of birthright citizenship clashed with the prejudice many Americans felt toward blacks as well as Indians. For the sake of legal and theoretical consistency, either principle or prejudice needed to prevail. The outbreak of the Civil War, according to Kettner, "removed obstacles that had long prevented Americans from achieving a consistent concept of citizenship" (1978, 334).[5] By force, the United States decided that the principle of birthright citizenship was to be the law and that state citizenship was subordinate to American citizenship.

With the Civil War over and the Union galvanized in its decision that the United States was not a "political community formed of separate sovereign peoples," it strove to make uniform citizenship laws within the boundaries of the nation (Kettner 1978, 334).

This push for legal uniformity extended inevitably into Indian Territory, especially in the case of the freedmen—not just in the Cherokee Nation but in other tribes as well (Littlefield 1977, 1978, 1980). The resulting pressure to conform to new citizenship standards also meant the erosion of tribal sovereignty and the eventual remaking of the tribal order as it had existed in the earlier part of the nineteenth century.

CHEROKEE SLAVEHOLDING

Extant work on the Cherokee freedmen is primarily concerned with historical nuance and placing them within the context of American colonialism or Reconstruction (Bailey 1972; Halliburton 1977; Littlefield 1978; Minges 2003). Little has been done to examine the political development of tribal citizenship as it relates to greater struggles for sovereignty and identity, especially in the case of the freedmen.[6] The legal, cultural, and political path trod by the freedmen and their posterity toward Cherokee citizenship, though unique in many respects, offers broader lessons on the nature of citizenship as it has evolved in the United States.

Slavery existed in parts of North America long before European settlers arrived. Though slaves were traditionally taken as prisoners of war, according to R. Halliburton, "there appears to have been a regular commercial traffic in some areas" as well. From the time of their earliest contact with Europeans, Cherokees had engaged in a practice of quasi-slavery and forced adoption among their Indian captives—a practice later used in the treatment of Caucasian and African prisoners as well (Lauber 1913, 49, 63, 136, 170). The term "quasi-slavery" here reflects the old Cherokee practice of claiming slaves from rival tribes as spoils of war—"most of the slaves [were] probably prisoners, [but] not all of the prisoners were slaves" (see Halliburton 1977, 4–6).

Although this quasi-slavery was widespread among the Cherokees at first contact, slavery as an institution did not exist prior to European settlement (Mooney 1900, 15–25). Once introduced by English traders, Cherokees were quick to accept the European brand of black slaveholding as one of the benefits of white civilization. English traders in the seventeenth century established themselves among the Cherokees through marriage and the spread of material wealth (Halliburton 1977, 6–7). The legacy of black slavery among them was passed down through a combination of cultural pressure, assimilation, and family heritage.[7]

The Cherokees also took to institutionalized slavery because of the benefits they received from stealing or returning runaway slaves. English and French colonists frequently urged Cherokees to sell them slaves stolen from the plantations or villages of their European opponents (Halliburton 1977, 6). In return, colonial powers typically promised Cherokees access to powerful weapons and ammunition. The return or barter of runaway slaves became so common that the Cherokees were often known colloquially as "slave catchers" (Corkran 1962). Whether through trade, theft, or personal benefit, black slavery gradually became a part of Cherokee society in a way that normalized the practice and invested many Cherokees in the European status quo. In everyday life, the addition of slaves was a boon for Cherokee women, who lacked the same level of farming skill as black slaves, and for Cherokee men, who could spend more time hunting, bartering, or at war. Yet once the Cherokee people had established themselves as invested in the institution of slavery, white settlers felt threatened and feared for their lives and property.

From the beginning, the Cherokee relationship to slaveholding was characterized more by "otherness" than by racism. The tension between Anglo-dominated slaveholding society and Native Americans has been well documented, but many tribes, including the Cherokees, felt a particular antipathy toward blacks as well (Limerick 1987; Minges 2003; Seagrave 2015). For whites, who harbored a racial animosity toward blacks and Indians alike, Indian slaveholding represented a potential alliance of natural enemies and threatened white civilization (Halliburton 1977). For the Cherokees, however, who did not possess a concept of race as such, foreignness determined their perceptions of outsiders (Perdue 1979; Minges 2003; Saunt 2004).

Since they had encountered blacks and whites at the same time, and typically with one another, Cherokees did not sharply distinguish between the two and considered them both inferior (Halliburton 1977; Perdue 1979; Minges 2003). There is in fact, according to Kenneth Porter (1971), no evidence that the northern tribes made any distinction between blacks and whites based on color until white society told them to. All were outsiders who, though bringing some benefits to the tribe, threatened the power of the sacred relationships between nature, kin, and community (Minges 2003). Those threats grew continually during the early half of the nineteenth century, until the U.S. government officially decided to remove Native Americans from their homelands to make room for the expansion of American settlements.[8]

Daniel Littlefield, in *The Cherokee Freedmen* (1978, 3–6), provides an account of how the Cherokees organized themselves and eventually coalesced into a cohesive government after removal. Two factions, with different immediate political and cultural interests, had formed over the issue of removal—those who supported it and those opposed. The "Old Settlers" had voluntarily relocated to Oklahoma before 1835 and the Ridge party, who supported removal, followed by 1838. According to Littlefield, these first two groups numbered roughly 6,000 (1978). The Ross party, fundamentally opposed to removal, was later forced to relocate and made to walk the Trail of Tears in 1838–39; they numbered approximately 16,000. In the dispute over governance that followed, the leaders of the Ridge and Old Settler parties were murdered, and John Ross was proclaimed chief of a united Cherokee Nation (Bailey 1972). By 1840 the Cherokee Nation had approved a constitution requiring officials to be blood Cherokee. This government existed with only minor factional infighting for the next decade with help from per-capita payments made by the United States as compensation for removal, and by 1860 the Nation had achieved a measure of stability under Chief Ross (Bailey 1972).

Throughout the 1840s and '50s, as the Cherokees settled into their new territory, the Nation found itself changing demographically (Littlefield 1978, 7–10). Tension slowly emerged as the "mixed blood" population grew and the number of "full-blooded" Cherokees shrank. According to Littlefield, to be a full-blooded Cherokee meant something more than simply racial pride; it meant standing up for traditional Cherokee values and resisting the impositions of white civilization. Full-blooded Cherokees also generally did not own slaves and largely disliked the practice. The slave owners among the Cherokees, who collectively owned more slaves than any other Indian nation, tended to be those with mixed ancestry for whom the practice had been beneficial as well as part of their family heritage.

The Cherokee Nation, amid its own infighting, was swept up into the Civil War, partially because of its location in the northeast of Indian Territory. Many in the Confederacy, especially Arkansas governor Henry Rector, wanted to shore up their western borders by securing the Cherokees as allies in the wars to come. When secession was brought up in Arkansas, Governor Rector appealed to Chief Ross as "natural allies in war and friends in peace," jointly invested in the "application of slave labor."[9] But, although Governor Rector tried to instill in Ross a fear of Lincoln and the Union, Ross determined to remain neutral in whatever conflict the United States was contemplating.

Pivotal social divisions had been growing within the Cherokee Nation during this time (Littlefield 1978; Minges 2003). While he was being pressured by Governor Rector to join the Confederacy, Chief Ross found himself caught between the pro-Union Keetoowah Society, comprising full-bloods, and the pro-Confederacy mixed-blooded Knights of the Golden Circle. These organizations represented social divisions that had been brewing for many years through the tensions brought on by mixing Cherokee and American social values and practices. The issue of slavery, as it had divided the United States, also affected the Cherokees, albeit in a different manner.

Debates over the Keetoowah Society's moral arguments notwithstanding, the Cherokees never seriously grappled with the moral ramifications of slaveholding, and according to Halliburton (1977, 11) no serious abolition societies were ever established.[10] As the Civil War drew closer, abolitionist missionaries in the Nation were often ostracized, and the abolitionist cause and troubles dealing with it were avoided (Halliburton 1977, 93–104). The locus of division among the Cherokees was over slavery in the sense that traditional values were being expunged by the acceptance of white culture and civilization; cultural purity was of greater concern (Littlefield 1978; Perdue 1979).

By October 1861, Albert Pike, Confederate liaison to Indian Territory, had convinced each of the Five Civilized Tribes to join the Confederacy.[11] The Confederacy's insistence, coupled with pressure and violence from the Knights of the Golden Circle, compelled Chief Ross to relent and sign a declaration of support for the Southern cause (Littlefield 1978; Minges 2003). The Cherokees, however, did not go wholeheartedly into the fray. In December of the same year, Union troops began to move in force through Cherokee territory, causing many Cherokees to defect to the Union side. Chief Ross himself followed suit, eventually fleeing to

Philadelphia (Littlefield 1978, 11). By the end of the war, a majority of the Nation had joined the Union side. The war, however, had been disastrous for the Cherokees; Indian Territory was devastated by 1865 (Gaines 1998).

In 1866 an official treaty between the United States and the Cherokee Nation was signed, granting amnesty to the Nation for joining the Confederacy (Abel 1925). That treaty essentially revoked and then restored many provisions of previous treaties, but one important thing had changed: the definition of citizenship. The new treaty defined citizenship of the Cherokee Nation as belonging to all native-born Cherokees, all Indians and whites legally adopted by members, all freedmen liberated by acts of masters, and all free blacks residing therein (Littlefield 1978, 28). The terms of the treaty, and the new legal definition of Cherokee citizenship, were set to affect those who could be declared residents of Cherokee territory within six months of the signing. This latter clause of the treaty would become the basis of an intense legal, social, and political conflict that continues to this day.

THE EVOLUTION OF CHEROKEE CITIZENSHIP: THE WAR OVER SOVEREIGNTY

Barbara Krauthamer contends that "we cannot fully understand the meanings and consequences of slavery, emancipation, and citizenship in the Indian nations without paying attention to the complicated history of Indian sovereignty" (2013, 1). That history reveals a Cherokee people in a state of semisovereignty. Unable to exert full authority over matters of criminal, civil, and citizenship law, the Cherokees yet retained the semblance of sovereignty throughout the nineteenth century, until the dissolution of the tribe in 1907.

The Cherokee Nation's status as a semisovereign organization extends back to the early nineteenth century. In 1831, Chief Justice John Marshall held in *Cherokee Nation v. Georgia* that Indian nations were "domestic, dependent nations" that were subject to the pupilage of the United States because of their condition (McGovney 1911, 326). From the view of the federal government, two things barred the Indian nation from full sovereignty—and U.S. citizenship. The U.S. restriction of tribal sovereignty was a response to the tribal organization of the natives and their refusal or inability to adopt American cultural habits, in many cases because of their practice of holding lands in common (Kettner 1978, 292; Stremlau 2011). The second reason was the supposed inferior intelligence of the Indians—natives were the "unfortunate children of the public" and thus doomed to extended pupilage (Kettner 1978, 293).

That the Cherokee way of life has traditionally been antithetical to liberal democratic ideals is not a new concept. The liberal tradition, by necessity, disenchants the ancestral and the traditional. Official Indian policy in the aftermath of the Civil War followed President Grant's example, laid out in his two inaugural addresses. In 1869, Grant favored any course that would lead to Indian civilization and ultimate citizenship. In 1873, Grant again, citing the American superiority of civilization and strength, argued that Indians should be made "useful and productive member[s] of society" via "teaching and treatment" (Strock 2010, 147). And though the Indian tribes were officially viewed as peoples in need of improvement, unofficially their American neighbors treated the Cherokees and others with a mixture of contempt and fear.

These Indian nations were, nonetheless, permitted to enforce their own laws upon their own people for the most part. True sovereign nations are generally understood to have jurisdiction over anyone who commits a crime within certain borders. But the Cherokees, and other Indian tribes, were always unique in their limited ability to enforce criminal law on outsiders (Rolnick 2014). It was often the case that the Cherokees were powerless to do anything, especially in instances where squatters and other ill-willed individuals strayed into Cherokee lands and violated their people (Littlefield 1978). These infractions occurred continuously throughout their history and often went unpunished (Smithers 2015).

The inherent prejudice, mixed with an authentic belief in the inability of Indians to participate in white civilization or adhere to American mores, kept the tribes in legal limbo (Kettner 1978, 293–95). When U.S. citizens wanted their lands in Georgia and elsewhere in the South during the 1830s, they forced the Cherokees to move (Limerick 1987).[12] When white civilization desired their possessions, they treated the Cherokees as a subjugated people. When Americans wanted nothing to do with them, they largely left the Cherokees alone. The Nation thus possessed varying degrees of sovereignty at different points in its history with the United States. Overall, Congress kept a firm hand on the Cherokees. "From the four corners of the Constitution and our constitutional history it appears that the tribal Indians were not included and not intended to be included" among the people of the United States (McGovney 1911, 327). Nor were they, as the Southern states had contended, separate sovereigns operating within the larger United States.

Given the legal restrictions placed on the Cherokee people, they often pressed back against the United States, retaining a belief in their own sovereign ability to fight for and celebrate their own peoples' cultural traditions (Littlefield 1978; Sturm 1998). Though issues of railroad development and escaped criminals/illegal settlers plagued the Nation in the 1870s and '80s, many tribal members clung to the notion of a unique tribal identity that coincided with Cherokee citizenship (Bailey 1972, 169–79). Unable to remove squatters legally, resist the development of new railroads, or deal with the crime railroad workers brought with them, the Cherokees stood their ground on citizenship when it came to the freedmen.

Fearing that the United States would attempt to dictate to the Cherokee people who could be considered Cherokee, the Cherokee National Council contended for the right to determine its own citizenship by citing justifications in treaties and other interpretations of U.S. law (Bailey 1972). In 1869, the Council passed an act empowering the Cherokee Supreme Court to sit as commissioners to pass judgment on citizenship claims. The Cherokees strictly interpreted the provision in the Treaty of 1866 that acknowledged the Cherokee citizenship of only those who returned to the Nation up to six months after the treaty had been signed. For years after the signing of the treaty, hundreds of freedmen and their families had slowly returned to the Nation. The Cherokees routinely refused them citizenship (Sturm 1998).

As the Cherokees set about asserting their authority to define their own citizenship, they quickly found that they could not handle the chaos caused by hundreds of people pouring into Cherokee territory, claiming previous residence (Bailey 1972, 178–79). Because the Nation lacked appropriate governing infrastructure to handle so many requests, many freedmen especially were either hastily denied or made to wait for long periods before action was taken. Those who were rejected for citizenship were periodically reported to the commissioner of Indian Affairs along with a request for removal—a provision present in long-standing treaties. The U.S. government, however, had other intentions.

As early as 1871, the Office of Indian Affairs began instructing Union agents in Indian Territory not to remove freedmen whom the Cherokees had classified as intruders (Bailey 1972, 180–81). The political situation in the Cherokee Nation was volatile. Cherokee public sentiment was deeply set against the United States interfering with Cherokee citizenship; the freedmen had become a politically dangerous issue that no Cherokee politician wanted to touch (Wardell 1938, 229–31). After over a decade of struggling with the Cherokee National Council, the freedmen circumvented tribal government and appealed to the United States instead. The Union Agency told the freedmen and others who had troubles with the Cherokee National Council to come to them directly, thus severely undermining tribal authority on the issue of citizenship.

The situation escalated when the time came to receive payment for Cherokee lands sold to the U.S. government. In 1883 the Nation quickly passed an act declaring that the money, some $300,000, should be distributed only among blood Cherokees (Bailey 1972, 182). The decision, passed over Chief Dennis Bushyhead's veto, excluded the freedmen from receiving any of the bounty. Desiring a share in the payment, many freedmen appealed to the Office of Indian Affairs directly, as they had been instructed in the past. Indian Affairs, having never viewed the Cherokee government as possessing actual power, began a larger political coup that led to the settlement of the issue of native sovereignty in the eyes of the U.S. government (Sturm 1998, 235).[13]

After numerous attempts by the freedmen to gain access to Cherokee citizenship and benefits, Congress began passing major legislation on the topic, culminating in the Dawes Act of 1887 and the Curtis Act of 1898 (Littlefield 1978; Sturm 1998). The Dawes Act began the process of converting the communally held lands within the Cherokee Nation to lots of individual ownership, hoping to modernize the Cherokees and make room for more white settlement on the leftover land (Sturm 1998, 235). The Dawes Act also established the Dawes Commission, which was sent to compile a roll of residents living in Indian Territory. The Cherokees opposed these measures and actively resisted efforts to count them (Littlefield 1978, 238; Sturm 1998).

Congress passed the Curtis Act of 1898 when it became clear that the Cherokees would not cooperate. The legislation gave the Dawes Commission authority to act without tribal consent, extended federal court jurisdiction over tribal land, and allowed the federal government to collect the tax payments of whites living within the Nation (Debo 1940; Sturm 1998). The Dawes Rolls broke down the residents of Cherokee land into three categories: Cherokees, whites, and freedmen. All told, the counted inhabitants of the Cherokee Nation numbered 41,798, including 4,924 freedmen (Littlefield 1978, 238). More than a thousand freedmen who had been citizens previously were, however, excluded from the Dawes Rolls—thanks to a mixture of clerical errors, inability to produce proof of citizenship, and racial profiling (Sturm 1998). In 1907 the Cherokee Nation ceased to exist as Oklahoma joined the Union.

Until 1907, the Cherokee Nation had been faced with political and practical problems that it was not given the authority or capacity to handle. Powerless to stop the inflow of settlers and business that followed the railroads, the Cherokees dug their heels in when it came to the issue of citizenship. By dissolving the Nation completely, and by granting all Cherokees and freedmen alike U.S. citizenship in 1924, the United States hoped to settle the issues of sovereignty and make citizenship uniform once and for all. Upon the restoration of tribal sovereignty in the 1970s, with the passage of the Five Civilized Tribes Act and the Principal Chiefs Act, the Cherokees again moved quickly to reassert their sovereign right to declare who was Cherokee, solemnly rejecting the American citizenship model by making tribal citizenship once again exclusive (Sturm 1998, 251).[14]

THE EVOLUTION OF CHEROKEE CITIZENSHIP: THE WAR OVER IDENTITY

It has been a continual struggle over time for Cherokees to determine what exactly it means to be Cherokee (Sturm 2002; Minges 2003, 1–3). Although "blood politics" has come again to the fore in recent decades, the journey of the Cherokees toward a definitive understanding of their greater political and private personal identities has been mired in racial politics. Having been denied full autonomy as a sovereign nation, Cherokees actively seek to assert control over their cultural and political identity wherever possible, especially on the touchstone issue of citizenship.

After regaining the ability to hold principal chief elections and exercise a wider range of self-government in the 1970s, the Cherokee people instituted a new citizenship policy: only those who could prove relation to someone listed on the Dawes Roll could partake in full citizenship (Sturm 2014). Former principal chief Ross Swimmer, discussing the 1975 Cherokee constitution, reflected that they "established, through the constitution, that one had to be either on—or a lineal descendant of—someone who was on the 1906 Dawes Roll. . . . So in order to be a member of the tribe one has to prove his ancestry back to a person on that roll" (Lemont 2006, 292). Swimmer further explained that the reason for this "somewhat arbitrary" method is that "there really is no way of determining what blood quantum is." To keep citizenship exclusive, the Cherokees moved from blood to the more practical Dawes Roll.

Sturm argues that, from the 1970s to the 1990s, Cherokees have expressed a contradictory consciousness; they resent racial discrimination yet use racially hegemonic concepts to legitimize social identities. Modern Cherokees regularly use blood, color, and race to demarcate sociopolitical community and distinguish themselves from other ethnic groups (Sturm 1998, 231). The ethnocentricity of the Cherokees, however, is not a new or surprising concept. In Halliburton's (1977, 139) telling, they had long viewed themselves as distinctly elevated above whites, blacks, and other Indians alike. Loathing the encroachment of white settlers on their lands, the Cherokees struggled continuously to carve out their own niche where they could realize their traditional way of life within their private communities.

Rather than being something new that, as Sturm attests, formed out of a pure racism, the Cherokee attempt to keep tribal citizenship exclusive by using the Dawes Rolls as a reference point was logical, given the historical tendencies of the tribe. Furthermore, the Cherokees never viewed slavery in quite the same manner as did their Southern white neighbors. Unlike white Southerners, the Cherokees never felt the need to justify slavery morally; slavery was merely a feature of white civilization adopted under the pressure to assimilate (Halliburton 1977, 143–44). Many Cherokees found it almost as easy to adopt slaves as it was to let them go, if it meant that white society would grant the tribe peace (Bailey 1972; Littlefield 1978).

Yet, despite the Cherokee historical tendency to resist assigning people to racial categories (Perdue 1979), many tribal members adopted the prejudices of white society as they eventually became Southerners by birth, marriage, economic ties, and lifestyle (Halliburton 1977, 141). But these new-found Southern sympathies did not negate the desire to exist as a cohesive and demarcated group. The emancipation of the Cherokee slaves was done under the impression that, since the Union government asked it of them, they would comply, if they could retain sovereignty and self-determination. These rewards for acquiescence, of course, were not realized.

What the federal government saw as a justly imposed uniformity, and the triumph of American inclusive citizenship, Cherokees saw as the destruction of their sacred kinship ties (Stremlau 2011). When Congress decided that freedmen, even those who had not intermarried with Cherokees and therefore had no blood connection, could be Cherokee citizens, it meant that Cherokeeness could be altered as a result. From the U.S. perspective, a citizen is one born of a territory and guaranteed all the privileges and immunities of that nation. For the Cherokees, citizenship means something much deeper; it means an identity stronger than national or legal ties normalized by the United States.

In 1996, Jason Tarrell, a member of the Cherokee Nation, attempted to explain what it means to be Cherokee. According to Tarrell, "You either are or you aren't. It's not a question of how many Europeans versus how many Cherokees one has in the [old] family tree. . . . It's not even about where you live. It is a question of loyalty. . . . It is a question of commitment. . . . it's the way you live and the way your family has lived." The editorial ended with "You can't suddenly become Cherokee. It's not a club."[15] Tarrell's sentiments are borne out by the history of the Cherokee people and how they and their politicians have reacted to attempts by the United States to redefine their tribal relationships.

Rose Stremlau's work on Cherokee communities after allotment further reinforces Tarrell's point. As the United States slowly transformed Cherokee communal lands into individual plots, the Cherokee people banded together with renewed determination to preserve their sacred ties and traditions. It was during the late nineteenth century, as the Dawes Commission was collecting data, that the Cherokees experienced a cultural revival. The Old Ways were once again studied, new stomp grounds were created throughout the territory, and spiritual leaders such as Redbird Smith gained public support in the efforts to preserve Cherokee heritage (Stremlau 2011, 165–70).

Today, the Cherokee Nation dedicates time and resources to spreading the message of what it means to be Cherokee (Cherokee Nation 2010; 2017). The work *Cherokee National Treasures*, a celebration of individuals who have become specialized in ancient Cherokee artwork, customs, or wisdom, argues that "it is not the color of our skins or the blood in our veins [that make us Cherokee]. Being Indian is a way of life, living and remembering our past" (Cherokee Nation 2017, 3). Threats to Cherokee tradition and custom over time have driven many in the Nation to reaffirm old practices and celebrate their unique cultural heritage.

After the Nation instituted the new citizenship policies in the 1970s and '80s, descendants of the freedmen fought back, attempting to regain the tribal benefits they and their families had previously held (Sturm 1998). After more than two decades of legal encounters, the Cherokee people finally amended their constitution via special election to exclude from citizenship all those who could not prove blood relation to someone on the Dawes Rolls.[16] Challenges to the amendment were seemingly put to rest by the Cherokee Supreme Court in 2011. Chief Justice Darell R. Matlock Jr. argued that "it stands to reason that if the Cherokee had the right to define citizenship" in 1866, then they would have the "sovereign right" to change it.[17]

In August 2017, however, U.S. District Court Judge Thomas Hogan ruled that the Cherokee Nation does not have the authority to deny citizenship to those descendants of their freedmen previously established in the Treaty of 1866.[18] As the results of Hogan's ruling indicate, Cherokee citizenship is legally defined as including all Cherokees, all white and others adopted, and all freedmen and their descendants—with reference to the Dawes Rolls. Legally, the United States' redefinition of Cherokee citizenship has prevailed. The 2021 Cherokee Court decision solidified Judge Hogan's ruling by altering the letter of the law, removing the words "by blood." Although the Cherokee Nation still retains sovereignty in other respects, the United States has expanded the scope of Cherokee exclusive citizenship.

THE IMPOSITION OF FREEDOM: CHEROKEE CITIZENSHIP DEFINED BY A FOREIGN POWER

The uniform application of national American citizenship, given to indigenous peoples in 1924, is a natural result of the conflict over citizenship in the Civil War. For the United States, the legal condition of citizenship represents stability and a confirmation of the sovereign power of the republic (Shklar 1991). Americans, dealing with their own racial prejudices, found it easier to impose unifying citizenship regulations on Indian tribes and compel them to adhere to American principles than to smooth out their own racial contradictions (Kettner 1978). In other words, the post–Civil War American citizenship project has focused on inclusion—at times forced inclusion (Temin 2017).

For the Cherokees, as their circumstances changed and they were forced to adopt aspects of white civilization, they found themselves less able to determine their own practices and cultural trajectory. Identity and tribalism were alternately threatened and undermined by the inevitable mixture of race and ethnicity that white civilization brought with it. Slavery was seen as a tool, first favored and then rejected by white society (Halliburton 1977). The Cherokees were shocked by the sudden request made of them to count those with whom they shared no kinship as brothers and sisters. They were especially incensed by the demands made by Congress that they share with their former slaves payment intended for Indians only.

For the freedmen and their posterity, who lived first as stateless, then as unwanted, and finally as marginalized people, Cherokee citizenship often represented a practical means for building a life (Sturm 1998; Saunt 2004). Cherokee citizenship granted exclusive access to universal tribal healthcare, educational scholarships, and, in the nineteenth century, a share in large government payments (Bailey 1972; Sturm 2002). The emphasis placed on citizenship by the freedmen and Cherokees offers us glimpses into the nature of the struggle over belonging in the United States and illuminates the role played by ethnic heritage in American history.

Freedmen's arguments for why they desire Cherokee citizenship are also couched in a need to be accepted in their unique cultural identity—and to participate in Cherokee exclusive citizenship. Marilynn Vann, president of the Descendants of Freedmen

Association (DFA), has stated her desire to ensure that freedmen are secure in their citizenship status with access to full citizenship rights.[19] Vann, in an August 2017 interview, explained why the freedmen desire Cherokee citizenship. She argued that, since her ancestors walked the Trail of Tears, labored to build Cherokee cities, and helped "make the tribe," the freedmen are an intrinsic part of Cherokee culture.[20] The freedmen not only reside among the Cherokee but also belong with the Cherokee as a single tribal family.

Along with the importance of cultural identity and belonging, Vann also indicated that modern descendants of freedmen desire the material benefits that come with Cherokee citizenship; these benefits include access to tribal healthcare, rental assistance, and other programs for the poor.[21] Other practical benefits to holding Cherokee citizenship today and historically have included access to federally funded programs, tuition waivers, government payouts, and land allotments (Littlefield 1978; Edwards 2006; Smithers 2015).

The freedmen push for Cherokee citizenship has used the language of inclusion to gain access to exclusive citizenship. To join the DFA as a full member, individuals must be able to "prove lineage to the 1898–1914 Dawes Freedmen Rolls."[22] The Cherokees have, in the modern era, also used the Dawes Rolls to establish tribal citizenship, albeit excluding the freedmen portion of the rolls. The DFA does not desire to open up tribal membership to anyone who wants it but rather seeks to maintain the exclusivity of Cherokee citizenship while asserting that freedmen have always been party to it.

Rogers Smith contends that "American political actors have always promoted civic ideologies that blend liberal, democratic republican, and inegalitarian elements in various combinations" to get elected (1997, 6). Though inconsistent in its own policymaking, the United States has been, in the case of the Cherokees, insistent that its liberal norms of citizenship be enforced. Alternately vilified and pitied from the beginning, Cherokees have been required to wrestle with American problems despite not having an intrinsic understanding of those problems (Smith 1997, 109). For example, Cherokees never struggled to justify slavery morally once it had been instituted by white colonies (Halliburton 1977). The United States did its part subsequently to instill in the Cherokees a fear of the Christian god and a remorse for having offended that god by adopting African slavery in the first place (Littlefield 1978; Smith 1997).

Wrapped up in the issue of Cherokee citizenship are the practical sovereignty needed to control tribal fate and identity, the drive to protect sacred cultural mores, and the desire to preserve the practical material benefits that come with legal belonging. Cherokee peoples have an idea, distinct from American politics, that the glue binding society is a mixture of blood, culture, and tradition (Sturm 2002). The United States has, over time, attempted to impose an inclusive understanding of citizenship on the Cherokee community. Yet, though the American brand of liberalism may instill certain benefits (Barber 2014), altering the view of what holds society together would likely destroy that which makes the Cherokee unique. The tension between the United States, and indeed other democratic nations, and indigenous peoples remains—a puzzle not easily solved (Kymlicka 1995; Tully 1995). This chapter aims to clarify that tension so that discourse on the subject may be grounded in a firmer understanding of what makes Cherokee political thought unique on the issue of citizenship.

Tensions between the United States and indigenous peoples remain relevant, not only because of the legal battles over Cherokee citizenship but also because of continued attempts to use tribal lands for industry. As recent stories such as the Standing Rock protest suggest, the struggle between the United States and Indian nations over issues of sovereignty has not been resolved. That the election of 2020 stirred up a renewed interest in national belonging may also be an indication that the situation in the Cherokee Nation is far more complicated than it may seem.

In 2007, Rep. Diane Watson argued that racial prejudice had prevented the Cherokee Nation from incorporating the freedmen and their families into full tribal citizenship.[23] But racial prejudice reveals only part of the story. Contrary to Sturm's (1998, 249) contention, echoed by Representative Watson, that the "Cherokee bias against dark skin" provides "the simplest explanation for their social treatment" of people with black ancestry, reality is more complicated. The Nation has resisted incorporation of the freedmen because of the impositions placed upon it by the federal government, systematically denying the Cherokees practical sovereignty and denying the importance of their cultural identity.

NOTES

1. In re: Effect of *Cherokee Nation v. Nash and Vann v. Zinke*, District Court for the District of Columbia, Case No. 13-01313 (TFH) and Petition for Writ of Mandamus requiring the Cherokee Nation Registrar to Begin Processing Citizenship Applications, Case No. SC-17-07.

2. A Bill to Sever United States' Government Relations with the Cherokee Nation of Oklahoma, HR 2824, 110th Cong., 1st sess., *Congressional Record* 153, no. 147, daily ed. [October 1, 2007]: H 11053.

3. The Treaty of 1866 redefined Cherokee citizenship by explicitly stating that formerly enslaved peoples once held by the Cherokees would thereafter be considered full Cherokee citizens, despite not being blood relatives of the Cherokees. The Cherokees were resistant to the treaty and agreed to sign with a stipulation that permitted only those residents of the Cherokee Nation within six months of the signing be considered citizens. Former enslaved peoples arriving after six months had passed could be legally excluded from Cherokee citizenship.

4. The standard of liberal American thought has changed over time. Though liberal citizenship at the founding may have entailed a contract between heads of families, derived from a perceived naturally hierarchical order, liberal citizenship in America today is more egalitarian in its emphasis on the individual, although illiberal elements remain (Dyer 2013).

5. For a full treatment of the development of American citizenship from the colonial period to the end of the Civil War, see Kettner (1978). Kettner elaborates in detail how the notion of individual consent and state citizenship was reconciled by force with the idea that U.S. citizenship was primary and state citizenship secondary. For a historical telling of the debate over sovereignty and citizenship during the Civil War, see Goodwin (2005).

6. For a more recent account of the struggle between the Cherokees and freedmen, see Smithers (2015, chap. 7).

7. For more detailed accounts of the origins of Cherokee slavery, see Halliburton (1977), Mooney (1900), and Lauber (1913). A full and accurate treatment of this subject, though interesting and important, is beyond the scope of this chapter. It should be noted as well that there is a dispute over how well Cherokees treated their slaves compared to Southern whites. See Littlefield (1978), Halliburton (1977), Perdue (1979), and Saunt (2004) for a better understanding of these competing views. For the present purpose, Halliburton's (1977) depiction, corroborated by Littlefield (1978), of Cherokee slavery as being much like Southern slavery in certain circumstances, especially after removal, is taken as authentic.

8. See Foreman (1932) for a detailed and thorough account of Indian removal in the nineteenth century.

9. Henry M. Rector to John Ross, January 29, 1861, 38th Cong., 1st sess., House Executive Document 1, pt. 3, 345; quoted in Littlefield (1978, 10).

10. Some scholars emphasize the abolitionist sentiments of the Keetoowah Society more than others. See Minges (2003) and Halliburton (1977) for a deeper look at these opposing viewpoints.

11. The Five Civilized Tribes, as they have come to be known, are the Cherokee, Choctaw, Chickasaw, Creek, and Seminole tribes, all of which inhabited the Oklahoma "Indian" Territory on the eve of the Civil War (Bailey 1972).

12. President Andrew Jackson famously said of Indian removal that white settlers "would gladly embrace the opportunity of removing to the west" in the manner forcibly undertaken by the Cherokees (quoted in Limerick 1987, 193).

13. For a thorough exploration of Indian/U.S. political struggles between 1866 and1907, see Littlefield (1978).

14. Principal Chiefs Act of 1970, Public Law 91–495, 91st Cong., 2d sess. (October 22, 1970). The legislation restored to the Cherokee Nation the ability to elect via popular ballot the office of principal chief. Widespread popular elections followed, imbued with a renewed sense of the importance of the Cherokee constitution and judicial system (Sturm 1998).

15. Jason Tarrell, "Editorial from a Member," *Cherokee Observer* 4, no. 4 (April 1996).

16. Cherokee Nation Registrar v. Raymond Nash et al., SC-2011–02 (Supreme Court of the Cherokee Nation).

17. Cherokee Nation Registrar v. Raymond Nash et al., SC-2011–02, 8.

18. The Cherokee Nation v. Raymond Nash et al. and Marilyn Vann et al. and Ryan Zinke, Secretary of the Interior, and the US Department of the Interior, 13-01313.

19. Will Chavez, "UPDATE: Freedmen Descendants Have Citizenship Restored and May Vote Sept. 24," *Cherokee Phoenix*, September 28, 2011.

20. Marilynn Vann, "Cherokee Freedmen Overjoyed by Federal Court Ruling Granting Citizenship," interview by Allison Herrera, PRI, August 31, 2017, audio, 4:40, www.pri.org/stories/2017-08-31/cherokee-freedmen-over joyed-federal-court-ruling-granting-tribal-citizenship.

21. Vann, "Cherokee Freedmen Overjoyed."

22. "Membership and Official Supporter Application," Descendants of Freedmen of the Five Civilized Tribes Association, accessed January 20, 2019, http://websites.godaddy.com/blob/b94b4dc8-e0df-448a-a658-31349283b956 /downloads/Descendants%20Membership%20Application%20revised%20 %208%2025%202014%20-%20revision%201%20(1).pdf?cb52130b&fbclid =IwAR3AgSQP2BQrNbIuVAZ5ZHC50igmbct2PAFIfWMhC39aQeLQCrF YchgRNbY.

23. A Bill to Sever United States' Government Relations with the Cherokee Nation of Oklahoma, HR 2824, 110th Cong., 1st sess., *Congressional Record* 153, no. 147, daily ed. [October 1, 2007]: H11053.

REFERENCES

Abel, Annie Heloise. 1925. *The American Indian under Reconstruction*. Cleveland, OH: Arthur H. Clark.

Awiakta, Marilou. 1993. *Selu: Seeking the Corn-Mother's Wisdom*. Golden, CO: Fulcrum.

Bailey, M. Thomas. 1972. *Reconstruction in Indian Territory: A Story of Avarice, Discrimination, and Opportunism*. Port Washington, NY: Kennikat Press.

Barber, Sotirios A. 2014. *Constitutional Failure*. Lawrence: University Press of Kansas.

Cherokee Nation. 2010. *Building One Fire*. Edited by Chadwick Corntassel Smith and Rennard Strickland. Norman: University of Oklahoma Press.

———. 2017. *Cherokee National Treasures: In Their Own Words*. Edited by Shawna Morton Cain, Pamela Jumper Thurman, and Betty Christine Frogg. Norman: University of Oklahoma Press.

Collins, Susan D. 2006. *Aristotle and the Rediscovery of Citizenship*. Cambridge: Cambridge University Press.

Conley, Robert J. 2005. *The Cherokee Nation: A History*. Albuquerque: University of New Mexico Press.

Corkran, David H. 1962. *The Cherokee Frontier: Conflict and Survival, 1740–1762*. Norman: University of Oklahoma Press.

Debo, Angie. 1940. *And Still the Waters Run: The Betrayal of the Five Civilized Tribes*. Princeton, NJ: Princeton University Press.

Dyer, Justin Buckley. 2013. *Slavery, Abortion, and the Politics of Constitutional Meaning*. Cambridge: Cambridge University Press.

Erman, Sam. 2018. *Almost Citizens: Puerto Rico, the U.S. Constitution, and Empire*. Cambridge: Cambridge University Press.

Foreman, Grant. 1932. *Indian Removal*. Norman: University of Oklahoma Press.

Gaines, Craig. 1998. *The Confederate Cherokees: John Drew's Regiment of Mounted Rifles*. Baton Rouge: Louisiana State University Press.

Goodwin, Doris Kearns. 2005. *Team of Rivals: The Political Genius of Abraham Lincoln*. New York: Simon and Schuster.

Halliburton, R., Jr. 1977. *Red over Black: Black Slavery among the Cherokee Indians*. Westport, CT: Greenwood Press.

Kettner, James H. 1978. *The Development of American Citizenship, 1608–1870*. Chapel Hill: University of North Carolina Press.

Krauthamer, Barbara. 2013. *Black Slaves, Indian Masters: Slavery, Emancipation, and Citizenship in the Native American South*. Chapel Hill: University of North Carolina Press.

Kruse, Line-Noue Memea. 2018. *The Pacific Insular Case of American Samoa: Land Rights and Law in Unincorporated US Territories*. London: Palgrave McMillian.

Kushner, Aaron. 2020. "Cherokee Political Thought and the Development of Tribal Citizenship." *Studies in American Political Development* 34 (2): 1–15.

Kymlicka, Will. 1995. *Multicultural Citizenship: A Liberal Theory of Minority Rights.* Oxford, UK: Clarendon Press.

Lauber, Almon W. 1913. *Indian Slavery in Colonial Times within the Present Limits of the United States.* New York: Longmans, Green.

Lemont, Eric D. 2006. *American Indian Constitutional Reform and the Rebuilding of Tribal Nations.* Austin: University of Texas Press.

Limerick, Patricia Nelson. 1987. *The Legacy of Conquest: The Unbroken Past of the American West.* New York: W. W. Norton.

Littlefield, Daniel F., Jr. 1977. *Africans and Seminoles: From Removal to Emancipation.* Westport, CT: Greenwood Press.

———. 1978. *The Cherokee Freedmen: From Emancipation to American Citizenship.* Westport, CT: Greenwood Press.

———. 1980. *The Chickasaw Freedmen: A People without a Country.* Westport, CT: Greenwood Press.

Mankiller, Wilma, and Michael Wallis. 1993. *Mankiller: A Chief and Her People.* New York: St. Martin's Press.

McGovney, Dudley O. 1911. "American Citizenship. Part II. Unincorporated Peoples and Peoples Incorporated with Less Than Full Privileges." *Columbia Law Review* 11 (4): 326–47.

Minges, Patrick N. 2003. *Slavery in the Cherokee Nation: The Keetoowah Society and the Defining of a People, 1855–1867.* New York: Routledge.

———, ed. 2004. *Black Indian Slave Narratives.* Winston-Salem, NC: John F. Blair.

Mooney, James. 1900. "Myths of the Cherokee." Smithsonian Institution, Bureau of American Ethnology, Washington, DC: Government Printing Office.

Moulton, Gary E., ed. 1985. "Editor's Introduction." In *The Papers of Chief John Ross:* Vol. 1, *1807–1839,* 3–11. Norman: University of Oklahoma Press.

Perdue, Theda. 1979. *Slavery and the Evolution of Cherokee Society, 1540–1866.* Knoxville: University of Tennessee Press.

———. 2000. "Clan and Court: Another Look at the Early Cherokee Republic." *American Indian Quarterly* 24 (4): 562–69.

Porter, Kenneth W. 1971. *The Negro on the American Frontier.* New York: Arno Press.

Rolnick, Addie C. 2014. "Tribal Criminal Jurisdiction: Beyond Citizenship and Blood." *American Indian Law Review* 39 (2): 337–449.

Ross, John. 1985a. *The Papers of Chief John Ross:* Vol. 1, *1807–1839.* Edited by Gary E. Moulton. Norman: University of Oklahoma Press.

———. 1985b. *The Papers of Chief John Ross:* Vol. 2, *1840–1866.* Edited by Gary E. Moulton. Norman: University of Oklahoma Press.

Saunt, Claudio. 2004. "The Paradox of Freedom: Tribal Sovereignty and Emancipation during the Reconstruction of Indian Territory." *Journal of Southern History* 70: 63–94.

Seagrave, S. Adam, ed. 2015. James Madison, "Memorandum on an African Colony for Freed Slaves." In *Liberty and Equality: The American Conversation*, 227–28. Lawrence: University Press of Kansas.

Shklar, Judith N. 1991. *American Citizenship: The Quest for Inclusion.* Cambridge, MA: Harvard University Press.

Smith, Rogers M. 1997. *Civic Ideals: Conflicting Visions of Citizenship in U.S. History.* New Haven, CT: Yale University Press.

Smithers, Gregory D. 2015. *The Cherokee Diaspora: An Indigenous History of Migration, Resettlement, and Identity.* New Haven, CT: Yale University Press.

Stremlau, Rose. 2011. *Sustaining the Cherokee Family: Kinship and the Allotment of an Indigenous Nation.* Chapel Hill: University of North Carolina Press.

Strock, Ian Randal, ed. 2010. Ulysses S. Grant, "Second Inaugural Address." In *The Complete Book of Presidential Inaugural Speeches: From George Washington to Barack Obama.* Brooklyn, NY: Grey Rabbit.

Sturm, Circe. 1998. "Blood Politics, Racial Classification, and Cherokee National Identity: The Trials and Tribulations of the Cherokee Freedmen." *American Indian Quarterly* 22 (1/2): 230–58.

———. 2002. *Blood Politics: Race, Culture, and Identity in the Cherokee Nation of Oklahoma.* Berkley: University of California Press.

———. 2014. "Race, Sovereignty, and Civil Rights: Understanding the Cherokee Freedmen Controversy." *Cultural Anthropology* 29 (3): 575–98.

Temin, David Myer. 2017. "Custer's Sins: Vine Deloria Jr. and the Settler-Colonial Politics of Civic Inclusion." *Political Theory* 46 (3): 357–79.

Tully, James. 1995. *Strange Multiplicity: Constitutionalism in an Age of Diversity.* Cambridge: Cambridge University Press.

Wardell, Morris L. 1938. *A Political History of the Cherokee Nation, 1838–1907.* Norman: University of Oklahoma Press.

West, Thomas G. 2017. *The Political Theory of the American Founding.* Cambridge: Cambridge University Press.

5

Divide et Impera

Immigration, Diversity, and the American Founding

Nicholas W. Drummond

Immigration and diversity were subjects of great interest to the men who designed America's constitution and debated its ratification. This included concerns about national unity and the cultural under-pinnings of republican government.[1] However, the topic of diversity was also a polemical debate about Montesquieu, territorial size, and the disrupting effect that heterogeneity would have on class warfare.[2] In this chapter, I merge these two areas of scholarship to further an understanding of America's constitutional design and the social forces that the founders anticipated interacting with this complex political system. I also introduce new textual evidence relating to the founders' views of immigration, culture, and ethnicity. The importance of such an investigation should be clear. If the United States has become far more diverse than the founders envisioned, then does this mean the American political system is no longer capable of operating as designed? More pointedly, does this mean today's political climate of division, plutocracy, and demagoguery is an inevitable outcome of ignoring what the founders considered to be the cultural requirements of the American constitution?

First, I discuss Montesquieu's influence on the American constitutional debate. Then, I investigate the benefits that John Jay, Alexander Hamilton, and James Madison associated with preserving America's cultural homogeneity, including national unity, the spirit of republicanism, and public vigilance against despotism.

Finally, I apply the key findings of this research to contemporary politics.

MONTESQUIEU, DIVERSITY, AND THE AMERICAN CONSTITUTIONAL DEBATE

During the period between drafting the Constitution and its ratification, two political camps emerged to debate the newly proposed government. Ironically, both sides would use the analysis of Montesquieu to support their clashing perspectives.[3] Montesquieu famously argued in *Spirit of the Laws* (1748) that a republic's territory must remain small and its people homogeneous so that patriotic virtue could be sustained.[4] He warned that citizens of large republics like ancient Rome and Syracuse lacked "mutual confidence" because they were divided by ethnicity, language, culture, and religion.[5] Large republics were also likely to suffer a polarization of wealth, which increased luxury and stimulated avarice among the affluent and envy among the poor.[6] All of these destructive influences would be compounded by the socioeconomic complexity of a large republic, which made it difficult for people to recognize the public good, let alone defend it against corrupt or incompetent rulers. The inevitable fate of a large republic was therefore to become a divided regime where "the public good is sacrificed to a thousand private views."[7] In this tumultuous political climate, "men of large fortunes" would oppress the republic unless the licentious multitude sought relief by supporting a populist demagogue who promised liberty but established tyranny instead.[8]

To make matters worse, Montesquieu warned that remaining geographically small was not a viable option for most republics because they were likely to be conquered by larger states with greater resources. Montesquieu's analysis offered two solutions, which the American framers synthesized into a new kind of republican government. The first option was for a small republic to expand its resources by federating with other small republics. This would equip member states with "the external force" of a larger state while mitigating "internal corruption" with a dual power structure.[9] Montesquieu's second solution was a complex government inspired by England's constitutional monarchy. The design of this political system offered three principal advantages to larger regimes: (1) class warfare was stabilized by incorporating the mixed orders of king, nobility, and commons; (2) democratic excesses were filtered through representatives better capable "of discussing public affairs"; and (3) power was strategically distributed among executive, judicial, and legislative branches of government so that "power should be a check to power."[10]

Both the Federalists and Anti-Federalists endorsed Montesquieu's tripartite political system, but the latter doubted the wisdom of humans to arrange coequal powers correctly or that such a system could operate effectively without the true mixed orders of king, nobility, and commons.[11] There was also a prevailing view among Anti-Federalists that America's large size would enable ambitious and wealthy elites to dominate the newly proposed government and engage in collusion rather than checking.[12] Swayed by Montesquieu's theory of the small republic, they wanted America to remain a decentralized confederation where member state governments had the sovereignty to govern themselves domestically in accordance with distinct interests and diverse cultural preferences. Anti-Federalists warned that ratification would "annihilate all the state governments" because of the Constitution's Supremacy Clause, the Necessary and Proper Clause, and the Common Defense and General Welfare clauses.[13] America would therefore be governed like a single consolidated nation and suffer the same fate of the Grecian and Roman republics when they "extended their conquests over large territories."[14] The country would either balkanize because of its diverse manners, laws, climates, and productions or succumb to "iron handed despotism."[15]

The Federalists countered this analysis with three principal arguments. First, Hamilton's *Federalist* 9 noted that Montesquieu favored the Lycian confederation because of its strong centralized government.[16] This meant the political scientist revered by so many Anti-Federalists would have endorsed the Constitution. Next, Madison's *Federalist* 10 theorized that a larger republic was "more favorable to the election of proper guardians" because size and diversity could impede the formation of overbearing majorities. Geographic separation would make it "more difficult for all who" felt a common motive "to discover their own strength, and to act in unison with each other." If a majority faction did overcome the spatial challenge, then it would likely be splintered by competing loyalties based on region, occupation, sect, economic class, or the demagoguery of popular leaders.[17] Finally, in *Federalist* 2 Jay asserted America to be culturally and ethnically homogenous, which distinguished it from the ancient republics informing Montesquieu's thesis about large republics. Instead of being a divided population destined for tyranny, the American people were a "band of brethren, united to each other by the strongest ties." What makes this third argument particularly important is that all three contributors to *The Federalist* believed America's culture to be sufficiently homogenous for the Constitution to function as designed. Moreover, they believed this homogeneity should be preserved.

JAY'S HOMOGENEOUS REPUBLIC

Jay authored only five *Federalist* essays, but he also wrote a separate pro-ratification essay, "Address to the People of the State of New York" (1788). In this article, he cautioned against having a new constitutional convention because it would be plagued by a new "set of politicians who teach, and profess to believe, that the extent of our nation is too great for the superintendence of one national government." Jay dismissed "this doctrine" as "mischievous in its tendency and consequences," and he argued that America could flourish as one nation because of its "fraternal affection, unsuspecting intercourse; and mutual participation in commerce, navigation and citizenship." Americans were essentially "a band of brothers" who should "have confidence in themselves and in one another."[18]

In *Federalist* 2, Jay had advanced these same arguments about kinship, communication, and social capital, but he explained in greater detail why these essential features of republican governance would subsist after ratification. First, the intercommunication and trade of the American people were enhanced by the "navigable waters" bordering the country and the "noble rivers" connecting the states. Second, Jay believed the kinship of Americans to be especially strong because of their homogeneity:

> With equal pleasure I have as often taken notice that Providence has been pleased to give this one connected country to one united people—a people descended from the same ancestors, speaking the same language, professing the same religion, attached to the same principles of government, very similar in

their manners and customs, and who, by their joint counsels, arms, and efforts, fighting side by side throughout a long and bloody war, have nobly established general liberty and independence.

Did Jay exaggerate the homogeneity of Americans? In terms of ethnicity, the most reliable data we have on the ancestry of white Americans during this period (1790) indicates that the English were an ethnic majority at nearly 60 percent; about 26 percent of white Americans traced their ancestry to Scotland, Wales, or Ireland; and most of the remaining whites hailed from other Western European nations.[19] Furthermore, according to census data from 1790, the U.S. total population was approximately 3,893,637, of which 3,140,207 were white (80.65 percent), 694,280 were slaves (17.83 percent), and 59,150 were free nonwhites (1.52 percent).[20] This means that of the total free population approximately 1.85 percent were nonwhite. Finally, because of voting restrictions, less than one million of America's mostly white citizenry were full members of the polity.[21]

In terms of culture, there were certainly sectarian differences among Americans as well as cultural variations associated with region, economics, and national origin.[22] However, it would be preposterous to argue an equivalence of heterogeneity between America today, an enormous country with an advanced industrialized society of nearly 330 million racially and culturally diverse citizens, and a significantly smaller, mostly agrarian country that had a dominant Protestant British culture and was populated by approximately 3.2 million citizens of mostly Western European descent, of which less than a million were enfranchised.

We should also note that Jay's *Federalist* 2 never said the American people shared one uniform culture. He said they were "very similar in their manners and customs," which meant the culture of Americans was sufficiently homogeneous for the American political system to operate according to its design. Jay also seemed hopeful in *Federalist* 64 that American unity would increase after ratification because of the emergence of "a national form and a national character," which would expand political concerns beyond the parochial. This interpretation corresponds with the message of *Federalist* 2 and his pro-ratification New York essay. Essentially, the cultural similarities of the American people coupled with the country's geographic connectedness would help facilitate a functioning union, which in turn would help forge and maintain a unifying national culture. However, this did not mean Jay thought America's national culture would become a self-perpetuating force that could survive independently of the cultural similarities he praised in *Federalist* 2.

Cultural homogeneity was so important for Jay that he once suggested erecting "a wall of brass around the country for the exclusion of Catholics."[23] His prejudice may have been personal. Jay's great-grandfather and grandfather were among the thousands of persecuted Huguenot Protestants who fled France for Britain, Holland, and America in the late seventeenth century.[24] However, Jay's anti-Catholicism also stemmed from political concerns about identity, unity, and republicanism. When he served on the Continental Congress, Jay wrote an official address to the British people in 1774 that repeatedly called the American colonists a British Protestant people. He also expressed concerns that the Quebec Act would swell the annexed Canadian territory with "Catholick emigrants from Europe," which would further disunite this region from the American colonists and provide the crown with a force to intimidate and oppress "the ancient, free, Protestant Colonies."[25]

In 1777, Jay said Catholics should be prohibited from voting or owning land until they swore an official oath that "no pope, priest, or foreign authority on earth" could absolve them from obeying political laws.[26] The implication of this recommendation is that cultural homogeneity was insufficient on its own to sustain a republic. Also important was the precise content of the shared culture. In this instance, Jay wanted all citizens to agree that political authority resided in government rather than ecclesiastic institutions. He nevertheless stated in 1816 that America was a "Christian nation" that preferred electing Christian leaders and benefited from doing so.[27] Seven years earlier, Jay also spoke approvingly of America and the Western Hemisphere being "gradually filled with civilized and Christian people."[28] The latter statement indicates support for European immigration, as does the concern he expressed in 1785 about emigration to America being discouraged by France.[29] However, that same year he also intimated the advantages of settling the continent with American emigrants rather than foreign immigrants: "They would transplant their love of liberty, their spirit of enterprise, and their attachment to republicanism."[30]

Jay's endorsement of French immigration in 1785 suggests that his anti-Catholicism had softened, but he still cautioned against foreigners holding political office. Indeed, a 1787 letter to George Washington may have prompted the "natural born citizen" clause of the presidency.[31] Nevertheless, in a 1794 letter to Hamilton he commented on European "war, discord, and oppression" and said: "I sometimes flatter myself that Providence, in compassion to the afflicted of these countries, will continue to leave America in a proper state to be an asylum to them." Although this was certainly an endorsement of European immigration, the people he seemed to have in mind were individuals of "rank and character."[32]

There is evidence that Jay viewed racial diversity more positively than cultural diversity. He grew up with household slaves and he purchased slaves as an adult, but he spoke harshly of "the horrors of slavery" and he was instrumental in establishing the New York Manumission Society.[33] This organization successfully advocated laws against the slave trade and petitioned for the gradual abolition of slaves. Jay's regard for America's indigenous peoples could also be amicable. In 1786 he said that "Indians" were treated harshly, including being "murdered . . . in cold Blood."[34] To improve upon this regretful history, he recommended a gradual extension of western settlements and the better management of Indian relations. However, in 1797 he bemoaned the difficulties of civilizing and Christianizing "savages" because of their cultural prejudice against things like work, noncommunal property rights, and in-door habitation.[35]

In summary, Jay thought America's culture was sufficiently homogenous for its political system to operate as designed. He favored natural population growth, but he also supported the immigration of European Christians of "rank and character" who shared the political values of Americans. There were occasions when he seemed optimistic about race relations, but the importance of ethnic and cultural homogeneity emphasized in *Federalist* 2 indicates that Jay would have opposed a truly diverse society.[36]

HAMILTON'S HOMOGENEOUS REPUBLIC

Early in his political career, Hamilton (an immigrant himself) favored skilled immigration and promoted religious tolerance. At the Constitutional Convention, he opposed residency requirements for members of Congress, arguing that Europeans "of moderate fortunes will be fond of coming here where they will be on a level with the first Citizens."[37] In *Federalist* 1 and the *Report on Manufactures* (1791), he criticized religious persecution and said that tolerance can benefit the economy because manufacturers will relocate to America for its "perfect equality of religious privileges." The *Report on Manufactures* also spoke approvingly of immigration "extending the population, and with it the useful and productive labour of the country."[38] Additionally, in a proclamation draft written for George Washington, Hamilton discussed a religious obligation "to render [America] more & more a secure & propitious asylum for the unfortunate of other countries."[39]

Scholars who reject the claim that America's political system requires cultural homogeneity also emphasize *Federalist* 12, where Hamilton postulated that gainful business relationships could intimately blend the interests of diverse professions and thus silence the "rivalships" of "agriculture and commerce." For example, Jay Cost argues that Hamilton's theory of "mutual economic gain" is applicable to diverse countries like America today.[40] This analysis ignores the possibility that rent-seeking behavior can be quite profitable for identity groups and their leaders.[41] Moreover, other than Hamilton's views on religious tolerance, there is scant evidence that he thought his theory could operate in a multicultural society. On the contrary, Hamilton indicated in *Federalist* 12 that unity via commercial activity would be facilitated by an "affinity of language and manners." He also offered the following perspective at the New York State ratifying convention (1788): "I acknowledge, that the local interests of the states are in some degree various; and that there is some difference in their habits and manners: But this I will presume to affirm; that, from New-Hampshire to Georgia, the people of America are as uniform in their interests and manners, as those of any established in Europe."[42]

Hamilton went on to argue that the diverse economic interests of the states would, "under the regular and gentle influence of general laws . . . be constantly assimilating, till they embrace each other, and assume the same complexion."[43] As for the diverse "habits and manners" of America's states, he said this heterogeneity would be problematic only if the "laws of the union . . . were . . . to alter, or abrogate at a blow, the whole of [any state's] civil and criminal institutions; were they to penetrate the recesses of domestic life, and controul, in all respects, the private conduct of individuals."[44] This analysis may seem disingenuous coming from a political thinker who consistently advocated an energetic national government. However, these viewpoints are reconcilable if Hamilton thought federal intervention into the social affairs of individual states was unnecessary because America's cultural landscape was sufficiently homogenized. Supporting this interpretation is a conversation Hamilton had the following year with British diplomat George Beckwith: "I have always preferred a connection with you, to that of any country, we think in English, and have a similarity of prejudices and of predilections."[45] Hamilton may have been wooing Beckwith with this statement, but he would hardly have attempted to ingratiate himself this way if such a claim was incredulous.

At the turn of the century, Hamilton's view of immigration would also significantly harden because of concerns about the national origin and political values of immigrant populations. During the Whiskey Rebellion of 1794, he called for the deportation of rebels and expressed great distrust of Irish immigrants.[46] Four years later, he supported a controversial law authorizing the president to expel aliens considered "dangerous to the peace and safety of the United States."[47] Aimed at Jacobins and their sympathizers, Hamilton said "the mass ought to be obliged to leave the Country," though merchants and "a few" well-behaved individuals deserved special consideration.[48] The following year, he expressed frustration that the Sedition Act was not being enforced against immigrant journalists from England, Scotland, and Ireland: "Renegade Aliens conduct more than one of the most incendiary presses in the [United States]—and yet in open contempt and defiance of the laws they are permitted to continue their destructive labours. Why are they not sent away?"[49] Finally, in *The Examination* (1802), he argued that America no longer required a steady flow of immigrants because "the natural progress of our own population is sufficiently rapid for strength, security and settlement."[50] Partisan politics may have influenced his thinking but, as I demonstrate below, Hamilton's case study analysis echoed Montesquieu's warnings about diversity.

The Examination was Hamilton's response to President Thomas Jefferson's first annual message to Congress. In this report, Jefferson argued that a trial period of residency for newcomers was unnecessary because, in most cases, the act of emigration itself would satisfactorily demonstrate the "general character and capabilities" required for good citizenship. Jefferson also raised humanitarian concerns and suggested that Americans had a debt to be paid forward to immigrants: "Shall we refuse to the unhappy fugitives from distress that hospitality which the savages of the wilderness extended to our fathers arriving in this land? Shall oppressed humanity find no asylum on this globe?"[51]

Hamilton flatly rejected Jefferson's "proposal to abolish all restriction on naturalization." Not only was this policy "at variance with the concurrent maxims of all commentators on popular governments," but it was also contradicted by Jefferson's *Notes on the State of Virginia* (1785).[52] In this text, Jefferson warned against mass immigration because most emigrants would originate from "absolute monarchies" and would therefore pollute America with their illiberal principles or succumb to "unbounded licentiousness, passing, as is usual, from one extreme to another." The *Notes* also suggested that "natural propagation" could sufficiently increase the country's population size. Jefferson surmised that restricting growth in this way would ensure that "our government be more homogenous, more peaceable, [and] more durable."[53]

Although Hamilton's nativist arguments in *The Examination* quoted heavily from the *Notes*, he further specified that foreigners are attached to their "particular customs and manners," which could "complicate and confound public opinion" and thus weaken the "the energy of a common National sentiment." He also raised the additional concern that foreigners lack "that love of country which will almost invariably be found to be closely connected with birth, education and family."[54] This was not the first time Hamilton made such an argument. At the New York state assembly in 1787, he said enfranchisement for naturalized citizens should require an oath of civil obedience, but this precaution was unnecessary for citizens "born amongst us, educated with us, possessing our habits, possessing our manners, with an equal ardent love of [their] native country."[55] Interestingly, the *Examination* also mentioned the fate of Rome and Syracuse, two case studies that informed Montesquieu's concerns about ethnic and cultural diversity.[56] Hamilton argued that both republics were ruined when "a great number of foreigners were suddenly admitted to the rights of citizenship."[57] Apparently, not even the new "science of politics" lauded in *Federalist* 9 or the commercialism praised in *Federalist* 12 could adequately mitigate this danger.

Hamilton believed Jefferson's "inconsistency" owed to gratitude and partisan politics rather than compassion. The president was "head of the American nation" because naturalized citizens had favored the Democratic Republicans in the previous election. Hamilton also thought his rival was propagating a false interpretation of history that portrayed Indians as unreservedly "humane and philanthropic." Hamilton entertained this narrative for the sake of argument, but he asked readers "to trace the history farther, and ask what has become of the nations of savages who exercised this policy?" Since their territory was now controlled by Europeans, the Indian example of hospitality offered Americans "a useful lesson."[58]

In spite of these observations, Hamilton may have viewed racial integration more favorably than cultural diversity. He owned or at least purchased slaves, but he was an important figure in the New York Manumission Society.[59] In 1779, Hamilton also sent Jay a letter in which he argued that blacks had "natural faculties . . . probably as good as [whites]."[60] However, his motive for supporting emancipation may have simply been an expedient enlistment of freed slaves into the Continental Army. Hamilton's commitment to integration is also disputed because his prolific journalist activities lacked "any clear, unequivocal exposition of the 'abolitionist' viewpoint."[61]

Hamilton's regard for America's indigenous peoples was likewise mixed. In *Federalist* 24 he said, "The savage tribes on our Western frontier ought to be regarded as our natural enemies." Yet he spoke favorably of trading "with the Indian nations" and elsewhere said, "It is our interest to make peace with the hostile Indians, whenever we can do it on proper terms."[62] He was also outraged by the violence of some frontiersmen toward Indians, though he likewise accused the latter of committing "injuries and provocations."[63] Most interesting of all, Hamilton was a trustee for a New York school that educated white and native children together.[64] Although some of these schools were designed to eradicate the cultural and spiritual heritage of Indian children, the native children at the Hamilton-Oneida Academy were taught both English and Indian languages.[65] Members of the Oneida tribe would actually write a letter to Hamilton referring to him as "a friend of every body—Indians as well as White people." The letter requested Hamilton's assistance in expanding the school's enrollment to include the children of other tribes because this "would serve to strengthen & brighten the Chains of friendship with those Nations."[66] There is no record of Hamilton replying to this letter, but the Oneida request may give us a better sense of the school's mission—to foster peaceful relations by educating diverse peoples together. Perhaps this was why Hamilton "cheerfully" accepted the trustee position and was willing to "afford it all the aid in his power."[67] However, there is no evidence that Hamilton wanted a full integration of America's indigenous peoples. On the contrary, he advocated policies that would—through payment or demographic pressure—gradually remove Indians from settlement territories.[68]

In summary, Hamilton concurred with Jay that America's culture was sufficiently homogenous for its political system to operate as designed. He thought the country had benefited from skilled European immigration, but the rapid immigration proposed by the Jefferson administration would pollute America republicanism with illiberal or licentious values. Mass immigration had also become unnecessary since America was meeting its own population needs. Finally, though Hamilton held views of race that were progressive for his time, these views were hardly the endorsement of a truly diverse society.

MADISON'S HOMOGENEOUS REPUBLIC

Madison at times seemed optimistic about cultural diversity. In a 1774 letter to William Bradford, he complained about Virginia's sectarian discord and pined for the religious tolerance of Pennsylvania. Much later in his life (1820), he wrote a response letter to a Savannah doctor praising Jewish integration. In both letters, Madison emphasized the importance of "equal laws" protecting the equal "rights of conscience," which produced desirable effects like commerce, learning, innovation, and "love of country." However, we should note that Madison's first letter said these benefits were acquired through "mutual emulation and mutual Inspection."[69] In other words, citizens learned from one another by critically evaluating different customs and by rejecting what they found to be harmful or unproductive. Diversity was beneficial because it was guided by a mutual goal of cultural improvement and cultural solidarity.

Madison also believed cultural divisions could be softened with education. In an 1822 letter to W. T. Barry, he recommended an education system that imparted knowledge of the "Globe we inhabit, the Nations among which it is divided, and the characters and customs which distinguish them." If people became acquainted with "foreign countries in this mode," they would experience a kindred effect that "[weakened] local prejudices" and "[enlarged] the sphere of benevolent feelings."[70] We might infer from this letter that Madison thought education could produce a similar effect within culturally diverse nations.

Perhaps the strongest evidence that Madison favored cultural heterogeneity is his thesis of the extended republic. In *Federalist* 10 and 51, Madison posited that the sectarian diversity of a larger republic could help mitigate the threat of majority faction. However, his recommendation to "extend the sphere" was not a call for boundless heterogeneity. Madison's analysis discussed political, regional, economic, sectarian, and demagogic forms of diversity, but even these had limits. In a 1787 letter sent to Jefferson, he explained that his mechanistic solution to majority factions would function only in "a sphere of a mean extent." If a republic was too small, then "oppressive combinations may be too easily formed against the weaker party," but if the republic was too large, then "a defensive concert may be rendered too difficult against the oppression of those entrusted with the administration." This meant the size of a republic could be larger than Montesquieu and Anti-Federalists calculated, but there was a limit to territorial expansion that if surpassed would enable the ruling elite to oppress the people via a strategy of *Divide et impera*.[71]

This thesis would resurface in the *National Gazette* essays Madison authored in the 1790s.[72] He repeatedly warned that ambitious elites and plutocratic forces were oppressing the people via a strategy of divide and rule.[73] He also frequently discussed the importance of public vigilance for securing liberty.[74] The emphasis on plutocracy was new, but Madison had always maintained that a republican citizenry must be actuated by a "vigilant and manly spirit."[75] Even his seminal essay *Federalist* 51 argued that the Constitution's distribution of powers was an "auxiliary" precaution because "dependence on the people" was "the primary control on the government."[76]

Madison's diminishing confidence in the extended republic in the 1790s owed primarily to America's increasing socioeconomic complexity, the growing influence of moneyed interests, and Hamilton's success at expanding the power of the national government.[77] Despite these challenges, Madison still believed effectual public vigilance was possible if "a general intercourse of sentiment" was facilitated by federalism, representatives traveling to and from the national government, "good roads, domestic commerce, a free press, and particularly a circulation of newspapers through the entire body of the people."[78] Patriotic education was also necessary, as was the censoring guidance of literati and the establishment of a true republican party that could unite the people against despotic threats.[79] He also recommended progressive taxation to mitigate class conflict.[80] But Madison never said the "sphere of mean extent" could operate in a republic of substantial cultural diversity. On the contrary, he concurred with Jay and Hamilton that America's culture had to be sufficiently homogeneous for its political system to operate as designed. To understand Madison's thinking, we have to consider the relationship he thought existed between national unity and the defense of liberty. In a 1791 *National Gazette* essay discussing the "interests and affections" of the American states, he said:

> The greater the mutual confidence and affection of all parts of the Union, the more likely will they be to concur amicably, or to differ with moderation . . . the less the supposed difference of interests, the greater the concord and confidence throughout the great body of the people, the more readily must they sympathize with each other, the more seasonably can they interpose a common manifestation of their sentiments, the more certainly will they take the alarm at usurpation or oppression, and the more effectually will they consolidate their defence of the public liberty.[81]

Madison never mentioned culture in this particular essay because the divisions worrying him in the 1790s were "all prejudices, local, political, and occupational, that may prevent or disturb a general coalition of sentiments."[82] Nevertheless, there is ample evidence that he thought cultural homogeneity was an important component of national unity. For example, Madison and Hamilton said in *Federalist* 19 that the Swiss cantons "kept together" because there were "few sources of contention among a people of such simple and homogeneous manners." However, religious heterogeneity "in three instances . . . kindled violent and bloody contests" and eventually "severed the league" into "Protestant and Catholic cantons." Religious diversity also "produced opposite alliances with foreign powers."

Speaking at the Philadelphia convention in 1787, Madison argued against the possibility of an oppressive combination of large states like Virginia, Massachusetts, and Pennsylvania. The similar "manners" and "religion" of these states, "which sometimes beget affection between different communities . . . were not more assimilated than the other states."[83] Two weeks later, he offered further clarification: "Altho' their climate varied considerably . . . the Govts., the laws, and the manners of all [states] were nearly the same."[84] Madison would, in one respect, consider America's cultural homogeneity a liability. He warned in 1799 that America was predominately British in "language . . . usages . . . & . . . manners," which rendered the country vulnerable to "foreign intrigues" from this particular country.[85]

Madison also thought Americans derived national unity from their ethnic solidarity and, presumably, the cultural kinship that often accompanies this connection. In a 1785 letter discussing western settlements, he claimed that the relationship between the new states and the Atlantic states would not mirror the relationship that exists "between the heterogeneous and hostile Societies of Europe." Instead of "[consisting] of a hostile or a foreign people," they would be populated by immigrants from the Atlantic states and would therefore "be a bone of our bones, and flesh of our flesh."[86] Madison reiterated this argument in an 1803 letter when he said, "Our Western fellow Citizens are bound to the union . . . by the ties of kindred and affection which for a long time will derive strength from the stream of emigration peopling that region."[87] The same language was used by Madison in *Federalist* 14 when he argued that the American people could be "mutual guardians of their mutual happiness" because they were "knit together . . . by so many cords of affection." This included the "kindred blood" flowing in their veins, which better enabled citizens to live "together as members of the same family." America's ethnic solidarity would help preserve national unity, which in turn would help facilitate a vigilant public defense of liberty against despotic forces.

This did not mean Madison opposed all immigration. While serving in the Virginia legislature, he drafted notes for a 1784 speech that warned against establishing a religious assessment because this oppressive law would provoke "emigrations from [the] State" and "prevent [immigration] into it as asylum."[88] He would reiterate this position in his "Memorial and Remonstrance" (1785), arguing for a continuation of "that generous policy, which, offering an Asylum to the persecuted and oppressed of every Nation and Religion, promised a [luster] to our country, and an accession to the number of its citizens."[89] At the Philadelphia convention, he said the Constitution would improve the country's "stability & reputation," which meant "great numbers of respectable Europeans: men who love liberty and wish to partake its blessings, will be ready to transfer their fortunes hither."[90] Several days later he said that "foreigners of merit & republican principles" should be invited to live among us because "America was indebted to emigrations for her settlement & Prosperity." Indeed, "that part of America which had encouraged them most had advanced most rapidly in population, agriculture & the arts."[91] Both speeches occurred during a larger discussion about requisite terms of citizenship for members of Congress. Madison warned against these restrictions because they would "give a tincture of illiberality to the Constitution" and "discourage the most desirable class of people from emigrating to the U.S."[92] He advised instead to "maintain the character of liberality which had been professed in all the Constitutions & publications of America."[93]

We must be careful about inferring too much from these statements. Madison's comment about rapid population growth indicates support for mass immigration, but he qualifies the type of immigrants he thought America should invite, namely, wealthy or skilled Europeans who were already favorably disposed toward America's political values. Madison would also intimate aversion to mass immigration in *Federalist* 43, where he warned that "the minority of CITIZENS" within an individual state "may become a majority of PERSONS, by the accession of alien residents." Madison was discussing the potential danger of "violent factions," but his analysis reveals a more general concern about immigration shifting the balance of power within states. Furthermore, when Madison was a member of the House of Representatives, he supported the country's first naturalization law with a speech that prioritized nationalist concerns rather than population growth: "It is no doubt very desirable that we should hold out as many inducements as possible for the worthy part of mankind to come and settle amongst us, and throw their fortunes into a common lot with ours. But why is this desirable? Not merely to swell the catalogue of people. No, sir, it is to increase the wealth and strength of the community."[94]

Madison concluded his speech by calling citizenship "a privilege" that should be offered to "[persons] of good fame that really meant to incorporate [themselves] into our society."[95] He never mentioned culture or national origin during this speech, but he offered no objection to the bill under review, which restricted naturalization to "free white person[s] . . . of good character."[96] He also supported the Naturalization Act of 1795, which similarly restricted naturalization to "free white [persons]" of "good moral character."[97]

Madison's support for both naturalization laws is significant for another reason. At this point, the reader might be asking why the Constitution itself did not restrict immigration if America's political system required cultural homogeneity. During the convention debate about citizenship requirements for members of Congress, Madison said constitutional restrictions were "unnecessary; because the [national legislature] is to have the right of regulating naturalization, and can by virtue thereof fix different periods of residence as conditions of enjoying different privileges of Citizenship."[98] He approved that this governing body could "confer the full rank of Citizens on meritorious" immigrants "by special acts of naturalization."[99] The implication of these statements is that Madison wanted naturalization laws to be flexible to the needs of the country rather than permanently fixed by the Constitution.

Finally, whatever Madison's concerns may have been about maintaining the liberality of the Constitution, he did not harbor this concern toward naturalization laws that restricted immigration racially. Madison was an ashamed slave owner who thought the solution to America's "original sin" was the recolonization of freed slaves.[100] Integration would ultimately fail because of white prejudice, black resentment, and the vices acquired by both races from the institution of slavery.[101] Moreover, in a major concession to the Anti-Federalists, Madison and Hamilton both worried that slavery was a polemical issue that divided the nation politically and culturally.[102]

Madison's regard for American Indians was nearly as skeptical as his view of American blacks: "Next to the case of the Black race within our bosom, that of the red on our borders, is the problem most baffling to the policy of our Country."[103] He also feared resettling freed slaves on the western frontier because such a settlement "would be destroyed by the Savages who have a peculiar antipathy to the blacks."[104] However, Madison believed a mutually beneficial trading relationship was possible if America's indigenous peoples assimilated European ways: "The benevolent provisions and steady efforts of the Government of the United States, to abolish the savage manners of those tribes, and to substitute the arts of Civilized life [are] not less conducive to their own happiness, than to the peace of our neighbouring settlements."[105] This did not mean Madison wanted a full integration with America's indigenous peoples, but he thought it possible to share the continent.[106]

In summary, Madison agreed with Hamilton and Jay that America's culture was sufficiently homogenous for its political system to operate as designed. Madison preferred natural population growth, but he also supported European immigration, so long as immigrants were skilled, wealthy, and shared America's political values. Finally, because he was deeply pessimistic about racial integration, he thought naturalization should be restricted to whites, and he recommended the resettling of freed slaves to Africa.

THE FOUNDERS AND DIVERSITY TODAY

The evidence I present in this chapter demonstrates that Jay, Hamilton, and Madison thought preserving a sufficient level of cultural homogeneity was necessary to bind the country together, sustain the spirit of republicanism, and facilitate a vigilant public defense of liberty against despotic forms of governance. All three men thought asylum should be offered to the persecuted, but they prioritized European immigrants of skill, wealth, and established character who shared America's political values. Since Jay, Hamilton, and Madison helped design our political system and secure its ratification, it behooves us to evaluate some of their concerns about mass immigration and cultural diversity in a contemporary context. The warnings of Anti-Federalists may also be relevant since America is now far more diverse than it was during the ratification debate.

Today, can we truly regard Americans, as Jay did, as "a band of brethren, united to each other by the strongest ties?" Or are we instead moving toward that which he sought most to avoid, the balkanization of the country into "unsocial, jealous, and alien sovereignties?"[107] The splintering of America into separate nations is difficult to imagine, but citizens today are self-segregating politically and racially.[108] There have even been efforts by states and cities to subdivide into distinct political entities, in some cases with racial motivations.[109] Nevertheless, a more likely scenario than balkanization would be for the country to remain connected by what one Anti-Federalist called "iron handed despotism."[110] America has already curbed liberties of speech, association, and privacy in response to cultural and racial tensions.[111] We have also seen the militarization of the police, the expansion of employee sensitivity training programs, and increasing efforts by the public and private sectors to socially engineer equality for designated identity groups.[112] Surely, there are times when efforts to secure order, protect vulnerable minorities, and facilitate equality are necessary. However, these measures do indicate that liberty becomes less of a priority in diverse republics like America.

Should we also heed Hamilton's warning about naturalizing immigrants from countries with autocratic governments? Mass immigration from authoritarian countries like China and illiberal democracies like Mexico might be changing (or at least shifting) the country's political values, which could forever alter America's government.[113] Such an outcome would not be unprecedented. Setting aside Hamilton's claim about immigration benefiting the Democratic Republicans, a more recent example of immigrant groups influencing American politics is the Irish and Eastern Europeans of the late nineteenth and early twentieth centuries. This wave of immigrants along with their progeny helped Franklin Roosevelt win the presidency and increase the power of the federal government.[114] For good or for worse, Asian and Latino immigration may similarly influence the country, especially given the electoral preference of these groups for the Democratic Party and "big government" programs.[115] Perhaps we should also heed Hamilton's counsel about limiting immigration because "the natural progress of [America's] population is sufficiently rapid for strength, security and settlement."[116] If experts are right that America's job market is going to endure major disruptions because of automation and artificial intelligence, then increasing our population size via immigration may not be prudent policy.[117]

Moreover, if Anti-Federalist warnings about diversity are correct, then perhaps Americans should be calling for a more decentralized political system. Consider the following provocative questions: Does a unified general interest still exist in multicultural America? And if not, then why do we tolerate a national government imposing uniform laws on diverse communities with distinct preferences? We might also ask why Hillary Clinton supporters should accept a political system forcing them to be governed by a president they regard as utterly hostile to their notion of "the good." Or had Hillary Clinton won the presidential election, why Donald Trump supporters should be willing to do the same. And relating to these concerns, why should Americans accept a political system whose national legislature scores such abysmal public approval ratings?

Finally, what are we to make of Madison's warning about ambitious and wealthy elites exploiting the political wedges created by diversity? Because of their cultural diversity the American people may be incapable of forming a defensive concert against despotic forms of governance. Moreover, if we also accept Montesquieu's political thinking, then citizens wanting to escape plutocracy could be seduced by demagogues into accepting tyranny. This analysis could help explain the appeal of populists like Trump and Bernie Sanders, both of whom have been labeled demagogues by critics.[118] What was especially fascinating about the 2016 election was the ideological overlap of Trump and Bernie supporters. Both groups believed that moneyed interests use the government to secure private interests unfairly, often to the detriment of the wider population.[119] To some extent, this overlap was a continuation of the ideological intersection of the Tea Party and the Occupy Wall Street movement. And yet, rather than uniting against the moneyed few, the American people remain intractably polarized by partisanship and identity. If Madison observed the state of our union, then perhaps he would tell us that we are being oppressed via a strategy of *Divide et impera*.[120]

NOTES

1. Previous research includes Walter Berns, "Constitutionalism and Multiculturalism," in *Multiculturalism and American Democracy*, ed. Arthur M. Melzer et al. (Lawrence: University Press of Kansas, 1998), 91–109; Thomas G. West, *Vindicating the Founders: Race, Sex, Class, and Justice in the Origins of America* (Lanham, MD: Rowman and Littlefield, 2000); Thomas West, "Immigration: The Founders' View and Today's Challenge," in *The Founders on Citizenship and Immigration* (Lanham, MD: Rowman and Littlefield, 2007), 75–113; Thomas West, *The Political Theory of the American Founding* (Cambridge: Cambridge University Press, 2017); and Michael C. LeMay, ed., *Transforming America: Perspective on U.S. Immigration* (Santa Barbara, CA: Praeger, 2013), vol. 1.

2. Previous research includes Lance Banning, "The Practicable Sphere of a Republic: James Madison, the Constitutional Convention, and the Emergence of Revolutionary Federalism," in *Beyond Confederation*, ed. Richard Beeman et al. (Chapel Hill: University of North Carolina Press, 1987), 162–87; Lance Banning, *The Sacred Fire of Liberty: James Madison and the Founding of the Federal Republics* (Ithaca, NY: Cornell University Press, 1995), 202–14; Colleen A. Sheehan, "The Politics of Public Opinion: James Madison's 'Notes,'" *William and Mary Quarterly* 49, no. 4 (October 1992): 609–27; Colleen A. Sheehan, *James Madison and the Spirit of Republican Self-Government* (New York: Cambridge University Press, 2009), 96–106; Tiffany Jones Miller, "James Madison's Republic of 'Mean Extent' Theory: Avoiding the Scylla and Charybdis of Republican Government," *Polity* 39, no. 4 (2007); and Teena Gabrielson, "James Madison's Psychology of Public Opinion," *Political Research Quarterly* 62, no. 3 (2009): 434.

3. For more on the influence of Montesquieu, see Donald S. Lutz, "The Relative Influence of European Writers on Late Eighteenth-Century American Political Thought," *American Political Science Review*, no. 78 (1984): 189–96; and Paul M. Spurlin, *Montesquieu in America 1760–1801* (New York: Octagon Books, 1969).

4. Charles de Montesquieu, *The Spirit of the Laws* (Amherst, MA: Prometheus Books, 2002), VIII.16 (hereafter cited as *SL*).

5. *SL*, X.3. See also *SL*, VIII.2 and note 3; Charles de Montesquieu, *Considerations on the Causes of the Greatness of the Romans and Their Decline* (Indianapolis: Hackett, 1965), IX (hereafter cited as *CR*).

6. *SL*, III.3, V.4, VII.2, VIII.16; *CR*, III, X.

7. *SL*, VIII.16. See also *SL*, IV.6–7.

8. *SL*, VIII.16. See also *SL*, VIII.2, 14, XI.13–14; *CR*, IV, VIII.

9. *SL*, IX.1.

10. *SL*, XI.4. See also SL, XIX.27; *CR*, VIII.

11. Centinel I, October 5, 1787, in *The Complete Anti-Federalist*, ed. Herbert Storing (Chicago: University of Chicago Press, 1981) (hereafter cited as

Storing), 2.7.7; An Old Whig V, November 1, 1787, Storing, 3.3.31; Patrick Henry, June 5, 1788, Storing, 5.16.8; and Patrick Henry, June 9, 1788, Storing 5.16.13. Examples of Federalist support for Montesquieu's distribution of powers include Alexander Hamilton, *Federalist* 9, in Alexander Hamilton, James Madison, and John Jay, *The Federalist Papers* (New York: Signet Classic, 2003). See also Madison, *Federalist* 10, 47, 51, and 63; and Jay, *Federalist* 64. Examples of Anti-Federalist support for the distribution of powers include Brutus XVI, April 10, 1788, Storing 2.9.197; Agrippa XVI, February 5, 1788, Storing, 4.6.73; and Federal Farmer XVII, January 23, 1788, Storing, 2.8.208.

12. Anti-Federalist concerns about America's large size enabling the "few" to prevail over the "many" can be found here: Federal Farmer XVII, January 23, 1788, Storing, 2.8.212; Brutus I, October, 18 1787, Storing, 2.9.18; Brutus IV, November 29, 1787, Storing, 2.9.46; and Samuel Chase V, April 1788, Storing, 5.3.20. Concerns about collusion can be found here: Federal Farmer VII, December 31, 1787, Storing, 2.8.97, 100; Federal Farmer XI, January 10, 1788, Storing, 2.8.146; Brutus IV, November 29, 1787, Storing, 2.9.47; and Samuel Chase V, April 1788, Storing, 5.3.20.

13. Brutus I, October 18, 1787, Storing, 2.9.4–21. See also Centinel I, October 5, 1787, Storing, 2.7.17–19; Centinel, "The Address and Reasons of Dissent of the Minority of the Convention of Pennsylvania to Their Constituents," December 18, 1787, Storing 3.11.16–17, 20–31; Federal Farmer I, October 8, 1787, Storing 2.8.14; and An Old Whig IV, October 27, 1787, Storing, 3.3.20, 24.

14. Brutus I, October 18, 1787, Storing, 2.9.12. See also An Old Whig IV, October 27, 1787, Storing 3.3.20; and A Farmer III, March 7, 1788, Storing, 5.1.53.

15. "The Address and Reasons of Dissent of the Minority of the Convention of Pennsylvania to Their Constituents," December 18, 1787, Storing, 3.11.17–8. The author is unknown but was most likely Centinel. See also Cato III, October 25, 1787, Storing, 2.6.12–20; Brutus I, October 18, 1787, Storing, 2.9.12–16; Centinel V, October, Storing, 2.7.94; and Patrick Henry, June 5, 1788, Storing, 5.16.2.

16. *SL*, IX.3.

17. Madison, *Federalist* 10, 51.

18. Jay, "Address to the People of the State of New York," in *The Correspondence and Public Papers of John Jay*, ed. Henry P. Johnston (New York: G. P. Putnam's Sons, 1890–93), III, 312–19 (hereafter cited as Johnston).

19. Thomas L Purvis, "The European Ancestry of the United States Population, 1790: A Symposium," *William and Mary Quarterly* 41, no. 1 (January, 1984).

20. 1790 Census: Return of the Whole Number of Persons within the Several Districts of the United States, United States Census Bureau, www

.census.gov/library/publications/1793/dec/number-of-persons.html (accessed February 2, 2019).

21. To arrive at this estimated figure, I have used the data of the 1790s census report and Robert Dinkin's finding that around 80 percent of adult white males were enfranchised in the late 1780s. See 1790 Census; and Robert J. Dinkin, *Voting in Revolutionary America: A Study of Elections in the Original Thirteen States, 1776–1789* (Westport, CT: Greenwood Press, 1982), 39. See also Donald Ratcliffe, "The Right to Vote and the Rise of Democracy," *Journal of the Early Republic* 33 (Summer 2014): 230.

22. Writing in 1989, David Fischer argued that early American culture was (and continues to be) divided by four distinct British cultures that "shared many qualities in common" like Protestantism but differed because of "British region, [sectarianism], rank, and generation," and because of distinct interactions with "the American environment, and the process of migration"; see David H. Fischer, *Albion's Seed: Four British Folkways in America* (New York: Oxford University Press, 1989), 6, 788. Barry Shain has argued that early Americans often formed exclusionary religious communities, but that America was predominately a Calvinist (or reformed Protestant) nation; see Barry A. Shain, *The Myth of American Individualism* (Princeton, NJ: Princeton University Press, 1994). For more on America's early religion, including data suggesting that Americans were less religious than often conceived, see Roger Finke and Rodney Stark, *The Churching of America 1776–2005* (New Brunswick, NJ: Rutgers University, 2014), 22–35.

23. Quoted by Morgan Lewis in conversation with Jared Sparks, August [no day], 1831, Letters, Sparks Manuscripts, quoted in Max M. Mintz, *Governeur Morris and the American Revolution* (Norman: University of Oklahoma Press, 1970), 75n19. The reader should also note that the date of Lewis's conversation with Sparks is given, not the date that Jay purportedly made this remark.

24. Walter Stahr, *John Jay: Founding Father* (New York: Diversion Books, 2005), 2.

25. John Jay, Address to the People of Great Britain, Johnston, I.

26. John Jay, "Convention Debate," March 20, 1777, in *Journals of the Provincial Congress, Provincial Convention, Committee of Safety and Council of Safety of the State of New York*, 1775–1777 (Albany, NY: Thurlow Weed, 1842), I, 844. See also David Sehat, *The Myth of American Religious Freedom* (Oxford: Oxford University Press, 2011), 23; and Stahr, *John Jay*, 78.

27. John Jay to John Murray Jr., October 12, 1816, Johnston, IV, 393. See also Sehat, *Myth*, 24.

28. John Jay to Reverend Dr. Jedediah Morse, August 16, 1809, Johnston, IV, 322.

29. Stahr, *John Jay*, 209. See also John Jay, Report re: Constitutional Convention, July 4, 1785, in *The Emerging Nation: A Documentary History of the*

Foreign Relations of the United States under the Articles of Confederation 1780–1789, ed. Mary A. Giunta et al. (Washington DC: National Historical Publications and Records Commission, 1996), III, 38–51.

30. John Jay to the Marquis De Lafayette, July 15, 1785, Johnston, III.

31. Stahr, *John Jay*, 246–47, 354–45. See also John Jay to George Washington, July 25, 1787, Johnston, III, 250; and John Jay to Timothy Pickering, May 13, 1798, Johnston, IV, 241.

32. John Jay to Alexander Hamilton, September 17, 1794, Johnston, IV.

33. Stahr, *John Jay*, 73; for more on Jay's view of slavery, see also 5, 73, 78, 94, 126, 171, 190, 193, 204, 223, 236–39, 284, 286, 332, 346–47, 370–72.

34. John Jay to Thomas Jefferson, December 14, 1786, Johnston, III, 224. See also John Jay to John Adams, July 4, 1787, Johnston, III, 249; and Jay, *Federalist* 3.

35. John Jay to Peter Thatcher, April 25, 1797, in Stahr, *John Jay*, 349, 450n27.

36. For more on this point, see Thomas Jefferson's First Annual Message to Congress, December 8, 1801, in The Examination Number I, note 1 [December 17, 1801]," in *The Papers of Alexander Hamilton*, ed. Harold C. Syrett (New York: Columbia University, 1961–79) (hereafter cited as *PAH*), XXV, 449.

37. Alexander Hamilton, "Constitutional Convention: Motion on Citizenship Requirement for Membership in the House of Representatives [August 13, 1787]," *PAH*, IV, 234.

38. "Alexander Hamilton's Final Version of the Report on the Subject of Manufactures," December 5, 1791, *PAH*, X, 254.

39. Draft of a Proclamation by George Washington, January 1, 1795, *PAH*, XVIII, 3.

40. Jay Cost, "We're Not on the Brink of Civil War. Here's Why," *National Review*, October 8, 2018.

41. With this possibility in mind, Hamilton's analysis of the "spirit of commerce" and relative gains in *Federalist* 6 may be more applicable to American identity politics than *Federalist* 12.

42. Alexander Hamilton, New York Ratifying Convention, Third Speech of June 21 (Francis Childs's Version), June 21, 1788, *PAH*, X, 57–58.

43. Hamilton, New York Ratifying Convention, *PAH*, X, 57–58. Madison or Hamilton offers a similar argument in *Federalist 56*; the authorship of this essay is disputed. See Alexander Hamilton, "The Federalist No. 18," February 16, 1788, *PAH*, IV, 524–27, n.1.

44. Hamilton, New York Ratifying Convention, 58.

45. Alexander Hamilton, "Conversation with George Beckwith," October 1789, *PAH*, V, 482. See also Ron Chernow, *Alexander Hamilton* (New York: Penguin Books, 2004), 294.

46. Chernow, *Hamilton*, 476–77.

47. "An Act Concerning Aliens," June 25, 1798, *Constitution Society,* http://constitution.org/rf/alien_ 1798.htm (accessed January 30, 2018).

48. Alexander Hamilton to Timothy Pickering, June 7, 1798, *PAH*, XXI, 495. For more on this topic, see Chernow, *Alexander Hamilton,* 571–72; and Michael P. Federici, *The Political Philosophy of Alexander Hamilton* (Baltimore: John Hopkins University Press, 2012), 174–76.

49. Alexander Hamilton to Jonathan Dayton, October–November 1799, *PAH*, XXIII, 604n15; and Chernow, *Alexander Hamilton,* 572.

50. Alexander Hamilton, The Examination Number VIII, January 12, 1802, *PAH*, XXV, 496–97.

51. Thomas Jefferson's First Annual Message to Congress, December 8, 1801, in The Examination Number I, note 1 [December 17, 1801]," *PAH*, XXV, 449.

52. Alexander Hamilton, The Examination Number VII, January 7, 1802, *PAH*, XXV, 491.

53. Thomas Jefferson, *Notes on the State of Virginia* (New York: W. W. Norton, 1972), Query XV.

54. Hamilton, Examination Number VIII, January 12, 1802, *PAH*, XXV, 496. See also Hamilton, The Examination Number VII, 491–92.

55. Alexander Hamilton, "New York Assembly. Remarks on an Act for Regulating Elections, January 24, 1787, *PAH*, IV, 23.

56. Montesquieu, *CR*, IX; *SL*, VIII.2 and n. 3.

57. Hamilton, Examination Number VII, 494.

58. Hamilton, Examination Number VII, 493–94.

59. Chernow, *Alexander Hamilton,* 215–16, 239, 581. See also Alexander Hamilton, Attendance at a Meeting of the Society for Promoting the Manumission of Slaves, February 4, 1785, *PAH*, III, 597. Evidence of Hamilton's purchase of slaves can be found here: Alexander Hamilton, Cash Book, March 1, 1782–1791, *PAH*, III, 21; and Alexander Hamilton to George Clinton, May 22, 1781, *PAH*, II, 642–43.

60. Alexander Hamilton to John Jay, March 14, 1779, *PAH*, II, 18.

61. Phillip Magness, "Alexander Hamilton's Exaggerated Abolitionism," *History News Network,* June 27, 2015, https://historynewsnetwork.org/blog /153639.

62. Alexander Hamilton, Conversation with George Beckwith, June 15, 1791, *PAH*, VIII, 476. See also Alexander Hamilton, Remarks on the Treaty of Amity Commerce and Navigation Lately Made between the United States and Great Britain, July 9–11, 1795, *PAH*, XVIII, 406.

63. Alexander Hamilton to George Mathews, September 25, 1794, PAH, XVII, 270–75. See also: Chernow, *Alexander Hamilton,* 337.

64. Federici, *Political Philosophy,* 32.

65. Chernow, *Alexander Hamilton*, 338. For an example of this type of schooling during the founding period, see Jon Reyhner and Jeanne Eder, *American Indian Education*, 2nd ed. (Norman: University of Oklahoma Press, 2017), 32.

66. Representatives of the Oneida Indians to Alexander Hamilton, January 15, 1794, *PAH*, XV, 642.

67. Joseph D. Ibbotson and S. N. D. North, eds., *Documentary History of Hamilton College* (Clinton, NY: Hamilton College, 1922), 57–58.

68. See, for example, Alexander Hamilton to George Clinton, October 3, 1783, *PAH*, III, 464–69; and Alexander Hamilton to Herman LeRoy, William Bayard, and James McEvers, March 4–18 July 18 1797, *PAH*, XX, 530–31.

69. James Madison to William Bradford, April 1, 1774, in *Papers of James Madison, Congressional Series*, 17 vols., ed. [by various] (Chicago: University of Chicago Press; and Charlottesville: University Press of Virginia, 1962–91) (hereafter *PJM*), I, 111–12; James Madison to Jacob De La Motta, [post–7] August 1820, in *Papers of James Madison, Retirement Series*, 3 vols., ed. David B. Mattern et al. (Charlottesville: University Press of Virginia, 2009–16) (hereafter cited as *PJMRS*), II, 81–82.

70. James Madison to William T. Barry, August 4, 1822, *PJMRS*, II, 555–58.

71. James Madison to Thomas Jefferson, October 24, 1787, *PJM*, X, 214. For "sphere of a mean extent," Madison also used the terms "practical sphere" and "practicable sphere." *Federalist* 14 and 51.

72. For more on this topic, see Douglas W. Jaenicke, "Madison v. Madison: The Party Essays v. Federalist Papers," in *Reflections on the Constitution*, ed. Richard Maidment and John Zvesper (Manchester: Manchester University Press, 1989), 116–44.

73. James Madison, "A Candid State of Parties," *National Gazette*, September 26, 1792, *PJM*, XIV, 371–72; James Madison, "Who Are the Best Keepers of the People's Liberties?" December 20, 1792, *PJM*, XIV, 426.

74. See, for example, James Madison, "Consolidation," *National Gazette*, December 3, 1791, *PJM*, XIV, 139; James Madison, "Public Opinion," *National Gazette*, December 19, 1791, *PJM*, 170; and James Madison, "Government of the United States," *National Gazette*, February 4, 1792, *PJM*, XIV, 218.

75. Madison, *Federalist* 57.

76. See also Madison, *Federalist* 63.

77. Some of these issues were anticipated by Madison in the 1780s; see *Federalist*, 43, 55, 56, and 62. For more on these topics, see Alan Gibson, "The Commercial Republic and the Pluralist Critique of Marxism: An Analysis of Martin Diamond's Interpretation of 'Federalist' 10," *Polity* 25, no. 4 (1993): 497–528; Drew McCoy, *The Elusive Republic: Political Economy in Jeffersonian America* (Chapel Hill: University of North Carolina Press, 1980),

120–32; Banning, *Sacred Fire*, 325–33, 343–57, 356; and Sheehan, *James Madison*, 19–27.

78. Madison, *Federalist* 14 and 51; Madison, "Public Opinion." For more on this topic, see Sheehan, *James Madison*, 80–81, 103–6, 167–70.

79. James Madison, Annual Message to Congress, December 5, 1810, in *The Papers of James Madison, Presidential Series*, Vol. 3, ed. J. C. A. Stagg et al. (Charlottesville: University Press of Virginia, 1996), 52; James Madison, "Notes for the National Gazette Essays," *PJM*, XIV, 168; Madison, "Candid State of Parties," 371–72; James Madison to Samuel H. Smith, November 4, 1826, in *Letters and Other Writings of James Madison* (Philadelphia: Lippincott, 1867), III, 533; James Madison et. al., Report of the Board of Commissioners for the University of Virginia to the Virginia General Assembly, August 4, 1818, *PJMRS*, I, 328–29; Madison to Barry, *PJMRS*, II, 555–58.

80. James Madison, Import Duties, April 17, 1789, *PJM*, XII, 86; James Madison, "Parties," January 23, 1792, *PJM*, XIV, 197.

81. Madison, "Consolidation," 138–39.

82. Madison, "Candid State of Parties," 372.

83. James, Madison, Rule of Representation in the First Branch of the Legislature, June 28, 1787, *PJM*, X, 80.

84. James Madison, "Apportionment of Representatives in the Legislature [11 July] 1787," *PJM*, X, 99.

85. James Madison, "Foreign Influence," *Aurora General Advertiser*, January 23, 1799, *PJM*, XVII, 214, 217.

86. James Madison to Marquis de Lafayette, March 20, 1785, *PJM*, VIII, 251.

87. James Madison to Robert R. Livingston and James Monroe, March 2, 1803, in *The Papers of James Madison, Secretary of State Series*, Vol. 4, ed. Mary A. Hackett, et al. (Charlottesville: University Press of Virginia, 1998), 366–67.

88. James Madison, Notes for Debates on the General Assessment Bill, PJM, X, 197.

89. James Madison, Memorial and Remonstrance against Religious Assessments [ca. June 20,] 1785, *PJM*, VIII, 295–306.

90. James Madison, Citizenship Qualifications for Senators, August 9, 1787, *PJM*, X, 141.

91. James Madison, Citizenship Qualifications for Representatives, August 13, 1787, *PJM*, X, 147–48.

92. Madison, Citizenship Qualifications for Senators, 141.

93. Madison, Citizenship Qualifications for Representatives, 147–48.

94. James Madison, Naturalization, February 3, 1790, *PJM*, XIII, 17.

95. Madison, Naturalization, *PMJ*, XIII, 17.

96. Michael LeMay and Elliot R. Barkan, eds., *U.S. Immigration and Naturalization Laws and Issues* (Westport, CT: Greenwood Press, 1999), 11.

97. LeMay and Barkan, *U.S. Immigration*, 12. See also James Madison to Thomas Jefferson, January 11, 1795, *PJM*, XV, 440.

98. Madison, Citizenship Qualifications for Senators, 141. Hamilton concurred with Madison that the legislature should have flexibility when it came to passing naturalization laws. Alexander Hamilton, Constitutional Convention. Motion on Citizenship Requirement for Membership in the House of Representatives, August 13, 1787, *PAH*, IV, 234.

99. Madison probably had in mind here individuals like the Marquis de Lafayette, whom multiple states naturalized in the 1780s. This included Virginia, which Madison spoke approvingly of in a letter to Jefferson. James Madison to Thomas Jefferson, January 22, 1786, *PJM*, VIII, 472–82. See also Robert Waln, *Life of the Marquis De La Fayette: Major-General in the Service of the United States of America, in the War of the Revolution* (Classic Reprint of Philadelphia: J. P. Ayres, 1825), 260–81.

100. James Madison to Lafayette, November 25, 1820, *PJMRS*, II, 158–60. See also James Madison, Memorandum on an African Colony for Freed Slaves, ca. October 20, 1789, *PJM*, XII, 437–38. For more on Madison's ownership of slaves and his criticism of slavery as an institution, see Ralph Ketcham, *James Madison* (Charlottesville: University of Virginia Press, 1990), 11–12, 148–49, 224–25, 315–16, 374–75, 551–52, 625–30.

101. Madison, Memorandum, *PJM*, XII, 437–38. See also James Madison to Lafayette, ca. October, 7 1821, *PJMRS*, II, 405–7. For more on the vices acquired from the institution of slavery, see James Madison, For the National Gazette, ca. December 12, 1791, *PJM*, XVII, 560.

102. See, for example, Cato II, Storing, 2.16.18. For more on this topic, see Chernow, *Alexander Hamilton*, 306–7; and David F. Epstein, *The Political Theory of the Federalist* (Chicago: University of Chicago Press, 1984), 103–5. Jay also discussed a North-South divide in *Federalist* 5.

103. James Madison to Thomas L. McKenney, February 10, 1826, *PJMRS*, III, 685–86.

104. Madison, Memorandum, *PJM*, XII, 438.

105. James Madison to James Monroe and William Pinkney, May 30, 1806, in *Papers of James Madison, Secretary of State Series*, Vol. 11, ed. Mary A. Hackett et al. (Charlottesville: University of Virginia Press, 2017), 625.

106. For more on Madison's view of Indians, see Jacob T. Levy, "Indians in Madison's Constitutional Order," in *James Madison and the Future of Limited Government*, ed. John Samples (Washington DC: Cato Institute, 2002), 121–33.

107. Jay, *Federalist* 2. See also Hamilton, *Federalist* 6.

108. "Spatial Polarization of Presidential Voting in the United States, 1992–2012: The 'Big Sort' Revisited," *Annals of the American Association of Geographers* 106, no. 5 (2016): 1047–62; Andrew Gelman, *Red State, Blue State, Rich State, Poor State: Why Americans Vote the Way They Do*, exp. ed. (Princeton,

NJ: Princeton University Press, 2009); Daniel T. Lichter, "Toward a New Macro-Segregation? Decomposing Segregation within and between Metropolitan Cities and Suburbs," *American Sociological Review* 80, no. 4 (2015): 843–73; John R. Logan, "Separate and Unequal in Suburbia," Census Brief prepared for Project US2010, December 1, 2014, www.s4.brown.edu/us2010.

109. See, for example, John Myers, "Radical Plan to Split California into Three States Earns Spot on November Ballot," *Los Angeles Times*, June 12, 2018, www.latimes.com/politics/la-pol-ca-california-split-three-states-20180612 -story.html; Sam Rosen, "Atlanta's Controversial 'Cityhood' Movement," *Atlantic*, April 26, 2017, www.theatlantic.com/business/archive/2017/04/the -border-battles-of-atlanta/523884; Jenny Jarvie, "In the Deep South, Residents of an Upscale Suburb Fight to Secede from Their Neighbors," *Los Angeles Times*, November 4, 2018, www.latimes.com/nation/la-na-georgia-eagles -landing-20181102-story.html; and Michelle Wilde Anderson, "Cities Inside Out: Race, Poverty, and Exclusion at the Urban Fringe," *UCLA Law Review* 55 (2007): 1095–160.

110. "The Address and Reasons of Dissent of the Minority of the Convention of Pennsylvania to Their Constituents," Storing, 3.11.17–8.

111. See, for example, A. J. Willingham, "The First Amendment Doesn't Guarantee You the Rights You Think It Does," *CNN*, September 6, 2018, www.cnn.com/2017/04/27/politics/first-amendment-explainer-trnd/index .html; Robert A. Levy, "Libertarianism and the Right to Discriminate," *Cato Policy Report*, March/April, 2016, www.cato.org/policy-report/marchapril -2016/libertarianism-right-discriminate; David E. Bernstein, "Context Matters: A Better Libertarian Approach to Antidiscrimination Law," *CATO Unbound*, June 16, 2010, www.cato-unbound.org/2010/06/16/david-e-bernstein/context -matters-better-libertarian-approach-antidiscrimination-law; William W. Keller, *Democracy Betrayed: The Rise of the Surveillance Security State* (Berkeley, CA: Counterpoint Press, 2017); Glenn Greenwald, *No Place to Hide: Edward Snowden, the NSA, and the US Surveillance State* (London: Macmillan, 2014); Nicolas Suzor, "Digital Constitutionalism: Using the Rule of Law to Evaluate the Legitimacy of Governance by Platforms," *Social Media + Society* 4, no. 3 (2018); and Tarleton Gillespie, *Custodians of the Internet: Platforms, Content Moderation, and the Hidden Decisions That Shape Social Media* (New Haven, CT: Yale University Press, 2018).

112. American Civil Liberties Union, *War Comes Home: The Excessive Militarization of American Policing* (New York: American Civil Liberties Union, 2014); Radley Balko, *Rise of the Warrior Cop: The Militarization of America's Police Forces* (New York: Public Affairs Publishing, 2013); Steven A. Holmes, "Fannie Mae Eases Credit to Aid Mortgage Lending," *New York Times*, September 30, 1999, www.nytimes.com/1999/09/30/business/fannie-mae -eases-credit-to-aid-mortgage-lending.html; Peter Wood, *Diversity: The Invention of a Concept* (San Francisco: Encounter Books, 2003); Richard Bernstein,

Dictatorship of Virtue: Multiculturalism and the Battle for America's Future (New York: Alfred A. Knopf: 1994).

113. In contrast to this speculation, two empirical studies have found that Latino immigrants embrace the specific American values of patriotism, hard work, and equal rights: Rodolfo O. de la Garza, Angelo Falcon, and F. Chris Garcia, "Will the Real Americans Please Stand Up?," *American Journal of Political Science* 40, no. 2 (May 1996); and Luis R. Fraga et al., *Latinos in the New Millennium: An Almanac of Opinion, Behavior, and Policy Preferences* (New York: Cambridge University Press, 2012), 56–75.

114. Jay Sexton, *A Nation Forged by Crisis: A New American History* (New York: Basic Books, 2018); G. H. Gamm, *The Making of the New Deal Democrats: Voting Behavior and Realignment in Boston, 1920–1940* (Chicago: University of Chicago Press, 1989).

115. George Hawley, "Immigration Status: Immigrant Family, Ties, and Support for the Democratic Party," *Social Science Quarterly*, March 28, 2019, https://onlinelibrary.wiley.com/doi/full/10.1111/ssqu.12621; Anna Maria Mayda, Giovanni Peri, and Walter Steingress, "Immigration to the USA: Problem for the Republicans or the Democrats?," *National Bureau of Economic Research*, no. 21941, 2016; "How Asian Americans Became Democrats," *American Prospect*, July 26, 2016, http://prospect.org/article/how-asian-americans -became-democrats-0; Russell Heimlich, "Hispanics Favor Bigger Role for Government," *Pew Research Center*, April 20, 2012, www.pewresearch.org/fact -tank/2012/04/20/hispanics-favor-bigger-role-for-government; Fraga et al., *Latinos in the New Millennium*, 277–90, 312, 315.

116. Alexander Hamilton, The Examination Number VIII, January 12, 1802, *PAH*, XXV, 496–97.

117. Mark Muro et. al., "Automation and Artificial Intelligence," *Brookings*, January 24, 2019, www.brookings.edu/research/automation-and -artificial-intelligence-how-machines-affect-people-and-places; Kevin Truong, "AI May Be Coming for Your High-Paying, White-Collar Job," *San Francisco Business Times*, April 10, 2018, www.bizjournals.com/sanfrancisco/news/2018 /04/10/ai-may-be-coming-for-your-high-paying-job.html; Erik Brynjolfsson and Tom Mitchell, "What Can Machine Learning Do? Workforce Implications," *Science* 358, no. 6370 (December 22, 2017): 1530–34.

118. See, for example, Katie Reilly, "Michael Bloomberg Blasts Donald Trump and Bernie Sanders in Commencement Speech," *Time*, April 30, 2016, http://time.com/4313436/michael-bloomberg-commencement-speech -donald-trump-bernie-sanders; and Scott E. Kaufman, "Paul Krugman Slams Bernie Sanders for Being as Big of a Demagogue as Donald Trump," *Salon*, March 11, 2016, www.salon.com/2016/03/11/paul_krugman_slams_bernie _sanders_ for_being_as_big_of_a_demagogue_as_donald_trump.

119. This concern is not unfounded. See, for example, Martin Gilens and Benjamin I. Page, "Testing Theories of American Politics: Elites, Interest

Groups, and Average Citizens," *Perspectives on Politics* 12, no. 3 (2014): 565; and Jacob S. Hacker and Paul Pierson, *Winner-Take-All Politics: How Washington Made the Rich Richer—and Turned Its Back on the Middle Class* (New York: Simon and Schuster, 2010).

120. Madison to Jefferson, October 24, 1787, *PJM*, X, 214.

6

What Publius Knew
and Didn't Know

James R. Stoner Jr.

Even the fondest admirers of *The Federalist* today—among whom I would be happily included—balk before claiming for the essays the encomium Thomas Jefferson immediately bestowed upon them in a letter to one of the authors: "the best commentary on the principles of government which ever was written."[1] Unlike Jefferson's Declaration of Independence, *The Federalist* contains no statement of first principles: nothing on natural rights or on duties to God, and only one mention of the law of nature, in the context of quoting the Declaration to justify the mode of ratification. These essays were written for a practical end—to encourage ratification of the proposed constitution—in dialogue through the newspapers with the plan's opponents, over the course of several months and at an impressive clip.

To be sure, their polemical edge is a part of their greatness, as the authors never lost focus and seldom digressed, exhibiting instead the depth of thought that went into the deliberations that produced the document and conveying the urgency of a right decision on the part of those they addressed. The suggestion in the first number—that the choice facing the state conventions in 1787 and 1788 would settle for all mankind "the important question, whether societies of men are really capable or not, of establishing good government from reflection or choice, or whether they are forever destined to depend, for their political constitutions, on accident and force"[2]—might have seemed rhetorical exaggeration, but it has been vindicated by events. In a small coastal city on the edge of the frontier of European civilization, the American founders invented a polity that not only changed the world but altered the way that politics itself was to be understood. Principles are indeed referred to throughout *The Federalist*—a simple search for the word "principle" yields 211 occurrences—and, though mention is often made of "principles of liberty" and especially "republican principles," often the reference is more mundane: to principles of compromise, or of discharging the nation's debt, or of navigation, or of policy, or simply, as Jefferson said, of government. In other words, as Michael Zuckert has argued and Harvey Mansfield has also explained, *The Federalist* is not a work of political philosophy but instead of political science, or at least its arguments rest upon what its authors call the "science of politics."[3]

Most modern political scientists are not so impressed by the founders' political science that they feel a need to engage it; they take the structure of our political system as generally fixed, studying variations in political behavior within it. One who does engage the founders' political science and probably sums up the assumptions of the others is William Galston, who has written: "Madison failed to understand fully the logic of his own creation: to function effectively, a constitution of divided powers and functions would need a party system to organize and channel the multiplicity of interest groups. And he was too confident that this multiplicity would generate enough centrifugal force to prevent the formation of large agglomerations that could make possible the dreaded tyranny of the majority."[4]

Although the two-party system of enduring coalitions seems not to have been anticipated—though ironically, it received its first incarnation in the decade after ratification thanks in no small part to James Madison and Alexander Hamilton themselves—Publius is acutely attuned to the human tendency toward partisanship throughout *The Federalist*. And he might point out in our current environment, could he see it, that modern political scientists are perhaps too sanguine in supposing the stability of the parties themselves.

In this chapter, I confront several more particular issues of institutional design where it seems that Publius got it wrong, that is, where his political science did not adequately anticipate how the system he advocated would function in practice, or where his arguments convey a deep ambiguity. The first concerns the separation of powers and in particular the observation that the legislative branch naturally predominates in a republican government. The second concerns the mechanism for the election of the president, now known as the Electoral College, and the question of the relation of the president to the people. The third and final concerns the eventual dominance of the central government over the government of the states, undeterred by the limits implicit in the enumeration of powers.

Of course, to speak of what Publius got "wrong" requires attention to what he claimed to get right. Here, despite the self-confidence exuded in the first number, one cannot help but be impressed by his caution and by the modesty of his claims. In *Federalist* 37, Madison writes at length about the uncertainty of all human knowledge, and particularly of knowledge about politics, identifying "three sources of vague and incorrect definitions; indistinctness of the object, imperfection of the organ of perception, inadequateness of the vehicle of ideas."[5] Later, in *Federalist* 82, Hamilton explains that, whatever can be determined at the moment of the founding, much remains to be worked out in the course of practice:

> The erection of a new government, whatever care or wisdom may distinguish the work, cannot fail to originate questions of intricacy and nicety; and these may, in a particular manner, be expected to flow from the establishment of a constitution founded upon the total or partial incorporation of a number of distinct sovereignties. Time only can mature and perfect so compound a system, liquidate the meaning of all the parts, and adjust them to each other in a harmonious and consistent WHOLE.[6]

Moreover, throughout *The Federalist*, literally from the first essay to the last, Publius indicates an awareness that partisan feelings are likely to distort or at least to color all political analysis, not excepting his own; practically he counsels a "spirit of moderation" to those who undertake to argue about forms of government, not in most fields the mark of a scientific disposition. In short, whatever Publius knew was qualified by the obscurity of political principles, the experimental nature of institutional design, and the clouds of partisan passion. To find that he got something wrong would more likely arch his brow than bruise his ego.

A NOVEL, CONTINENTAL REPUBLIC

There is a central difficulty in Publius's argument that leads to significant consequences, directly or indirectly. This difficulty involves the legislative power of Congress and the character of federal representation, a chief complaint of the Constitution's opponents. To understand the difficulty, one needs first to recall the novelty of the form of government established by the Constitution. The model of the Articles of Confederation that preceded the Constitution was simple enough: Each state had a government, formed of and by the people, which possessed sovereign power and divided its functions among various institutions as it chose. These governments sent delegates to a gathering, literally a congress, which had responsibility and authority for matters of external sovereignty—fighting wars, making treaties—but had no sovereign power domestically. Congress could not raise taxes but could merely requisition funds from the states, who alone had authority to tax. Congress had no executive authority and no courts, except an ad hoc tribunal designed to settle disputes among the states. As was discovered after the revolution, even the enforcement of Congress's treaties was subject to judicial determinations in the states. Strictly speaking, under the Articles Congress had no legislative authority at all over individual citizens, unless ancillary to its foreign powers and only if exercised in tentative, restricted ways.

The Constitution meant to change all that. Now the central authority would be a general government, fully sovereign in the matters accorded to its care—republican, to be sure, like the states, only extended like an umbrella over top of them. This new general government would derive its power from the people (hence the importance of ratification by popular conventions in the states, rather than by the state governments) and would be able to act directly upon the people, rather than only upon the states in their corporate capacity. It could tax; it would have its own courts; it would have an executive power headed by a commander-in-chief, an officer somewhere between a governor and a king. Its legislative branch would be clearly granted the power to make laws on a variety of subjects, as well as to tax and of course to borrow and spend money (the latter were things even the Articles Congress could do, until they ran their credit dry). To illustrate this shift, it is noteworthy that not until the Committee of Detail issued its report to the federal convention on August 6, 1787, was the name "Congress" revived to describe the new legislature, which had been simply called the National Legislature in the Virginia Plan.

When the Anti-Federalists referred to a "solecism" in politics or the Federalists to the unexampled novelty of the form they had devised, they meant precisely this: that a central government with sovereign power was to be laid upon the preexisting state governments, with sovereignty divided as to areas of responsibility, but not as to the degree of authority. Both were empowered to tax, to regulate, to punish, to settle conflicting claims, and to call forth the public force, at least within their spheres of responsibility. Naturally it was understood that the spheres would interface, that the laws of each would be consulted in the courts of the other, but they trusted to the Supremacy Clause and to the logical capacities of the judiciaries, federal and state, to sort out the details. Imagine a feast with different service crews responsible for the food and the drink— or better, a simultaneous feast with thirteen separate kitchens preparing and serving the food, but a single sommelier and his team serving wine to all—and of course two tabs and two tips. There would certainly be challenges in coordination, but nothing beyond American ingenuity, and the kitchens might even learn to compete for guests.

REPRESENTATIVE REFINEMENT

The Constitution, then, sought to institute a republican government over all thirteen states rather than retain the confederation of thirteen distinct republics. This raised an important question: Would republican government writ large be the same as republican government in the familiar dimensions of a state? Is size an accident, or is the right size an essential ingredient in republicanism? Here is where Publius is, I think, deeply ambiguous and problematic. On the one hand, according to the familiar argument he makes in *Federalist* 10, size matters quite a lot: government over an extended sphere breaks the violence of faction, by incorporating more interests and affinities and by making combination among them in any scheme to oppress or to profit more difficult. "A coalition of a majority of the whole society could seldom take place upon any other principles than those of justice and the general good," writes Publius confidently.[7] This is not an automatic effect but comes about in part because the federal government will attract a different sort of legislator than the states. In *Federalist* 10 he explains that "the proportion of fit characters" available for election will be greater in a large republic than a small, since the electorate increases in size more than the representative assembly possibly could, favoring the happier consequence of representation—"to refine and enlarge the public views, by passing them through the medium of a chosen body of citizens, whose wisdom may best discern the true interest of their country, and whose patriotism and love of justice, will be least likely to sacrifice it to temporary or partial considerations"— and discouraging the "inverted" triumph of factious politicians.[8]

Moreover, the tasks of legislation being different, he later explains, the kind of knowledge required for the job would be different as well. On the one hand, the knowledge of a federal legislator must be more extensive, justifying more than an annual term; that legislator must know the laws and the circumstances of the several states, as well as foreign affairs and the laws of other nations. Some of this knowledge can be "acquired in a man's closet," Publius writes, but some depends on "a practical application to the subject, during the period of actual service in the legislature."[9] Several essays later, however, he makes anew the case for closet knowledge. Explaining why it is safe for federal representatives to have only a limited acquaintance with all the "interests and circumstances of his constituents," he appeals to the limited purview of federal power, saying a representative's knowledge need only be proportionate to his regulatory authority; for example, "a skillful individual in his closet, with all the local codes before him, might compile a law on some subjects of taxation for the whole union, without any aid from oral information."[10] To be sure, soon afterward he appeals again to refinement and enlargement: it is likely, he writes, that members of Congress will have served in the legislatures of their states, enabling them to bring to Congress all the others need to know about their home states, even as it takes time for them to learn about the others.

In short, though members of Congress may once have sat in the legislatures of their states, Publius anticipates that Congress will be a very different place than a state legislature. The Anti-Federalists complained that the general government could never be truly republican because the people could never be represented at such a distance; there are too few federal representatives to reflect the people in their full variety and array, and they are too distant to be appraised of everyday concerns and to receive timely communication. Publius admits that federal representation will not be the same as state representation, that the connection of Congress to the people will not be organic and comprehensive as is representation in the states. He thinks this is in some respects a good thing; as the people's agents for limited purposes, they are less apt to succumb to the factious ways of a body that more faithfully represents the multitude. It is at any rate not a bad thing; Congress is still republican because, at least in its popular branch, it is elected directly by the people, indeed by constitutional design the same electorate that chooses the popular branch of the legislature in the states.[11]

But here is the catch, or what I referred to earlier as an ambiguity: although Publius speaks of Congress as different from the legislatures of the states—thanks to its limited agenda, larger districts, longer term lengths, and the indirect election of senators—when treating the separation of powers Publius assumes the federal legislature will act the same way state legislatures do because they will draw on the same sympathy of the people:

> In a representative republic, where the executive magistracy is carefully limited, both in the extent and the duration of its power; and where the legislative power is exercised by an assembly, which is inspired by a supposed influence over the people, with an intrepid confidence in its own strength; which is sufficiently numerous to feel all the passions which actuate a multitude; yet not so numerous as to be incapable of pursuing the objects of its passions, by means which reason prescribes; it is against the enterprising spirit of this department, that the people ought to indulge all their jealousy, and exhaust all their precautions.[12]

The ambiguity is not in the size of the body. Madison explains very clearly in the essays on the House that there is an optimum size beyond which no chamber should go; that the larger the body is, the fewer are those who control it; and that there is a psychology of crowds that affects even the most rational man: "Had every Athenian citizen been a Socrates, the Athenian assembly would still have been a mob."[13] These arguments seem to apply identically at the state and federal levels. Rather, the ambiguity concerns

Congress's supposed connection with the people, the "intrepid confidence" that comes from shared identity. Why should this be supposed to exist in the Congress he describes, whose representatives tend to be scholars or to make use of scholars, whose class background is confined to the wealthier or better educated or at any rate the more ambitious, whose remoteness from the people, or at least the less refined among them, is seen as a virtue or a likely cause of or support for virtue? If Congress will be less unruly, then it has less need to be confined, or, at any rate, it may not be the chief source of popular danger. If it has been designed to be at some remove from the immediate will of the people, there is reason to doubt it will enjoy the same confidence of the people that gives rise to legislative predominance in the states.

In *Federalist* 51, after repeating his observation that "in republican governments, the legislative power necessarily predominates," Publius explains: "The remedy for this inconveniency is, to divide the legislature into different branches; and to render them, by different modes of election, and different principles of action, as little connected with each other, as the nature of their common functions, and their common dependence on society, will admit."[14]

When discussing the Senate, Publius reiterates this rationale of dividing the chambers to diffuse their natural strength. He apologizes for the departure from the principle of proportional representation by population as a 'necessary compromise between the larger and the smaller states in "a spirit of amity." He adds that there is a happy consequence, namely, that, with different bases of organization, there will be "an additional impediment . . . against improper acts of legislation," since "the facility and excess of lawmaking seem to be the diseases to which our governments are most liable." After eschewing a theoretical defense of equal representation of the states in the Senate, he nevertheless follows with a good one: "The equal vote allowed to each state is at once a constitutional recognition of the portion of sovereignty remaining in the individual states, and an instrument for preserving that residuary sovereignty"—his point being, I suppose, that this principle is one the small states demanded, not one he embraces.[15]

In the subsequent discussion of what makes the Senate distinctive, however, Publius goes beyond pragmatic considerations, appealing to experience—"History informs us of no long lived republic which had not a senate"—and making the case for experience in government, to ensure both legislative skill and "national character" on the world stage, the lengthier term of senators promoting these virtues and allowing senators to interpose to protect the people against themselves when "stimulated by some irregular passion, or some illicit advantage, or misled by the artful misrepresentation." And in this context Publius makes what is probably his boldest, most antidemocratic statement in *The Federalist*: the superiority of American over ancient republics "lies in the total exclusion of the people, in their collective capacity."

In the account of Congress, then, despite the concern expressed about legislative predominance rooted in the members' connection to the people, Publius emphasizes all the ways the House and the Senate place a brake on popular passion and prejudice. Of course, his point is that Congress does not thwart the popular will but rather refines it; as he writes in relation to the Senate, "How salutary will be the interference of some temperate and respectable body of citizens, in order to check the misguided career, and to suspend the blow meditated by the people against themselves, until reason, justice, and truth, can regain their authority over the public mind."[16] At the same time, even in the same essay, he expresses the contrary concern, namely, that the people "may possibly be betrayed by the representatives of the people."[17] On the one hand, this nicely expresses the sense of balance, prudential rather than mechanical, that permeates *The Federalist*. But it does raise a question: in this new Constitution, with a legislature less immediately tied to the people, might the people seek a different champion?

PRESIDENTIAL POPULARITY

Neither the admirer nor the critic of the framers and the authors of *The Federalist* will deny that the provision of the Constitution least anticipated in its effect is Article II, Section 1, on the manner of electing the president and vice president: the selection, "in such manner as the legislature [of each state] shall direct," of a number of electors equal their total delegation in Congress who in turn each vote for two candidates, with the winner of a majority becoming president and the runner-up the vice president (and with the election thrown to the House if no outright majority is won). With its process of voting modified after only four elections by the Twelfth

Amendment, principally separating the vote for the two offices after the appearance of slates and a consequent tie, what has come to be called the Electoral College (the term is not used in the Constitution itself) remains a source of controversy and perplexity to the present day. Hence it is surprising to contemporary readers that Publius has such confidence in the original design, writing that it "affords a moral certainty, that the office of president will seldom fall to the lot of any man who is not in an eminent degree endowed with the requisite qualifications. . . . It will not be too strong to say, that there will be a constant probability of seeing the station filled by characters preeminent for ability and virtue."[18] Perhaps these sentences—carefully hedged as they are, if one reads closely—are simply part of Publius's rhetorical strategy for introducing the presidency, an office he knows might be seen as an elective monarch barely a decade after the Americans threw off the British crown. The concluding essays on the Senate, immediately before the numbers on the president, discuss its role as a court in impeachment proceedings, checking the office, as it were, before it is even announced, and the first essay of the series is an indignant attack on the distortions in its treatment by Anti-Federalists. Still, why did Publius express such admiration for the electoral system, and how does it fit with his presentation of the office taken as a whole?

Publius gives five reasons for the excellence of the presidential electoral system: first, that "the sense of the people should operate in the choice"; second, "that the immediate election should be made by men most capable of analyzing the qualities adapted to the station, and acting under circumstances favourable to deliberation, and to a judicious combination of all the reasons and inducements that were proper to govern their choice"; third, to avoid "tumult and disorder"; fourth, to prevent "cabal, intrigue and corruption"; and finally, to ensure "that the executive should be independent for his continuance in office, on all but the people themselves." The third, fourth, and fifth desiderata are achieved by the electors being themselves selected solely for a single day's voting and meeting in the capitals of the several states, not in the capital of the union. Modern textbooks commonly teach that the second was the true reason for the system—except when they suggest the aim was to magnify the vote in the slave states—but recent scholarship has noted what readers of Madison's *Notes of Debates in the Federal Convention* have always known, that the Electoral College was a practicable device to move election of the executive out of the legislature, where the Virginia Plan and the practice of a number of the states had placed it, to the people, or to as close a replication of the people as could be devised.[19] Publius's mention of "men most capable" follows soon after his discussion of the Senate and seems in the same vein, but the Constitution even as amended does not specify how the electors are to be chosen, leaving that determination to the legislatures of the states.

As it happened, some of the states at the beginning, most of them by the 1820s, and all of them after the Civil War established popular election of electors, the system suggested by Publius and still in place. The election of slates of electors in the states pledged to the national candidate of their political party developed as early as the 1830s, and, though it was not precisely anticipated by the framers or by Publius, it would not likely have surprised them and perhaps not even disappointed them, at least insofar as party officials proved themselves most capable of assessing that combination of qualities, circumstances, reasons, and inducements likely to win.[20] The twentieth century's innovation of popular presidential primaries in the states no doubt adjusted the balance of popular sense and politicians' assessment, but the underlying principle has remained the same: the highest officer is elected by the same sovereign who can amend the Constitution itself, namely, the people in the states.

Publius does not emphasize the organization of the vote by states, referring to them only in passing and neglecting to mention the role of the state legislatures in deciding how electors are chosen, but the role of the people is the first and the last thing he mentions, in the final mention referring implicitly to reelection, an issue he discusses with conviction a few essays later. There he insists that reeligibility "is necessary to enable the people, when they see reason to approve of his conduct, to continue him in the station, in order to prolong the utility of his talents and virtues" and asserts: "There is an excess of refinement in the idea of disabling the people to continue in office men who had entitled themselves, in their opinion, to approbation and confidence."[21] Whatever the role of the knowledgeable in proposing candidates for an open seat or for a challenge, when the question is reelection the people can come to a decision on their own.

Subsequently, of course, from Jefferson and Jackson to the Roosevelts and Reagan and beyond, presidents have successfully made themselves advocates of the people and have won, if not uniform affection, at least reelection. Would Publius be surprised, or disappointed? These are not easy questions to answer. On the one hand, he insists the president is a constitutional officer, in contrast even to a constitutional monarch, not to mention a despot or tyrant. This does not necessarily imply that the president will be an opponent of the people, who after all are authors of the Constitution, but it appears as a constraint on the virtue of energy Publius identifies as the key to executive success, not to mention on his ambition, which is thus tamed to seek its rewards within the law, not by transgressing it.

On the other hand, by promoting the unity of the executive in order to promote his energy (and ensure his responsibility), Publius suggests an implicit if not explicit identification with the people, precisely if they are to be considered a single whole. Although he supports a Senate, he impugns the idea of a council that would share executive authority (in the colonies, the governor's council had effectively served as upper house to the assembly); in the president, representation of the people is complete. As in the discussion of the Senate, Publius here distinguishes between the people's immediate demands and those "extensive and arduous enterprises for the public benefit" that a president might undertake, promising the people's gratitude to "the men who had courage and magnanimity enough to serve them at the peril of their displeasure."[22] "It is one thing to be subordinate to the laws, another to be dependent on the legislative body," Publius reminds his readers; even a popular president is required to be the first, but popularity is probably forfeited by the second.

What character does Publius actually expect presidents to have? Despite the "moral certainty" of "characters preeminent for ability and virtue" in *Federalist* 68, we find in *Federalist* 76 only "the great probability of having the place supplied by a man of abilities, at least respectable."[23] Energy is described as the leading characteristic of a good executive, but perhaps he means this more as a formal attribute of the office than a human trait. Publius writes in *Federalist* 72 that "the love of fame [is] the ruling passion of the noblest minds," but a page later he is describing both the avarice and the ambition of a president, taming them by the prospect of continuing in office after a single term. Indeed, by the end of the paper he imagines an incumbent of "irregular ambition" in whom "his passion for power and pre-eminence had acquired the force of habit."[24] In the matter of appointments, the subject of the concluding essays in the presidency series, Publius defends the presidential power of nomination because "the sole and undivided responsibility of one man, will naturally beget a livelier sense of duty, and a more exact regard to reputation," while explaining the necessity of Senate confirmation to deter "a spirit of favouritism in the president, and . . . appointment of unfit characters from state prejudice, from family connections, or from a view to popularity."[25] So tepid is Publius's endorsement of presidential virtue—and so great the risk of a president's appeal to the people against lawful order—that he supposes "the consent of [the Senate] will be necessary to displace as well as to appoint," the clearest error in *The Federalist* in predicting the actual way in which constitutional practice will unfold.[26] In short, whatever may subsequently have been bequeathed to the office by its first incumbent, known to have been probably such by the authors who formed Publius, *The Federalist* itself treats the presidency as it treats all other positions in government: an office in which virtue is hoped for and which in fact offers to great virtue a wide field of memorable exercise, but which can survive not only human foibles but occasional vice. Publius neither expects the president to be the people's tribune nor denies that populists might sometimes win the presidency. He expects the president to serve the people, as every republican officer ought to do, and he aims to constrain those who exceed their charge.

CENTRALIZING THE STATES

Publius's use of the term "energy" in relation to the president is its second appearance in *The Federalist*; the first is in *Federalist* 23, on "the necessity of a constitution, at least equally energetic with the one proposed, to the preservation of the union." His official position, repeated throughout the essays, is that the federal government and the states have separate spheres of competence, each being sovereign and powerful in its sphere, and moreover that state responsibilities are "numerous and indefinite," federal powers being "few and defined."[27] But the Constitution is clear, in its Supremacy Clause, that if the powers of the governments should conflict federal authority will supersede. The argument of *Federalist* 23 is that, when an object is given to the federal government, such as defense of the country against outside foes, there can be "no constitutional shackles"[28] on that government's means to its ends, by which he seems to intend that there be no interference or interposition by the states that hinders the federal government from following through: tax collection rather than requisition of funds; judicial enforcement in federal court rather than, for example, the enforcement of the treaty requiring repayment of prerevolutionary debts only through the courts of the states. In *Federalist* 33 and 44, one by each of the major authors who penned the essays, the Necessary and Proper Clause is expounded liberally to permit the means arguably needed to secure the ends, in one case referred to as the "sweeping clause," in the other explained as essential to federal authority and to remove a pretext that would undercut it. As explained earlier, Publius declined to assert in his own name a recognition of state sovereignty as a justification for equality of votes in the Senate. In *Federalist* 45 his national sentiments are evident in a rhetorical appeal. He asks whether blood was spilt and money spent in the revolution for the sake of preserving attributes of sovereignty in "the governments of individual states [and] particular municipal establishments," rather than to secure the "peace, liberty, and safety" of "the people of America." He then concludes that "as far as the sovereignty of the states cannot be reconciled to the happiness of the people, the voice of every good citizen must be, let the former be sacrificed to the latter."[29]

Perhaps on no subject is Publius's power of prediction more acute than on the question not of constitutional authority but of actual power between the federal government and the states, both on the immediate likelihood of state predominance and the eventual cause of federal ascendancy. In part, he argues, the general tendency among historic federations is toward disunion, not centralization; he gives both ancient and modern examples and alludes to the tradition of jealousy concerning local prerogatives that fueled the American revolution.[30] In part, he refers to the immediacy of the objects of state government in the day-to-day lives of the people—their "ordinary administration of criminal and civil justice," their "guardian[ship] of life and property," "the great cement of society—as well as the natural affection most men feel toward the familiar and their own."[31] In part, he notes the constituent role of the states in forming the federal government: to this day, the states conduct all elections, and the election of all legislative representatives through the states suggests that local interests will never be ignored, even if they do not always predominate.

There are two principal causes that might reverse this ordering of affection, however, leading the people to favor the general government over the states. The first is war: "The operations of the federal government will be most extensive and important in times of war and danger; those of the states in times of peace and security."[32] The second is the possibility of "manifest and irresistible proofs of a better administration," suggesting that the two levels of government will compete for the people's affection.[33] Publius anticipates that war will be infrequent—a prediction borne out in the nineteenth century, though not in the twentieth, nor actually in the twenty-five years following the Constitution's adoption but for the policy of Washington that kept the United States neutral and aloof from the wars occasioned by the French Revolution, at least until their latter days. And though he might have hoped for superior federal administration, he can hardly have supposed federal advantage in the competition, at least until the passage of the Sixteenth Amendment ensured clearly superior federal access to the people's wealth. He would thus not be surprised that popular affection tended toward the states in the early years of the republic, nor that amid the twentieth century's global challenges, military and economic, it shifted toward the center.

In *Federalist* 56, while discussing representation in the House, Publius makes a prediction about the future course of American development: the states will grow more assimilated in their interests—more differentiated within themselves, more similar to one another.[34] This is not an accident, nor is the prediction a flash of insight. Rather, it was a deliberate purpose of the union and an anticipated outcome of a strengthened federal government able to promote and protect commercial growth, "an unequalled spirit of enterprise [being] the genius of the American merchants and navigators, and which is in itself an inexhaustible mine of national wealth."[35] But the states' growing more similar to one another poses a significant challenge to the famous argument for the extended sphere, which supposes a wider disparity of interests spread across the continent than in any local community as a means of moderating the excesses of faction. As the nation becomes more homogeneous in its interests and culture, Publius's argument that "the regulation of the mere domestic police of a state . . . hold[s] out slender allurements to ambition"[36] for national officials becomes increasingly questionable. Such domestic issues, like slavery in the nineteenth century or the "social issues" today, no longer seem isolated but repeat state by state and assume national significance. A homogeneous extended republic has effects not only on the balance of power between the states and the central government but also on the separation of powers within the latter. Will the national legislature grow more to resemble the legislatures in the states, as their members' concerns grow more similar, and what will be the consequences for the equilibrium of the branches on the federal level that the framers adroitly designed and Publius intricately defended?

CONCLUSION: *THE FEDERALIST* AND AMERICAN POLITICAL DEVELOPMENT

To ask such questions is at once to indicate the limits of what Publius could know and to suggest that implicit in the arguments he makes is a way of thinking about American political development that deserves further exploration. In a sense, the emerging field of "APD" within political science is a study of how time has matured, perfected, elucidated, and adjusted the constitutional system devised by the founders, to borrow the language of *Federalist* 82, accounting as well for demographic, economic, and geopolitical change. Even these latter forms of change are not unanticipated by Publius; as just mentioned, he anticipated and encouraged the growth and development of American society and meant for the system to support it, and his awareness of history makes clear that, however constant he thought human nature, he expected the world outside America would change. As for changes in the religious or the intellectual life of the people, it is harder to say, since Publius seemed content to leave these in the hands of a free people, indeed to consider such latitude constitutive of their freedom.

Concerning our contemporary political polarization, he would hardly be surprised. Although it is often noted that he did not anticipate the two-party system as it unfolded, once regular parties came to be seen as legitimate players in republican government rather than a threat to its persistence, *The Federalist* is so attuned to the ubiquity of partisanship—from the first number to the last, in the famous discussion of *Federalist* 10, and in the description of both Congress and the president—that Publius ought to be seen as one who contributed to the legitimization of partisanship by recognition of its necessity rather than as one who longed for its eradication. That he nevertheless recognized its dangers makes him more, not less, useful today. As at the moment of the founding, Publius might explain to us that we lack not republican government but good government, and he might be more disappointed than surprised that we have apparently forgotten the difference between the two.

NOTES

1. Thomas Jefferson to James Madison, November 18, 1788, *Founders Online* (National Archives), https://founders.archives.gov/documents/Madison /01-11-02-0257 (accessed January 13, 2021).

2. Alexander Hamilton, John Jay, and James Madison, *The Federalist*, ed. George W. Carey and James McClellan (1788; reprint, Indianapolis: Liberty Fund, 2001) (hereafter cited as *Federalist*), no. 1, 1.

3. Michael Zuckert, *The Natural Rights Republic* (South Bend, IN: University of Notre Dame Press, 1997); Harvey C. Mansfield Jr., *America's Constitutional Soul* (Baltimore: Johns Hopkins University Press, 1991); *Federalist* 9, 38.

4. William Galston, "Constitutional Surprises: What James Madison Got Wrong," in *What Would Madison Do? The Father of the Constitution Meets Modern American Politics*, ed. Benjamin Wittes and Pietro Nivola (Washington, DC: Brookings Institution, 2015), 48. For a more thoroughgoing critique, see Edward C. Banfield, "Was the Founding an Accident?," in *Saving the Revolution: The Federalist Papers and the American Founding*, ed. Charles Kesler (New York: Free Press, 1987). Together these volumes are a good introduction to those political scientists who do take the political science of Publius seriously.

5. *Federalist* 37, 183.

6. *Federalist* 82, 426. This anticipates what political scientist Keith Whittington calls "constitutional construction," in *Constitutional Construction: Divided Powers and Constitutional Meaning* (Cambridge, MA: Harvard University Press, 2001).

7. *Federalist* 51, 271.

8. *Federalist*, 10, 46–47.

9. *Federalist*, 53, 280.

10. *Federalist* 56, 292–93.

11. Nor is this a matter of a difference between the authors writing as Publius. Madison is writing *Federalist* 53–58, yet in *Federalist* 35 Hamilton likewise makes it clear that the members of the federal legislature are likely to be a more select group than the full range of types to be found in the states, precisely by the voters' choice: large landowners will be picked to represent all the landed interests, merchants to represent manufacturers as well as themselves, and lawyers will abound.

12. *Federalist* 48, 257.

13. *Federalist* 55, 288.

14. *Federalist* 51, 269.

15. *Federalist* 62, 320–21.

16. *Federalist* 63, 327.

17. *Federalist* 63, 328.

18. *Federalist* 68, 354.

19. See Christina Villegas, "Electing the People's President: The Popular Origins of the Electoral College," *Perspectives on Political Science*, 47 (4): 201–9.

20. Madison did apparently endorse proposals for electoral reform in private correspondence in the 1820s. See Alexander Keyssar, *Why Do We Still Have the Electoral College?* (Cambridge, MA: Harvard University Press, 2020), 89–90.

21. *Federalist* 72, 375, 378.

22. *Federalist* 72, 375; *Federalist* 71, 371.

23. *Federalist* 76, 392.

24. *Federalist* 72, 375–76, 378.

25. *Federalist* 76, 392, 394.

26. *Federalist* 77, 396; the Liberty Fund edition includes a footnote from the 1818 Gideon edition, apparently written by James Madison, explaining that "this construction has since been rejected by the legislature; and it is now settled in practice, that the power of displacing belongs exclusively to the president," without mentioning that he himself had insisted on this against Hamilton in the first Congress.

27. *Federalist* 45, 241.

28. *Federalist* 23, 113.

29. *Federalist* 45, 238.

30. See *Federalist* 18, 19, and 46.

31. *Federalist* 17, 82.

32. *Federalist* 45, 241.

33. *Federalist* 46, 244.

34. See especially *Federalist* 56, 293–94.

35. *Federalist* 11, 52.

36. *Federalist* 17, 80.

7

Turgot, Adams, and the Federalist–Anti-Federalist Debate

Timothy W. Burns and Kevin J. Burns

An extended debate between Anne Robert Jacques Turgot, Baron de Laune (1727–81), and John Adams had a fateful effect on the debates over ratification of the constitution proposed for America in 1787. Turgot was a French political economist who served briefly as Louis XVI's finance minister and was an advocate of what we would today call classical liberal economics and classical liberalism. In a 1781 letter responding to the *Additional Observations on Civil Liberty* (London, 1777) of Dr. Richard Price, the English champion of American independence, Turgot criticized the thirteen American states for slavishly following the British in having different branches of government, with checks and balances on these class-based branches.[1] To Turgot, this division of government was out of place in the egalitarian American states, for it mimicked a class system in which a monarch served as chief executive, aristocrats occupied the upper house of the legislature, and commoners held the lower house. Such class-based systems, which rested on deep longings for political ambition and greatness, belonged to the past, Turgot believed, as liberal ideas and modern commerce were undermining class and hierarchical distinctions in favor of radical egalitarian commercial republics, republics that promoted finance and trade rather than glory and honor.

Turgot's letter provoked an extended response from Adams, published as *Defense of the Constitutions of the United States* in 1786–87. Adams sought to defend the thirteen state constitutions by insisting that, contrary to Turgot's claim, the American system of separation of powers was beneficial; rather than slavishly copying the British system, the American system of separation of powers allowed the representation of three natural classes, classes that have been manifested throughout human history and not only in England. Thus, whereas Turgot envisioned a future in which modern commercial republics would transcend traditional classes, Adams believed that the United States would continue to rely on these classes to check each other. In effect, Turgot envisioned an egalitarian future created by modern commerce and a liberal regime that protected individual rights and encouraged acquisitiveness, whereas Adams saw in American constitutionalism simply a more modern version of Aristotle's mixed regime. The disagreement between Adams and Turgot reveals two quite profoundly different understandings of the new science of government directing the proponents of the modern, commercial republic and the new understanding of human beings on which it rests.

In this chapter we explore this public disagreement as well as its effect on the ratification debate in the United States (1788–89). Because Adams's response to Turgot missed the radical nature of the enlightened, commercial republic Turgot sketched—its attempt to wipe out deep longings that give rise to both political ambition and religious devotion—Adams unwittingly misled the Anti-Federalists in the debate over ratification of the Constitution, convincing them that the proposed constitution, like the thirteen state constitutions, embodied a system that guaranteed representation for the three natural classes in the House of Representatives (democratic), Senate (aristocratic), and executive branch (monarchic). In contrast, as we show, the Federalists understood the new, tripartite representative government much more along the lines of Turgot and his illustrious predecessors, recognizing, as he did, that it would subvert classes and turn citizens from the passions attached to regime-level classes and religion to the softer and more pacific attachments created by the bonds of free commerce. Although *The Federalist* did not fully embrace Turgot's argument, its authors proposed a radical understanding of America's constitution, one that viewed property rights and modern commerce as critical for overcoming the challenges of democracy and creating a stable, liberal regime. Misled by Adams, the Anti-Federalists never fully grasped this critical argument, believing instead that the proposed constitution would maintain a class-based system of representation. By considering the heretofore unexplored impact of the Turgot-Adams debate, we hope better to understand the ratification debate and more fully grasp the radical nature of the American regime as envisioned in *The Federalist*.

To make our case, we first sketch the arguments by which Turgot's predecessors in modern political philosophy, Locke and Montesquieu, had made private property, acquisitiveness, and the promotion of commerce the ends of government, and to what purpose they had done so. We then explain how Adams's public response to Turgot convinced the Anti-Federalists that the American system of separation of powers was based on a tripartite class system. Finally, we turn to *The Federalist* to show both Publius's implicit rejection of Adams's class-based argument and the Federalist embrace of the modern commercial republic.

LOCKE AND MONTESQUIEU: PROPERTY RIGHTS AND PASSIONS

The Declaration of Independence's famously Lockean second paragraph declares that "to secure . . . rights, Governments are instituted among Men." This is, perhaps, the single shortest statement of the goal of liberal political theory, and two of its chief influences on both Turgot and the American founding were Locke and Montesquieu. Their emphasis on rights, and especially property rights, profoundly affects the way government operates and the ways in which the citizenry behave. By emphasizing individual rights and promoting capitalism and commerce, Locke and Montesquieu not only limit government, directing it toward the protection of property rather than the classical goal of the promotion of virtue, but also seek to limit human nature, directing humankind's passions away from religion and virtue and toward profit making.

In contrast to his protoliberal predecessor Thomas Hobbes, who, though the first to argue for inalienable, prepolitical natural rights, proclaims man's life in a *violent* state of nature to be "solitary, poor, nasty, brutish, and short,"[2] Locke stresses the *penury* of the original state of nature and emphasizes the creation of government as a significant step to escaping this penury.[3] Yet even before he turns to the discussion of the creation of political society (*Second Treatise*, chaps. VII–VIII), Locke shows that all persons in the state of nature are capable of relieving their penurious condition. The means at each person's disposal are, in the first place, human labor, encouraged by guarantees of the right to private property; second, money, as the means of overcoming the natural spoilage limitation on goods and thereby vastly increasing the desire for gain in humans; third, the spread of the "arts and sciences," as supplying additional "remedies" for the pains and oppressions from a harsh and penurious nature; and fourth, markets in which both wages and the prices of goods and services are determined by the laws of supply and demand (rather than by an alleged "natural wage" or "natural price"), as the means of rationally distributing the goods and services that "industrious and rational" (*ST*, §34) humans produce through their labor, physical and mental.

So where Hobbes had defined the end of government as security and peace (*Leviathan*, XVII, 1 and 5), Locke defines it as "the regulating and preserving of property" (*ST*, §3). "Freedom" means for Locke primarily freedom to protect and preserve one's material private property (which, as he defines it, includes one's life and liberty, *ST*, §§85, 87). And in the fifth and most important chapter of the *Second Treatise*, Locke lays down the moral foundation of what came to be called capitalism. Here he claims that justice, or the common good of all humanity, requires a society to devote itself chiefly to encouraging every individual to pursue the limitless, self-interested acquisition of ever more and more private material possessions and economic buying power (money), so long as each person respects the right of every other person to do likewise. In other words, Locke wholly rejects the arguments of Aristotle and St. Thomas that subordinate property to the good life and see it as a mere tool while disdaining unlimited acquisition (see, e.g., Aristotle, *Politics*, I, chaps. 8–9; Aquinas, *Summa Theologicae*, IIa IIae 78, Art. 1). Locke becomes the first to argue that peacefully competitive greed is the core of a just and moral society.

Since our natural condition is one not of abundance but of penury, or one in which uncultivated land is "waste land" (*ST*, §36), reason tells us to subdue the earth, by labor. And the invention of money overcomes the natural limitation of spoilage that had made boundless acquisition appear to be irrational (*ST*, §37). It thereby gives people a great incentive to enclose and cultivate through labor the land given by nature. And the productivity of that land improves by a factor of ten, or one hundred, or even one thousand; as Locke eventually puts it, all value is from human labor, nature supplying in truth "almost worthless materials" (*ST*, §§37, 43). Since such productivity through human labor and scientific manipulation of nature "increases the common stock of mankind" quite dramatically, moreover, the pursuit of wealth is shown to improve the lot of everyone, lowering the prices of essential goods and services and thereby serving a genuine common good (*ST*, §§41, 47, 49). Though such a system will result in vast inequalities, these inequalities are justified because they vastly elevate the material condition of even the lowest rung of society; in Locke's developing society, all boats rise together, even those of poor wage earners.

As a result, property becomes the key right in Locke's political theory, and the government's role in protecting rights turns increasingly to emphasizing the protection of private property and thereby promoting the constant increase of private property. As Locke puts it, "The increase of lands, and the right employing of them, is the great art of government," and a wise prince will be sure "by established laws of liberty to secure protection and encouragement to the honest industry of mankind" (*ST*, §42). Government should strive to enhance incentives for the working rich and poor— to make everyone see that they can hope by hard work to become more and more prosperous. In the face of the barrenness of nature, we recognize that *the* great engine of a real common good is acquisitiveness that expresses itself in honest labor and endless accumulation. Such acquisitiveness is not exploitative, for in fact the greatest benefactors of humankind are the rationally self-interested, the acquisitive who are industrious.[4]

But though Locke provides this great moral justification and goals and structure of government that is to protect and promote economic rationality through practicing the "great art of government," he leaves the elaboration of this art to his successors, greatest among whom was Montesquieu.

Building upon the theoretical defense of capitalist economics provided by Locke, Montesquieu elaborates on the effects of commerce on society and the benefits the state may derive from these effects. One of commerce's chief effects is "softness," that is, the dissolution of severe, strict, disciplined habits ("prejudices") and a corresponding encouragement of indifference to vice and attachment to bodily pleasures and comforts. "It is almost a general rule," writes Montesquieu, "that wherever there are soft ways of life there is commerce; and wherever there is commerce, there are soft ways of life."[5] Instead of being devoted to one's fatherland, to glory, or to the next life, one is inclined by dint of the flourishing of commerce to become attached to one's material security, comfort, and refined pleasures—to one's body rather than to anything above it. In short, when private acquisition is available through trade, one becomes, as Thomas Pangle neatly summarizes it, "hard-working, tolerant, and peace-loving."[6]

Moreover, commercial intercourse with foreigners and their habits similarly weakens attachment to one's own manner of life as the one right way, causing each individual to understand his own customs as simply one way among many. Strong or unbending attachment to one's own particular way of life comes to appear to be the result of mere narrowness or lack of exposure to other ways. Commerce in this way enhances the belief that good and evil, noble and base, beautiful and ugly are no more than declarations of a person's subjective utilitarian preferences.[7] By encouraging the acceptance of this principle, commerce encourages a cosmopolitanism based on a recognition of what comes to sight as the true, universal needs of humans: material security and comfort. The movement of commercial nations trading with one another is thus not only toward peace, it is toward homogeneity. As nations increasingly emphasize their mutual material needs and the pursuit of money—the means to satisfy those needs—they become similar to one another (XX, 2). In fact, coming to be guided by the pursuit of wealth, all come, in Montesquieu's striking formulation, "to be but a single State, of which all societies are members" (XX, 23).

But to attain this homogeneity to which commerce, manufacture, riches, and luxury lead, it is necessary to *destroy* the "pure morals" or virtue at which classical republicanism aims (XX, 1; cf. III, 3). Commerce corrodes moral virtue, commodifying and setting a cash price on all goods and services formerly done out of grace, generosity, hospitality, or attachment to high-mindedness (see XX, 2). It does so all the more wherever vanity and all that comes in its train ("luxury, industry, the arts, fashions, politeness, taste") drive work and exchange of goods and services to new heights (XIX, 9). This corroding of moral virtue is not an unfortunate side effect of commerce; it is the very end sought by Montesquieu's promotion of commerce, for he holds such moral virtues to be at odds with genuine human freedom and prospering.

As the commercial republic will bring about the atrophy of classical virtues—and with them the end of the ambition for honor, glory, and virtuous deeds—so too it is intended to bring about the atrophy of faith in revealed religion. In the heart of the two chapters on religion in *The Spirit of the Laws* one finds Montesquieu's extraordinary statement that "religion can be most successfully attacked" not by persecution but "by favor, by the conveniences of life, by hope of fortune . . . by that which makes one forget . . . [and] throws one into lukewarmness, when other passions act on our souls, and those which religion inspires are in silence" (XXV, 12). Economic cooperation for satisfying the material wants and needs of pacified individuals, rather than principled stands taken on the basis of stern virtue or religious devotion, is the aim of Montesquieu's modern commercial republic.

THE TURGOT-ADAMS DEBATE ON COMMERCE, HOMOGENIZATION, AND CLASSES

Following Locke's and Montesquieu's lead, Turgot envisioned a withering of political ambition, or the hunt for glory, the privatization and softening of stern moral and religious life, and the eclipse, by economic life, of political life understood as the life devoted to the cultivation of virtues.[8] He hoped that the republics being set up in America would eventually be the end of what he considered the deep, deluded longings that had hitherto animated political life. Turgot's letter to Price presents a judgment of the state constitutions in America that encapsulates this desire to see an American republic emerge that will be governed "by nature, by reason, and by justice"—that is, he looks for a government in accord with modern Lockean-Montesquieuean principles. But he finds the state governments that Americans have produced to be deficient.

The American states, he complains, have thoughtlessly imitated the British system of separation of powers by adopting bicameral legislatures and an independent executive. This system, he argues, should be seen for what it truly is: a result of accidental historical circumstances under which the king is balanced by parliament, and in parliament itself the nobles and people balance each other.[9] The American states, in which all citizens are equal, have foolishly adopted a class-based system and created divisions and instability

where they would not normally exist. The American states' constitutions, Turgot contends, have given insufficient attention to the
fact that there are but two *natural* classes: propertied and nonpropertied. Other classes, he argues—and this would include the classes
of the virtuous, the wise, kings by divine right, the clergy, noble families, and serfs—are artificial and should be accorded no specific
place in any constitutional arrangement. He claims that the constitutions that will bring about the death of all artificial classes are
those that build on the natural class distinction between propertied
and nonpropertied.

Finally, Turgot complains that the American states are foolishly
attempting to regulate commerce among themselves rather than
instituting free trade, which should be seen as a corollary of the
natural right to property (280–81). Turgot sees, quite correctly, that
his argument has a momentous consequence. In a word, the nation-
state is finished if the corollary concerning free trade is fully understood. For, as he suggests, commerce and the private property on
which it is based, when left to themselves, produce a natural homogeneity among peoples, and an equality of economic progress.
Leaving each state to regulate its commerce with others will, on the
other hand, perpetuate an artificial division of states, with diverse
laws and manners and opinions. As Locke had attacked sacred customs,[10] and as Montesquieu had championed the homogeneity
wrought by commerce, so does Turgot find that nature, which speaks
universally, will when followed eliminate diversity of customs, laws,
manners, and opinions and lead to a salutary, rational homogeneity.
The nation has no exalted end; it must simply preserve the freedom of its citizens and protect those individuals' property against
domestic and foreign threats. The nation should therefore recognize that it has only a "pretended" interest in other things: in conquest, glory in "arms" or even a more pacific desire for the glory of
excelling in "arts and sciences." If the interests of a nation are "pretended interests," as Turgot repeats (281), it is because the territory
of the nation belongs not to the nation but to the individual proprietors of the soil. The state exists to serve those proprietors.

Thus, Turgot takes the Montesquieuean thesis very far, showing the possibilities of transcending artificial national divisions and
delusional national desires for glory and turning instead to rely on
property rights and free trade to promote rational, peaceful cooperation. Just as Montesquieu showed the possibility of eradicating

deep longings after piety, virtue, or glory in individuals and replacing them with a desire for commercial gain, Turgot shows that states, like individuals, can be reduced to a level of promoting bodily comfort through commerce; states *and* the individuals composing them must be turned away from problematic desires and see those desires replaced with the softer and more rational desire for commercial comfort. Here then, in the work of its early proponent, as in its later nineteenth-century state (when Tocqueville observed it),[11] and as we see it today in its most advanced state in the European Union, the liberal order favors peace over war, prosperity over glory, and physical satisfaction of needs over spiritual responses to higher callings.

ADAMS'S RESPONSE TO TURGOT: "NATURAL" CLASSES AND MIXED REGIMES

It is against this background of the commercial republic that we can best understand and assess the counterarguments of John Adams's *Constitutions of the United States* and their effect on the debate between the Anti-Federalists, who followed Adams, and the Federalists, who were much closer to the thought of Locke, Montesquieu, and Turgot.

If Turgot is among the most progressive critics of American constitutionalism at the time of the founding, Adams is with good reason considered one of the more conservative, and devoutly Christian, of the American founders in matters of religion and morals.[12] In contrast to Turgot's belief that commerce can soften human nature, undermining rigid virtues and class structures and producing a remarkable homogeneity and equality, Adams had faith in an older vision of political order to produce virtuous citizens and balances between what he saw as the three permanent natural classes.

Unlike Turgot, Adams believed that human progress was seen especially in "progress in education and society, in knowledge, and in virtue" (284); and this progress, Adams claimed, has come about because of advances in the "theory and practice of government": checks and balances, an independent judiciary, and the protection of rights to conscience, speech, and petition. To put Adams in context, we might say that he viewed the modern science of politics as seeking the very same ends as the ancient or classical had sought (the good life and virtue), but as employing new political means to attain them (constitutional-institutional arrangements).

Virtue, as Adams (and Montesquieu) well knew, had been the goal of small, ancient regimes—of small republics, not large despotisms. Though Adams acknowledges that such republics have hitherto been short-lived, he also believes that the modern science of free government can remedy this problem—by introducing modern notions of representation, checks and balances, and a balance of powers in the government, in three branches. And the three "branches of government" brought into being by the new science of politics are an executive, a senate, and a house of representatives. With this argument Adams intends to show that the branches and the checks on each branch seen in the American states are not a merely accidental part of British government adapted in slavish imitation of them. They are instead based on a correct understanding of human nature. By improving ancient political arrangements with the modern understanding of politics, Adams believes, new regimes can both produce virtue in their citizens and maintain themselves for a more extended period of time.

The modern science of government may excel at extending the lives of such republics, Adams argues, primarily by recognizing and balancing the three natural, permanent classes of men. The balance to which Adams refers is not between "powers" (executive, legislative, judicial) but instead between proponents of regimes: aristocrats, democrats, monarchists. These members of three grand, *permanent* parties that promote these three types of rule and, indeed, three ways of life, through legislation, are for Adams the center of the focus of the new science of politics, whose progress consists in understanding how best to balance them in their legislative capacities. Human nature will indeed remain the same, and there will indeed ever be aristocratic and democratic (as well as monarchic) parties. But, claims Adams, human nature can be controlled in a way that the ancients did not see, by balancing the three permanent political parties.[13] Ironically, Adams's understanding of checks and balances relies not on the modern understanding of separation of powers but on the ancient understanding of the mixed regime. For by relying on three separate classes to balance and check each other, Adams essentially proposes a version of Aristotle's mixed regime.

The American states have, according to Adams, created constitutions that balance parties, affording members of each a share in rule. Just as a king and his nobles may check the people, and the people and the nobles may together check the king, so too Adams sees the American executive and bicameral legislatures functioning as a complex mixed regime, one he dubs a "democratical mixture" (see 288–90, 583). Adams's understanding can be seen most clearly by his view of the senates, the upper chambers. Whereas other American founders, such as Jefferson and Madison, conceive of the senate as a chamber of sober second thought, Adams envisions it as composed by men of the highest merit and talents and hence becoming the home of a scheming, ambitious aristocratic party, a place to which problematically ambitious men can be ostracized (290–91).[14]

Thus, we see that Adams actually agrees with Turgot's fundamental premise: the branches of our governments do indeed reflect and represent three different orders of people—three classes. But where Turgot had argued that classes (and with classes, nations) are disappearing owing to the securing of individuals' right to private property, Adams finds that the constitutions are already, as Turgot had hoped, based on nature and reason. He denies, that is, that there soon will be a universal, rough equality in talents and ambition among humans, and a reduction of classes to two economic ones. He argues with particular vigor that there will always be public ambition, always human beings of an aristocratic bent who argue that the best deserve to rule. It is this ambitious type above all that must be checked, he argues, for the sake of preserving the popular voice and thereby preserving the balance needed for free government. Unlike Turgot, Adams does not at all envision a withering of the hunt for glory, nor the privatization of moral and religious life,[15] nor the eclipse of the political by the economic as the driving force of life. He does not see, or does not think, that the republics that are being set up in America will end those deep longings that have hitherto animated political life, as Turgot had argued all modern republics would. It is in part because Adams sees the end of government not simply as liberal, not simply as is stated in the Declaration, but as having as ends the securing of the "lives, liberties, properties, *and characters* of the citizens" (585, emphasis added) that he sees a natural place for "merit," or considerations of worth or desert, as enduring in the new type of government.

If Turgot and Adams are both heirs of the arguments of Locke, Turgot has grasped and wishes to promote the radical, novel end of

Locke's argument. In his promotion of the new science of politics, Adams is either an unaware foot soldier of the radical enlightenment promoted by Turgot or a quiet critic of that enlightenment who is intent on maintaining within the modern world a vision of the classical Christian republic, a free government now fortified by the new doctrines of representation, separation, and balance.

THE ANTI-FEDERALISTS, THE CLASSICAL REPUBLIC, AND THE THREE CLASSES OF MEN

Adams's *Defense of the Constitutions of the United States* was fateful, for it was widely read by the Anti-Federalists. The letters of "Centinel," "Federal Farmer" (2.8.54), and "John DeWitt" (4.3.14), as well as the speeches of Luther Martin in the Maryland assembly (2.4.38) and Melancton Smith in the New York ratifying convention (6.12.22), explicitly cite Adams's argument, viewing the *Defense* as an explanation of the proposed constitution's system of separation of powers.[16] However, although they agreed with Adams that a regime balanced by "three co-equal orders" would be beneficial, the Anti-Federalists did not believe that the Constitution would produce such a balanced regime (2.7.7). Many Anti-Federalist authors—notably, Federal Farmer, Brutus, the signatories of the Pennsylvania minority report, Agrippa, and Melancton Smith—agreed with Adams in theory, arguing that the aristocratic elites and the democratic yeomanry should each be represented in different branches of the government, balancing each other's worst impulses and helping to promote good government (see 2.8.25, 2.8.54, 2.9.42–43, 2.9.46, 2.9.49–52, 2.9.200, 3.11.35, 4.6.43, 6.12.15–17).[17] But because none of the Anti-Federalist authors believed that the Constitution would actually create such a balanced class system in practice, they rejected it for its failure to guarantee the "first of all among the political balances," the preservation "in its proper station [of] each of these classes" (2.8.97).

Although we emphasize the Anti-Federalist desire for a government that balances the three "natural classes," it is worth noting that the Anti-Federalists also sought small republics, in which a homogeneity of mores and the promotion of virtue were possible—indeed, these desires form the basis of their rejection of a large, extended republic.[18] These oft-noted Anti-Federalist concerns for elements of a classical or premodern republicanism of virtuous self-rule are suffused with a less-often-noted dependence on Adams's understanding of different classes or "orders of men," causing the arguments to take on a quite different tone. Of course, it is true that the Anti-Federalists also broadly accepted many Lockean political teachings, including the principle tenets of modern political rationalism. They accepted the principle of the original "state of nature," of individual "natural" rights, of the social compact that frees humans from the state of nature and creates a government in order to protect their rights. It is in fact in part on these modern, Lockean grounds that the Anti-Federalists oppose the proposed constitution's Supremacy Clause, demand a bill of rights, and oppose Congress's control of the purse strings and the executive's control of the sword.[19]

But it was on the basis of Adams's *Defense*, looking for a new federal constitution that ensured the balance between democratic and aristocratic factions called for in it, that the Anti-Federalists predicted that the proposed constitution would actually create an aristocratic government, favoring great wealth and even tending toward hereditary offices. The Senate, it was widely acknowledged, would lean toward aristocracy by its prominence and position, and the president would presumably come from the same upper crust of American society. Moreover, these two aristocratic institutions would be further united by their common functions, for the Constitution requires close cooperation between the president and Senate on federal appointments and the ratification of treaties (2.8.29).

Although the aristocratic and monarchic orders would be represented in the Senate and in the person of the chief executive, they argued, the common people would not be represented as a class. Even large states would send fewer than a dozen members to the House, thereby guaranteeing that only "the first men in the state" (2.9.42) would gain election, whereas the people would be excluded from office (see variously 2.8.25, 2.8.54, 2.8.60, 2.8.97, 2.8.98–99, 2.9.42–46, 2.9.200, 3.11.35, 4.6.43, 5.1.72, 5.16.8, 6.12.17–18). Thus, America's "democratic" middle class would be shut out of government, and the aristocrats, only rarely coming into contact with the common man, would be detached from the day-to-day concerns and economic interests of their constituents (2.9.49, 6.12.17). As Brutus concluded, although the House was purported to be the democratic branch, in truth it offered little more than the "shadow of representation" (2.9.43, see also 2.9.50, 5.16.8). The federal city would be filled with "the great and mighty of the earth" (2.9.200), and these "lordly and high minded" rulers (3.11.49) would willingly sacrifice the public good to advance their own interests and perpetuate their positions (2.9.47).[20]

Because they accepted Adams's argument and believed that the government would represent classes of people, rather than the people as a whole, the Anti-Federalists demanded that the common yeoman be more suitably represented in Congress than the Constitution provided. The people would be well represented only if they could "chuse men from among themselves, and genuinely like themselves" (2.8.97), so representatives should "resemble those they represent; they should be a true picture of the people" (6.12.15). The resulting involvement of the yeomanry would, they insisted, yield tremendous benefits. By bringing them into government, the community would benefit from the solid, middling virtues that marked it. The states, as small republics and schools of virtue, encouraged "manly virtues," the virtues of a free people: good morals, religion, temperance, a moderate healthy ambition, and avoidance of corrupting "foreign mixtures" (4.6.34, 6.12.17). The Anti-Federalists believed that these virtues would come to fruition primarily in "the substantial yeomanry of the country" (6.12.17), whereas the first men of the community would be "licentious, assuming, and overbearing" (2.8.63).[21]

Moreover, the Anti-Federalists argued that only if the governing and the governed held the same interests would good government be possible. Unless the middle class was suitably represented in the legislature, the government would be wholly aristocratic, and its members would neither understand nor sympathize with their constituents' interests. A legislature made up of aristocrats would naturally pursue policies favoring the aristocracy. But if the government, or at least one branch of it, represented the common man, then the yeomanry's representatives would enact policies that would benefit the middle class. In this way—and only in this way— could the rulers be counted on to promote the good of the people; their passions and self-love would drive them to enact policies benefiting themselves, and they would thereby (almost incidentally) benefit their fellow citizens. Sympathy and attachment were the keys to good government.

Finally, the Anti-Federalists linked suitable representation to lawfulness, patriotic virtue, and the maintenance of free government. In this context, the Anti-Federalists were clearly influenced by Montesquieu's arguments, particularly those from the early parts of *The Spirit of the Laws*, that virtue was the "spring" of a popular republican state (III, 3).[22] But Montesquieu also suggested that genuinely republican regimes must be small (VIII, 16 and 19; especially *Federalist* 9 and 10 rejected this argument and adopted a more complex understanding of Montesquieu's teaching); because a larger regime would necessitate a strong central authority to enforce the law throughout the realm, an extended territory must be ruled by a single person (Montesquieu, VIII, 19, cf. especially Storing, 2.7.18, 2.7.94). Similarly, the Anti-Federalists argued that small regimes allowed a largely homogeneous people to elect rulers similar to themselves, rulers who would write laws beneficial to the people's interests. As a result of such elections, they expected widespread patriotic virtue; the common man would be attached to the rulers and the regime and would willingly obey the law, thereby limiting the government's need to employ coercion and force. Conversely, the Anti-Federalists predicted that in a large republic this tie of sympathy between the people and their rulers would be missing, and with it patriotic virtue. Thus, relying on Montesquieu they predicted that a large regime would find it necessary to enforce the law by means of a powerful standing army, obedient to the central government—all but ensuring that despotism would eventually arise (see 2.6.15–17, 2.8.18, 2.8.24, 2.8.93–95, 2.9.17–18, 3.6.21).

In short, the Anti-Federalists supported Adams's proposed system of institutionalized and balanced representation of classes; as a result, they rejected the Constitution, because they recognized that it would fail to achieve this goal. The government would not adhere to the "true principles" (2.8.97) of representation, for the three "natural classes" would not be represented (2.8.97, see also 2.9.44, 3.11.35). And without suitable representation for all three classes, the Anti-Federalists predicted unfair, class-based legislation and a quick decline into despotism.

THE FEDERALIST ON REPRESENTATION AND COMMERCE

From Adams and the Anti-Federalists, we must turn now to *The Federalist* and Publius's response to these charges of aristocracy and despotism. In answering these charges, Publius did not take the obvious course of action—to defend American republicanism by insisting that the Constitution would ensure full representation of both the aristocratic and democratic classes. Instead, he chose to focus on the issue of representation more broadly. It is easy to miss the import of this turn in the argument. Publius's refusal to address the question of class directly was in truth a rejection of the terms of debate proposed by his opponents. He not only rejected their view of representation, but he ultimately rejected their theory of government, arguing for a truly radical understanding of the proposed constitution, based on a Lockean-Montesquieuean conception of commerce and modern government. If the Anti-Federalists accepted certain aspects of Lockean political thought while remaining convinced by the classical view of government espoused by Adams, Publius clearly sets himself apart, embracing an understanding of government far closer to Turgot's than to Adams's.

Thus, in rejecting the Anti-Federalist claims that the new government will promote a class-based aristocracy, Publius attacks their understanding of representation at its core. He rejects their contention that the House should directly represent "all the different classes of citizens . . . to produce a due sympathy between the representative body and its constituents."[23] The Anti-Federalists emphasize the shared sympathies of the three regime-level classes, but Publius looks beyond this outdated notion, arguing that a modern commercial regime would allow individuals to transcend narrow class interests and create unity across classes. Most critical, Publius shows that modern commerce will unite all citizens around a single goal of making money, thus creating broad-based, shared economic interests. Not class interests but financial interests will create unity in the new American republic.

Unlike Adams and the Anti-Federalists, who assume that the proposed constitution will incorporate significant aspects of classical politics through what they view as a class-based system of separation of powers, the argument set out in *The Federalist* embraces much of the Lockean-Montesquieuean argument, proposing a system that overcomes the weaknesses of classical republicanism and striving to bring about the leveling equality and peace and stability that comes with a modern commercial republic. As Publius writes in *Federalist* 9, the United States has learned from the "history of the petty republics of Greece and Italy," which, despite the "fleeting brilliancy" of their nascent republican governments, were continually plagued by "domestic faction and insurrection" (66). The modern "science of politics" has developed "models of a more perfect structure," relying on principles of government "not known . . . or imperfectly known to the ancients" (67). These great improvements of the new science of politics are separation of powers, legislative checks and balances, an independent judiciary, representative government, and, most important, "the ENLARGE-MENT of the ORBIT" (67), the extended sphere of government so famously expounded in *Federalist* 10. In embracing the enlarged orbit—looking toward an *extended* republic rather than one constrained by the size of the traditional polis—Publius acknowledges that the new American constitution rejects a "blind veneration for antiquity," looking instead to a regime "which has no parallel in the annals of human society" (99–100). Critical to this new experiment is the role of free commerce, which helps to avoid the petty factional conflicts of the ancients precisely by turning everyone from the deep-seated desire for virtue, glory, or moral excellence and toward the lower—and yet infinitely safer, from Publius's perspective—desire for profit.

The proposed constitution, which *The Federalist* so ably defended and promoted, does not speak directly to the issue of economic policy, but it does clearly lay the groundwork for a commercial republic. Prior to the addition of the Bill of Rights, the sole mention of "rights" in the unamended document was with reference to Congress's power to promote "the Progress of Science and useful Arts" by protecting patents and copyrights (Article I, Section 8, Clause 8). The economic powers granted to Congress, in combination with the powers specifically denied the states, all but guarantee free trade and promote centralized control over the nation's economy. Congress is given broad tax powers to impose duties on imports, the power to regulate interstate and foreign commerce, to fix standard weights and measures, to coin money and regulate its value, and to enact uniform rules for bankruptcies (Article I, Section 8). The states, in contrast, lose the authority to coin or print money, lay duties on imports or exports (except in very limited circumstances), or impair the obligations of contracts (Article I, Section 10). Finally, the Constitution forbids taxes or duties on the exports of states and bans preferential regulations that would benefit one state or its shipping over another (Article I, Section 9). As

Forrest McDonald has pointed out, these powers "enshrine[ed] in fundamental law . . . a broad, modern conception of contracts," allowed Congress to "promote manufacturing through protective tariffs," and ensured that, "no matter what system of political economy was adopted, internally the United States would be the largest area of free trade in the world."[24]

The commercial implications of the Constitution were not lost on Publius, who pointed to the many benefits of a single, united government with broad powers to control foreign and internal commerce. A strong national government capable of setting a single unified trade policy would allow more advantageous trade relations with Europe, promote a robust, diversified American economy, and have sufficient power to ensure American access to the Great Lakes and the Mississippi River (*Federalist* 11 and 12, 80, 82, 84–85, 88–90). Moreover, a union that encompassed commercial unity would discourage jealousy and harmful rivalry among the states while encouraging increased trade: "unrestrained intercourse between the states" would guarantee that the "veins of commerce in every part will be replenished and will acquire additional motion and vigor from the free circulation of the commodities of every part" (*Federalist* 11 and 12, 84; see also 87), advancing trade at home and abroad.[25]

Tellingly, these commercial benefits were central, not ancillary, to the new constitutional project. Indeed, promotion of commerce would become one of the national government's primary objects; as Publius recognizes, in the realm of modern politics the "prosperity of commerce" has become a "primary object of . . . [the] political cares" of "enlightened statesmen"; like Locke, Publius holds that promotion of commercial success is a significant part of the modern "great art of government" (*Federalist* 10 and 12, 86, also 74–75; cf. Locke, *ST*, §42). Notably, Publius explicitly aligns this great art with the project of unleashing humankind's greed. The union of the states, in addition to the freedoms and property rights guaranteed by the Constitution,[26] encourage a beneficial acquisitiveness: "By multiplying the means of gratification, by promoting the introduction and circulation of the precious metals, those darling objects of human avarice and enterprise, [commerce] serves to vivify and invigorate all the channels of industry and to make them flow with greater activity and copiousness" (*Federalist* 12, 86). It is by promoting this gratification of human avarice that the country is benefited, as the "unequaled spirit of enterprise . . . [and] the genius of the American merchants and navigators" are unleashed through modern commerce (*Federalist* 11, 12, and 60; see generally 83–87, 367).

Publius's Lockean praise of enterprise-promoting money is striking, but equally important is what the commercial republic is said to mean concerning the "orders of men." Adams's three orders or classes are quietly replaced by "the assiduous merchant, the laborious husbandman, the active mechanic, and the industrious manufacturer" (*Federalist* 12, 86). Everyone, that is, is working—for money; there is no leisured aristocratic or monarchic class in this new republic. And each "order" is defined by its job classification. Economic interests are to replace what Adams had considered permanent classes.

It is because of the uniting interest in profit, which undermines traditional class distinctions, that Publius may so easily disregard the Anti-Federalist demand for mirrored representation. Whereas the Anti-Federalists insist that representatives must share a common way of life with their constituents, in *Federalist* 35 Publius contends that the people do not even wish to vote for men like themselves but will consistently choose their superiors in political ability, those most capable of navigating the legislative process. Manufacturers and mechanics will not support the election of other manufacturers or mechanics but will naturally "be inclined . . . to give their votes to merchants in preference to persons of their own professions or trades. . . . [They know] their interests can be more effectually promoted by the merchant than by themselves. . . . They are sensible that . . . influence and weight and superior acquirements of the merchants render them more equal to a contest . . . [in] the public councils" (210–11). Publius does not expect a mechanic, for example, to promote the good of another economic interest at the expense of his own, but he does predict that a mechanic may recognize that he will benefit more by the election of a merchant skilled in the political arts than by the election of another mechanic. Interest may drive men, but skill is needed to advance interest.

Even more important, Publius sees that the issue goes far beyond the skill of the political candidate in parliamentary procedure. A mechanic might vote for a merchant, recognizing that the merchant's trade makes him more suited to a spirited public debate.

But the mechanic will trust the merchant to advance his interests because he knows that their economic interests are intertwined. Representatives, without holding the very same interests as their constituents, will nevertheless have "interests . . . intimately blended and interwoven" (*Federalist* 12, 86) with those of their constituents, thereby all but guaranteeing that their self-interest will drive them to protect both their own economic interests and the interests of those they represent (*Federalist* 35, 211).[27] Thus, *The Federalist* partially agrees with the Anti-Federalists, seeing that self-love and interest will help to promote good government. Nevertheless, Publius shows that the Anti-Federalists have an unduly limited conception of interest, one so focused on class interests that it fails to account for a complex modern economy in which various commercial interests are closely connected and interreliant.

The process of transcending regime-based divisions begins by showing that all humans are united by a common interest (money) and moves forward to show how a modern commercial republic intimately intertwines various *modes* of money making to further complicate the process. *Federalist* 10 famously elaborates on this argument concerning control of factions by extension of the sphere of popular government. For Publius, the factional conflict based on deep-seated longings that most threatens a modern regime may be combated by modern commerce, by the commerce that relies on avarice to soften human pride and encourages homogeneity at the expense of rigid principles of virtue.

Although *Federalist* 10 is remembered for its emphasis on property-based factions, it is other factions, factions based on deep longings, which trouble Publius the most. Attachment to a particular "religion . . . [form of] government . . . [or] to different leaders" creates dangerous factional conflicts, inflaming the citizenry with "mutual animosity" and enkindling the "most violent conflicts" and oppression (73–74). As Martin Diamond has observed in his magisterial work on *Federalist* 10, it is these sorts of factional conflicts—those based on deep-seated, impassioned views that rest on a foundation prior to or beyond reason (e.g., prerational attachments or an attachment based on faith *and* reason)—that Publius believes arouse the most violent internecine conflicts. For all his trepidation about property-based factional conflict, he also recognizes that multiplying the number of economic, commercial interests through a large-scale republic will draw upon the pacifying nature of trade to ameliorate these more deadly forms of factional conflict.[28]

Thus, as Diamond contends, Publius desires to direct humankind away from *these* sorts of conflicts to a safer and more manageable form of factional conflict, one based on property. These economic factions, as we know, will be less dangerous in part because they are so many in an extended sphere. The great genius of *Federalist* 10 is not that it will do away with factions but that it shows how America may choose which factions it will encourage—thereby directing its citizens away from religious, regime-based, or leader-based factions and toward economic factions.[29]

Notably, Publius relies heavily on the work of Locke and Montesquieu, showing that property-based factions are the most manageable precisely because they rely on what Montesquieu and Locke would call rational self-interest. Factional conflict based on wealth, based on strife between those who have more and those who have less, is simplified by the fact that both sides want the same thing—wealth—and by the economic growth that patents, copyrights, and private property make possible. As Publius argues, the uniting factor between various classes or orders is love of wealth: "All . . . look forward with eager expectation and growing alacrity to this pleasing reward of their toils" (*Federalist* 12, 86). And neither side must, in order to attain that wealth, devote itself to the destruction of the other; the rich want simply to remain rich, the poor want to join the rich in their success. And it is this factor, this common love of lucre, which creates a common ground for cooperation between economic factions. All factions seek money; all may accumulate more through vigorous modern commerce, "the faithful handmaid of labor and industry in every shape" (*Federalist* 12, 87). Cooperation, rather than bloodletting, is the proper outlet for the energies of commercial competitors. And modern commerce, as opposed to an older conception of mercantilism based on zero-sum gain, promises the gratification of that longing: all boats may rise together.

Thus, in order to avoid the threat of tyranny posed by a majority faction, Publius relies on an extended republic that will ensure a plurality of small, *economic* interests. Yet he also recognizes the benefits that flow from the vast fluidity and interconnectedness of a modern economy. This fluidity would allow Publius to show the

great impact of commerce on reducing the dangers of factional conflict. Not only will the *membership* of these classes change as individuals shift between them and new generations and circumstances
alter the relative influence of each, but the *alliances* between classes
will vary over time. Publius's emphasis on the intertwined economic
interests seen in a modern commercial republic shows that the fluidity of a modern economy will allow a vast variety of constantly
shifting coalitions—coalitions formed by both "the possession of different *degrees*" of property and the possession of different "*kinds* of
property" (*Federalist* 10, 73, emphasis added). A laborer working
in manufacture will recognize his common interest with other
laborers in every field. But he will also recognize that he is intimately tied to the interests of everyone engaged in manufacture,
from his employer to moneyed investors or wealthy carriers of man-
ufactured goods.[30] Publius proposes, essentially, factions that can
form both horizontal and vertical alliances, overcoming the traditional "class" distinctions between the rich and the poor by both
uniting and dividing individuals on various planes. The fluidity and
complexity of the modern commercial economy will undermine
both rigid classes and rigid factions, creating shifting coalitions of
economic interests, interests that will form the many small diverse
factions *Federalist* 10 famously predicted would block each other
and prevent majority tyranny (73–77; also *Federalist* 35, 210–12).

In his argument for a modern commercial republic, Publius
clearly reflects the thought of Locke and Montesquieu and shows
himself to be closer to Turgot than to Adams. As Martin Diamond
points out, Publius envisioned a society in which "men will tend to
think in terms of their various immediate economic interests; that
is, to think as members of an 'interest group' rather than of a class."[31]
Classes, as understood in an older and more traditional sense, would
disappear. Every man, regardless of his economic interest, would be
essentially equal as a member of "the great body of the people" (*Federalist* 57, 349; also *Federalist* 35, 213). By replacing social classes
with economic and interest-based groups, Publius rejects Adams's
argument and suggests that Turgot was at least partially correct, for
the United States would overcome the old classes and allow greater
social mobility and economic freedom. In its hope to see widespread
commerce overcome traditional class divisions and unite humans
in a pacific love of gain, *The Federalist* clearly places itself in the
modern camp, aligning itself with modern understandings of

rational self-interest as the cornerstone of politics and rejecting classical notions of political life. The new science of politics, and especially the enlarged orbit, will protect and maintain republican liberty and individual rights (especially property rights), but *The Federalist* does not promise that the new constitution will find a way to protect republican virtue (*Federalist* 10, 72–73). Indeed, it would not be an exaggeration to say that Publius plans to sacrifice traditional notions of virtue for liberty and stability.

Yet if *The Federalist* arguments are distinctly modern, they never go as far as Turgot. Most notably, Publius does not predict that commerce will lead to any transcendence of the nation-state. To the contrary, in *Federalist* 11 he bases his hope for America's "dangerous greatness" (80) on its rising commercial and maritime power and, in language that points toward the Monroe Doctrine (and even the "Roosevelt Corollary"), looks forward to a day when the United States will control "all transatlantic force or influence" and be capable of "dictat[ing] the terms of connection between the old and the new world!" (*Federalist* 11, 86, also 82). Commerce will unite America, but it will also strengthen it as an independent nation-state, allowing it to take up its separate and equal station among the powers of the earth.

CONCLUSION

The discourse between Turgot and Adams points to two extreme positions that exerted significant influence over the ratification debate of 1787–89. Adams's argument, which failed to distinguish between a complex government in which separate *powers* checked each other and a regime in which separate *classes* maintained an equilibrium, looks back to an ancient understanding of politics, more reminiscent of Aristotle's mixed regime than Locke's or Montesquieu's understanding of the separation of powers. On the other hand, Turgot's radical faith in the ability of commerce not only to overcome class divisions but even to eliminate the importance of national borders looks beyond the arguments of Locke and Montesquieu. Although neither of these positions can be said fully to represent American thinking during the ratification debate, both influenced the arguments presented by the friends and enemies of the proposed constitution.

Because of Adams's misunderstanding of American constitutionalism, the Anti-Federalists presented lengthy diatribes against a perceived threat of aristocratic government. Yet in this they were misled, and their critique missed the point. For *The Federalist* rejected the notion that the "natural" classes were permanent, believing instead that the new "science of politics" would provide a novel and more stable foundation for free government. Publius asserts that a modern commercial republic will unleash the acquisitiveness of human beings, overcoming traditional class boundaries and replacing them with the complex relationships that come with economic deal making and competition. Thus, *The Federalist* fundamentally rejected the terms of the debate laid down by the Anti-Federalists, emphasizing a new, emphatically modern order in which regime-level classes would have no place. Class interests would be replaced by economic interests as a result of the economic freedom promised by the new constitution.

This more radical argument, depending so heavily on free trade, economic mobility, and individual initiative, clearly underlies the argument of Publius but was never fully understood or grasped by the Anti-Federalists. Had the Anti-Federalists more fully understood what was at stake, had they better understood Turgot's critique and seen how much of his argument for a modern, classless, commercial republic had been accepted by *The Federalist*, they might have presented a different argument, more pointed in its critique of luxury, trade, and intermixture with foreign nations. Though it goes beyond the scope of this chapter to prove it, had the Anti-Federalists better understood the *Federalist* argument, they might have been able to produce a keen critique of Publius's praise for the modern commercial republic; indeed, they might even have won the debate.

NOTES

1. Excerpts from the letter appear in *Defense of the Constitutions of Government of the United States*, in *The Works of John Adams*, ed. Charles Francis Adams (Boston: Little, Brown, 1856), vol. 4. All parenthetical page references appearing in this section are to this edition.

2. Thomas Hobbes, *Leviathan*, ed. Richard Tuck (Cambridge: Cambridge University Press, 1996), XIII, §9 (hereafter cited in the text by chapter and page).

3. John Locke, *First and Second Treatises of Government*, ed. Peter Laslett (Cambridge: Cambridge University Press, 1988), §32 (hereafter cited internally).

4. See Thomas L. Pangle and Timothy W. Burns, *Key Texts of Political Philosophy: An Introduction* (Cambridge: Cambridge University Press, 2014), 276–306.

5. Montesquieu, *The Spirit of the Laws*, ed. Anne Cohler, Basia Miller, and Harold Stone (Cambridge: Cambridge University Press, 1989), Book XX, chap. 1 (hereafter cited internally by book number and chapter).

6. Thomas L. Pangle, *Montesquieu's Philosophy of Liberalism: A Commentary on* The Spirit of the Laws (Chicago: University of Chicago Press, 1973), 200–259, especially 204. For an excellent contemporary defense of Montesquieu's strategy, see Steven Kautz, *Liberalism and Community* (Ithaca, NY: Cornell University Press, 1995). For an account of some difficulties with that defense, see Timothy W. Burns, "Virtuous Liberalism," in *Political Science Reviewer* 28 (1999): 272–314.

7. As Montesquieu puts it in another work, "The terms beautiful, good, noble, great, perfect, are attributes of objects which are relative to the beings that are considering the objects. It is very important to keep this principle in mind. It is the sponge that erases most prejudices." Montesquieu, *Pensées*, no. 2162, quoted in Pangle, *Montesquieu's Philosophy*, 230. See also Hobbes, *Leviathan*, VI, 7–8.

8. The following two sections are taken, with revisions, from Timothy W. Burns, "Adams, Turgot, and the New Science of Politics," in *Classical Rationalism and the Politics of Europe*, ed. Ann Ward, chap. 11 (Cambridge, UK: Cambridge Scholars, 2017).

9. Anne Robert Jacques Turgot, Baron de Laune, "Letter to Dr. Price," in John Adams, *Defense of the Constitutions of Government of the United States*, in *The Works of John Adams*, ed. Charles Francis Adams (Boston: Little, Brown, 1856), vol. 4, 279, middle (subsequent references appear parenthetically in the body of the text).

10. "When Fashion hath once Established, what Folly or craft began, Custom makes it sacred." (*First Treatise*, §58).

11. Consider in this light Tocqueville's summarizing comparison and contrast between the aims and inclinations of life in the old regime versus life in the newly emerging liberal democracies: "If, finally, the principal object of a government, according to you, is not to give the most force or the most glory possible to the entire body of the nation, but to procure the most well-being for each of the individuals who compose it and to have each avoid the most misery, then equalize conditions and constitute the government of a democracy." *Democracy in America*, trans. and ed. Harvey C. Mansfield and Delba Winthrop (Chicago: University of Chicago Press, 2000), vol. 1, pt. ii, chap. 6, 235. Consider also Thomas Pangle's presentation of Nietzsche's critique of the

human type thus fostered in *The Ennobling of Democracy: The Challenge of the Postmodern Era* (Baltimore: Johns Hopkins University Press, 1992), 81–82.

12. Adams himself was aware of this position vis-à-vis other founders. Consider for example his letter of July 3, 1776, to Abigail Adams (in *Colonies to Nation: A Documentary History of the American Revolution*, ed. Jack P. Greene [New York: Norton, 1975]) in which he tells his wife that it is "the will of Heaven" that America and Britain should be sundered forever, that the coming "furnace of affliction" will "inspire us with many virtues" that we *now lack* and may bring a needed "purification from our vices," and in which he looks forward to future Independence Day celebrations that will "be commemorated" not only with fireworks and games and parades but "as the day of deliverance, by solemn acts of devotion to God Almighty" (296). Consider also his "Thoughts on Government" in the same collection. It begins by declaring best what any liberal of the time might declare best, "the form of government which communicates ease, comfort, security, or in one word, happiness, to the greatest number of persons" (307). But having brought in arguments concerning human dignity, patience, humility, moderation, honor, and wisdom, Adams is soon speaking instead of a society's happiness as found in "ease, its safety, its *freedom*" (309, emphasis added). Finally, having brought in the need to attend, in the governance of a free people, to "the dignity and stability of government in all its branches," "the morals of the people," the liberal education of youth, sumptuary laws ("the very mention of which," he declares, "will excite a smile," 310), "great, manly, and warlike virtues," and "elevation of sentiment," he concludes by speaking of "the happiest governments *and the best character* of a *great* people" (311, emphasis added).

13. Adams excerpts a portion of Thucydides's description of the Corcyrean civil strife (3.81–82), but upon reaching Thucydides's statement that "such things will ever be . . . so long as human nature continues the same," he interrupts the quotation to say: "But if this nervous historian had known a balance of three powers, he would not have pronounced the distemper so incurable, but would have added—*so long as parties in cities remain unbalanced.*" Adams, *Defense*, vol. 4, 285.

14. In America, of course, the *aristoi* are not merely conventional—not founded and sustained by primogeniture—but "natural" (380, 382). It is these natural *aristoi* whom Adams intends when he speaks of "the few" (382) and when he says, in his conclusion, that their foundation is in nature (579).

15. Adams directly addresses the question of religion in his *Defense of the Constitutions of the United States* and agrees in part with Jefferson's outlook (291–93). He presents every republic of the past as having been founded on a fraudulent appeal to a god or gods, and the United States as the only country in which this will never be the case (291, 292, 293). He argues that the enlightenment of the people has protected them from the "monkery of priests, or the knavery of politicians" (293). Yet one sees in his writings no hope that human

beings will become tamed in their religious deeds or speech or have their hitherto apparently strongest longings atrophy through their pursuit of commercial success. In fact, over and against the authority of "the monkery of priests, or the knavery of politicians," Adams presents "the authority of magistrates and the obedience of citizens" in America as "grounded on reason, morality, *and the Christian religion*" (293, emphasis added).

16. For works of the Anti-Federalists, see Herbert Storing, *The Complete Anti-Federalist* (Chicago, University of Chicago Press, 1981), 2.7.6–10.

17. The response to Adams was not uniform. Centinel, likely the harshest of Adams's Anti-Federalist critics, insisted that Adams, for all his historical erudition, had "not been able to adduce a single instance of such a government" existing in practice (2.7.7). A (Maryland) Farmer was perhaps most sympathetic to Adams's claims. Taking the argument to its logical conclusion, he insisted that the House should be democratically elected, but that the president and senators should serve life terms; thus, rather than merely represent a wealthy gentry (a "subaltern aristocracy," as he called it), these two institutions ought to be openly aristocratic (5.1.72–73).

18. See Storing, *Complete Anti-Federalist*, 2.8.41–43, 2.9.8–21 (citing *Spirit of the Laws*, VIII, 16), 2.9.50–52, 2.9.100, 2.9.119–20, 2.9.186–94, 3.11.28–29, 3.11.49–54, 4.6.19–20, 5.14.7–9, 5.16.22–23. In thus arguing for homogeneity of mores in each state, the Anti-Federalists intend the very opposite of what one finds in Turgot. They intend by it not a universal or cosmopolitan, commercially induced, and potentially worldwide homogeneity but homogeneity within each state, owing to each state's self-rule and its promotion of republican virtue.

19. The Anti-Federalists' Lockeanism is, one might add, why the Federalists were able to win many of them over with the promise of a bill of rights, which protected so many Lockean rights. See Storing, *Complete Anti-Federalist*, 2.8.15–20, 2.8.49–50, 2.8.74–80, 2.8.200, 2.9.22–30, 4.6.26 (cf. 4.6.31 on commerce), 5.14.2.

20. The Anti-Federalists frequently predicted that the Constitution would create an aristocracy, though descriptions of the means by which this aristocracy would rise were left vague. Brutus suggested that senators would rely on their reputations and political influence to guarantee reelection, eventually creating a presumption that members of the upper body would be retained for life (2.9.201). The signatories of the Pennsylvania minority report saw a more dangerous option, predicting that the members of Congress would use their power to control the time, place, and manner of holding national elections to "prolong their existence in office, for life, by postponing the time of their election" (3.11.25, also 3.11.36; for variations, see 4.6.4, 4.18.1).

21. The virtue of the middle class did not come from the "intrinsic superiority" of the common man, for the Anti-Federalists conceded that the "same passions and prejudices govern all men" (6.12.17; also 2.7.105–10,

5.1.56–58, 6.9.19). The key was not the desires of the classes, which were essentially identical, but the means each class had to attain their desires. Whereas the aristocrats of the state would often wield the power and influence necessary to achieve their ends, the middle class would face fewer temptations; their modest way of life and circumstances typically inclined them "to set bounds to their passions and appetites," and if this was not sufficient "the want of means to gratify [their desires] will be a restraint" (6.12.17). Even if every person was driven by self-interest, circumstances could tame their passions and prejudices and promote real virtues in the middling class. Storing, "What the Anti-Federalists Were *For*," in *Complete Anti-Federalists*, I.18. Compare Niccolo Machiavelli, *Discourses on Livy*, trans. Harvey C. Mansfield and Nathan Tarcov (Chicago: University of Chicago Press, 1996), 18.

22. See especially Martin Diamond, "The Ends of Federalism," in *As Far as Republican Principles Will Admit* (Washington, DC: AEI Press, 1992), 149.

23. Publius, *The Federalist Papers*, ed. Clinton Rossiter (New York: Signet Classic, 2003), 210 (hereafter cited internally as *Federalist*, with page numbers from this edition).

24. Forrest McDonald, *Novus Ordo Seclorum* (Lawrence: University Press of Kansas, 1985), 266, 273, see also 265–66, 270–73.

25. In *Federalist* 14, James Madison laid out an ambitious set of policies by which the national government could facilitate trade. Whatever his later Jeffersonian tendencies, in 1787 Madison proposed a system that sounds strikingly like Henry Clay's American System, replete with national roads, a system of interior canals, fostering of "communication between the Western and Atlantic districts," and "interior navigation" throughout the Atlantic seaboard (98).

26. Consider especially Congress's ability to protect property by controlling patents and copyrights (Article I, Section 8, Clause 8) and the guarantee of equal "Privileges and Immunities" to citizens of the several states (Article IV, Section 2, Clause 1). On the latter, see Justice Bushrod Washington's opinion in Corfield v. Coryell, 6 Fed. Cas. 546, no. 3, 230 C.C.E.D.Pa. (1823); and, for an excellent explanation of the rights (especially to make contracts and buy, sell, and use property freely) Congress intended to protect by similar language in the Fourteenth Amendment, see Michael Zuckert, "Fundamental Rights, the Supreme Court, and American Constitutionalism," in *The Supreme Court and American Constitutionalism*, ed. Bradford P. Wilson and Ken Masugi (New York: Rowman and Littlefield, 1998), 129–56.

27. Indeed, even the landed element—which Publius separates from the mechanic-manufacturer-merchant element in *Federalist* 35 (210–11)—is seemingly integrated into a single complex modern economy in *Federalist* 12 (86) and 60 (368).

28. Martin Diamond, "Ethics and Politics: The American Way," in *As Far as Republican Principles Will Admit*, 349–51. As Diamond notes, speaking

emphatically of *modern* legislation and its focus on interests, Madison argues that "the regulation of these various and interfering interests forms the principal task of modern legislation, and involves the spirit of party and faction in the necessary and ordinary operations of the government" (*Federalist* 10, 74).

29. Diamond, "Ethics and Politics," 351.

30. See especially Martin Diamond: "Notes on the Political Theory of the Founding Fathers," Working Paper No. 10, Center for the Study of Federalism, January 1971, 46; and Martin Diamond, *The Founding of the Democratic Republic* (Itasca, IL: F. E. Peacock, 1981), 74–75.

31. Diamond, "Ethics and Politics," 352.

8

American Constitutional Exceptionalism Revisited

Judicial Review and the Postwar Paradigm

Sung-Wook Paik

In his radio address celebrating the 150th anniversary of the ratification of the Bill of Rights, President Franklin D. Roosevelt proclaimed, "There is not a single Republic of this hemisphere which has not adopted in its fundamental law the basic principles of freedom of man and freedom of mind enacted in the American Bill of Rights. There is not a country, large or small, on this continent and in this world which has not felt the influence of that document, directly or indirectly."[1] FDR's statement exemplifies the essence of American constitutional exceptionalism today. National mythology places this sacred text as the centerpiece of what makes the U.S. Constitution a model from which other postwar democracies have drawn inspiration.

The standard account in academic discourse has not strayed too far from this popular perception. Scholars have echoed the sentiment that the Constitution is at the crux of the "American way of life, both descriptively and prescriptively." Those "fundamental principles of political life enunciated both in the Declaration of Independence and the Constitution itself" encapsulate two hundred years of accumulated history and practice, forming a "crucial component of the national ideology."[2] The acclamation of the Constitution has been associated with a corresponding narrative regarding judicial review as "an innovation of the American constitutional order that has become a norm of democratic constitution writing" during the second half of the twentieth century.[3] Writing in the direct aftermath of World War II, Carl Friedrich commented that "the idea of making the courts, or at least a judicial body, the guardian of the constitution" was an "important feature of American constitutionalism that has taken hold of Continental European theorists to an unprecedented extent."[4] Many scholars today continue to assume that the judicial guardianship of fundamental rights is America's "most distinctive and valuable contribution to democratic theory."[5]

Mainstream discourse has never fully come to terms with how American constitutionalism has taken important cues from the development of constitutional trends abroad.[6] Most scholars tend to vacillate between two conflicting attitudes when analyzing the American constitutional experience in relation to that of other liberal democracies. On the one hand, they crudely assume the "pervasive influence" of American constitutionalism in the shaping of "postwar liberal democracies and . . . international rights-protecting instruments." When the arrow is reversed, however, they display a defensive attitude that isolates the "indigenous, historically based" foundations of the American constitutional experience from external influence.[7] This duality is symptomatic of the way in which legal scholarship has contributed to a romanticized and misguided notion of American constitutional exceptionalism.

In this chapter I argue that the orthodoxy of America's presumed contribution is inadequate for understanding constitutional change in the twentieth century. Accordingly, I illustrate how the political and ideational factors that informed constitutional reforms abroad both during and after World War II have influenced the remaking of judicial review into the archetype it is today. The analysis further addresses what this suggests for purposes of understanding contemporary constitutional development, which has converged on a strikingly uniform trajectory toward judicial guardianship during the postwar era.

JUDICIAL REVIEW PRIOR TO THE TWENTIETH CENTURY

The mythology of the American model of judicial review rests on a combination of two related but separate assumptions. One concerns the necessity of a centralized judicial power that is sufficiently robust to assert the finality of decisions over all levels of government, whether vertical or horizontal. The second is an antimajoritarian interpretation of rights meant to serve as a bulwark against democratic assemblies. Since the mid-twentieth century, the Supreme Court has assumed that these two pillars have been canon in American constitutional development. In *Cooper v. Aaron*, the Warren court delivered a unanimous opinion tracing the historical and doctrinal roots of judicial supremacy back to *Marbury v. Madison*. Drawing upon Chief Justice Marshall's declaration that the judiciary's role is "to say what the law is," the Court interpreted this statement as establishing "the basic principle that the federal judiciary is supreme in the exposition of the law of the Constitution." According to this version of history, the principle has "ever since been respected by this Court and the Country as a permanent and indispensable feature of our constitutional system."[8]

The second assumption, that constitutional rights serve a side-constraint to political majorities, is best captured in Justice Jackson's statement in *West Virginia State Board of Education v. Barnette*: "The very purpose of a Bill of Rights" has been to withdraw the protection of fundamental rights "[above] the vicissitudes of political controversy" and "beyond the reach of majorities and officials." That these rights "may not be submitted to vote" or "depend on the outcome of . . . elections" implies a substantive limit on the decisions made by democratic assemblies even when the laws themselves are enacted legitimately.[9] The historical accuracy of these claims has been a source of heated debate among constitutional scholars. Revisionist studies have long suggested that the origins of the contemporary practice of judicial review cannot be traced back to the founding era.[10] Though the framers may have laid down the basic framework from which judicial review has evolved, these studies point out that they neither intended nor anticipated the expansive role of courts portrayed today.

One reason why judicial review continues to attract protracted debate is that Article III does not make any explicit reference to this function.[11] Although the framers created the federal judiciary as an independent branch of government, a plain textual reading of this omission at most suggests that the three branches exercise coequal authority to interpret and uphold the Constitution. Because the text itself offers little guidance in clarifying the framers' intentions, one must turn to *Federalist* 78 to infer what may have been the implied scope of this power. Alexander Hamilton argued that the life tenure of federal judges was necessary for exercising the "right of courts to pronounce legislative acts void."[12] There are, however, questions as to whose legislative authority the framers believed judicial review was designed primarily to constrain.

In light of the failures of the Articles of Confederation, the founders were deeply concerned with the "political conditions in the states" where "legislative abuses" were rampant.[13] Thomas Jefferson expressed concern that there was "no barrier . . . provided between the several powers" within the states.[14] In most cases, state legislatures controlled the process in which governors were selected. Stripped of traditional prerogatives, the governor served as an executive official in the strictest sense limited to administering the rules made by legislatures. Many state legislatures also assumed a quasi-judicial function mimicking the royal courts during the colonial era. For example, the state legislature of Massachusetts was named the General Court and served as an appellate tribunal similar to the British House of Lords in its function as a court of first instance for the trials of peers as well as a court of last resort. At the time, it was not uncommon for legislative assemblies in the several states to hear individual petitions concerning the redress of grievances.[15] The "impetuous vortex" of state legislative powers was sufficiently alarming to be seen as a threat to the preservation of the union.[16] The historical context lends support to the view that judicial review was designed as a counterbalance against legislative abuses in the states.

The Anti-Federalists' criticism of the federal judiciary shares this outlook. In Letter XI, Brutus expressed concerns that the Supreme Court would "operate to a total subversion of the state judiciaries, if not, to the legislative authority of the states." Due to the Court's authority to "determine all questions that may arise . . . on the meaning and construction of the constitution," the Anti-Federalists worried that constitutional provisions such as the Necessary and Proper Clause or even the Preamble's commitment to the "general Welfare" would be a means to arm Congress with "general and indefinite" powers.[17] In this regard, the Federalists and Anti-Federalists were in agreement that judicial review would primarily function to legitimize federal supremacy over the states. Whether this unelected branch possessed the authority to challenge Congress was a more sensitive issue, for it involved a horizontal dynamic between coequal branches. Though *Federalist* 78 does in fact suggest that the Court would likely wield this power, Hamilton stated that legislative acts of Congress would be challenged only when in violation of "the *manifest tenor* of the constitution." At most, the

Court would be responsible for keeping Congress "*within* the limits assigned" when there was a very clear violation of its enumerated powers.[18] This was a far cry from the Herculean courts
portrayed in the contemporary narrative.

The fact that the framers objected to the inclusion of a Bill of
Rights further reinforces the limited scope of judicial review of federal legislation. In *Federalist* 84, Hamilton insisted that specific
constitutional protections for individual rights were "unnecessary"
and "dangerous." He maintained that the best way to limit government power was through the dynamic interaction among its institutions. That the "Constitution is itself . . . a Bill of Rights" highlights
the framers' belief that the protection of liberty is best achieved
through a well-defined process that can structurally counterbalance
abusive authority.[19] In response, the Anti-Federalists' demand for
the inclusion of a charter of rights was intended to preserve state
autonomy by constraining the scope of federal powers more than
it was for the active protection of individual liberties covered by
state constitutions. In Letter XV, Brutus "venture[d] to predict" that
the role of state governments will be diminished "if [the Constitu-
tion] is adopted without amendments, or some such precautions
as will ensure amendments immediately after its adoption."[20] The
disagreement over the Bill of Rights illustrates how the primary
focus of constitutional politics during the founding era was driven
by structural concerns.[21]

For the most part, legal development prior to the early twentieth century was a continuation of this intellectual debate as the
Supreme Court struggled to maintain its position in balancing federal and state authority. The Court exercised judicial review much
more sparingly, especially during the antebellum period. The first
time the Court declared an act of Congress unconstitutional was
of course during the landmark decision *Marbury v. Madison*.
Although the decision famously asserted that "courts, as well as
other departments, are bound by that instrument" whenever a law
is declared void, the actual decision involved the Marshall court dis-
missing Marbury's petition to avoid a head-on collision with the
Jeffersonians who had taken control of the political branches of the
federal government. Prior to the 1850s, the Court declared federal
law unconstitutional just once in contrast to the twenty-nine
instances it had struck down state or local statutes.[22] Even after
the ratification of the post–Civil War amendments, the Court

primarily dedicated its attention to policies emanating from the states. The marked increase of social and economic legislation challenged during the late nineteenth and early twentieth centuries was an extension of the structural dynamic that defined constitutional politics during the antebellum period. It is not uncommon to characterize this era as reflecting the ongoing efforts of a conservative judiciary interested in promoting laissez-faire economics, but Howard Gillman points out that the justices were in fact struggling to ascertain the scope of the states' police powers in the midst of accelerated socioeconomic changes.[23] What is important about constitutional politics throughout this period is that grand efforts to expand judicial power had always been met with a backlash from the political branches, as demonstrated by the reversal of *Dred Scott* through the post–Civil War amendments or in the reversal of the judicial protection of the freedom of contract during the New Deal. Unlike what we see today, elected officials were far less likely to acquiesce to the Court's decisions as the final word on the Constitution.

It was not until the twentieth century that the dominant understanding of judicial power dramatically changed. There is a noticeable disjunction between the Court as an enforcer of federalism and the Court as an activist institution involved in the settlement of fundamental rights across both liberal and conservative agendas today. The Supreme Court's reputation as the guardian of the Constitution and as a national policymaker is in this regard very much a contemporary creation, as is the legacy of *Marbury* as a foundation of judicial supremacy. The turbulent history of judicial power throughout the first 150 years of American political development falls short of explaining how it would eventually "become a norm of democratic constitution writing" after World War II.[24]

THE CENTRALIZATION OF JUDICIAL POWER

Constitutional politics during FDR's presidency was in many ways the turning point for the reimagining of judicial review. Prior to 1932, the Supreme Court had been heavily criticized as being a "prætorian guard" that protected the interests of propertied minorities in "strik[ing] down radical state legislation that might aim at economic democracy, and . . . federal legislation that might hurt the hegemony of the corporation." The early New Dealers were heavily influenced by this progressive attack against the role of unelected justices. The Court's "veto power" had been criticized as a "bottleneck of legislative policy" and ultimately a major hindrance to FDR's proposed reforms.[25] One of the New Dealers' priorities was to reverse precedents such as *Lochner v. New York* to ensure that the national government would be authorized to resolve the national economic crisis politically without interference from courts.[26] This challenge was rooted in a broader philosophical commitment regarding the importance of the democratic process in addressing constitutional questions. The chief intellectual proponent of this view was John Dewey, who offered a theory of communication and education as a means to instill democratic habits into the moral fiber of the people. It was a program that emphasized the active engagement of the citizenry as responsible agents of the public affairs of the state. In the absence of politics driven by a robust democratic culture, Dewey warned, the institutions of government would be dominated by the "modern economic régime," as was the case during the Gilded Age.[27] Though concerns over political and civil liberties were not completely neglected, the thrust of progressivism came from the belief that the final bulwark of liberty did not come from courts but from the unflinching conviction of empowered citizens.[28]

Embracing a majoritarian vision to defeat the specter of *Lochner*, however, also meant that the Supreme Court would have to be reduced to a passive role in its review of federal legislation. Justice Robert Jackson, who was otherwise one of the most ardent supporters of the New Deal, confessed uneasiness about the implications that followed from retracting the Court's authority. On the eve of the Supreme Court's reversal of all pre–New Deal era limitations on the use of the Commerce Clause, Jackson expressed concerns in a memorandum to his law clerk: "I don't see how we can ever sustain states' rights again as against a Congressional exercise of the commerce power. . . . It is perhaps time that we recognize that the introduction of economic determinism into constitutional law of interstate commerce marked the *end of judicial control* of the scope of *federal activity*."[29]

The dilemma concerning the judicial role during the New Deal era was foreshadowed by Austrian jurist Hans Kelsen, who wrote extensively about the limits of the American model of judicial review in coping with the changing political realities of the time. Similar to the American founding, one of the most pressing concerns during the drafting debates for the Austrian constitution of 1920 was its reconstruction into a federal state. Kelsen believed that a federal system suffers from an innate structural instability concerning the consistent application of its laws across (semi-)autonomous subunits of governance. The judicial cacophony caused by a decentralized system in which state courts share in the review of the constitutionality of federal laws as in the United States was considered a fundamentally destabilizing force. He wrote:

> The disadvantage of this [the American] solution consists in the fact that the different law-making organs may have different opinions with regard to the constitutionality of a statute, and that, therefore, one organ may apply the statute because it regards it as constitutional whereas the other organ will refuse the application on the ground of its alleged unconstitutionality. The *lack of a uniform decision* of the question as to whether a statute is constitutional, i.e. whether the constitution is violated is a great danger to the authority of the constitution.[30]

Kelsen viewed the constitutional crises over slavery during the Civil War and, later, over the regulation of the economy during the Great Depression as rooted in a structural deficiency in which no single branch was able to provide authoritative settlement on matters of critical importance. As a legal theorist, he was most concerned with the stability and congruity that was demanded by the rule of law. "The problem of legality (*Rechtsmäßigkeit*)," for Kelsen, was in maintaining "the 'relation of correspondence' between the lower and higher levels . . . found in the hierarchy beneath the constitutional level."[31] The challenge was to adopt the appropriate institutional means for ensuring the uniformity between federal and *Länder* legislation designed to avoid the pitfalls of American-style judicial review. His proposed solution was the creation of a specialized tribunal, called the constitutional court, armed with the *centralized* power to synchronize the application of laws throughout the nation. He understood that there was a practical justification in "coordinat[ing] for the common good the self-interested and strategic behavior of individual officials." If the role of settlement was left to politics alone, the constitution would inevitably be subject to multiple interpretations, thereby causing "interpretive anarchy."[32] For this reason, a constitution demanded a preconstitutional commitment in which a centralized judicial body could provide authoritative settlement on disputes whose interpretation was binding upon all entities within its reach. These insights served as the basis for the emergence of a postwar paradigm that elevated the judicial role beyond what was envisioned in early American constitutional development. The Supremacy Clause of the U.S. Constitution does provide the formal justification for maintaining the primacy of federal over state laws, but the text leaves open at which level and by whom this determination is made. As a result, in a decentralized system such as the United States, "all judicial organs" are granted the "power to determine the constitutionality of legislation." Any judge deciding a case where the legislation in question is in tension with the Constitution "must disregard the former and apply the latter."[33] The fact that different interpretations may lead to inconsistent results on politically close questions is what Kelsen understood as the unavoidable source of conflict in American politics.

Another necessity for centralizing judicial power emerged from the rise of the "social state" (*Sozialstaat*). Europe had, since the mid-nineteenth century, been experiencing a radical political transformation in response to changing economic realities that necessitated greater centralization of government powers. There was a drastic shift in the traditional doctrine of separation of powers, due to the creation of administrative agencies that functioned as "not only law-applying but also law-creating organs." The necessity of the executive to share in the legislative function was an inevitable yet alarming by-product of the *Sozialstaat*. Kelsen believed that there was a constant "danger that administrative organs will exceed the limits of their power," which warranted an extra layer of checks. For this reason, he maintained that the judicial review of administrative rules would carry an even higher priority than that of statutes. These changes predated the birth of the New Deal administrative state, which Kelsen understood would inevitably trigger the expansion of judicial power in the United States. He observed that America had yet to confront this new reality fully, which is why judicial power was underdeveloped. He predicted that "as soon as the administrative organs of the United States in the course of actual political and economic evolution will have attained a similar legal position as the administrative organs of the European Continent, the problem of the constitutionality of ordinances will play a much more important role in this country than it does today."[34]

Kelsen's outlook proved to be prescient, for America eventually had to come to terms with the expansion of federal power in embracing the finality of judicial review. New Dealers were initially torn about this prospect. In his book published during his final year as attorney general (which also became his first year as associate justice), Robert Jackson identified "the vice of judicial supremacy" in its "progressive closing of the avenues to peaceful and democratic conciliation of our social and economic conflicts." However, he acknowledged that the crisis of the time demanded "constitutional litigation [to be] an essential part" of American democracy and that "the sovereign power of judicial review of constitutionality of legislation" ought to be centralized to "a court of finality" rather than being scattered among the lower courts.[35] After spending years on the bench, Justice Jackson would eventually champion the view that "the supremacy and uniformity of federal law are attainable only by a centralized source of authority," which he understood as a practical necessity for maintaining stability: "Reversal by a higher court is not proof that justice is thereby better done. There is no doubt that if there were a super-Supreme Court, a substantial proportion of our reversals of state courts would also be reversed. We are not final because we are infallible, but we are infallible only because we are final."[36]

The New Deal's embrace of the Supreme Court's finality expresses strong Kelsenian overtones in what would become the core premise that contributed to the remaking of American judicial review in its contemporary image. By the time the justices had confronted this dilemma, there were plenty of frontrunners abroad to support the Supreme Court's repositioning of itself into a more centralized tribunal. Judicial review emerged as a critical institution of American democracy in a way that was sharply different from the past. Edward Corwin observed in 1938 that the importance of the Supreme Court as an agent of constitutional interpretation was "contingent on public opinion, and seems likely to remain so." American constitutional development has retained a tension between what he calls the "juristic conception" versus the "political conception" of judicial review. The former view entails giving finality to the Court's pronouncement, which then attaches a fixed meaning to the Constitution. The latter regards the Constitution as an instrument of popular government and hence stresses the role of public opinion in steering the Court's function. At the time, Corwin believed that the juristic conception had "never assumed a sufficiently authoritative shape to put it beyond the reach of important challenge" by the political branches.[37] This projection quickly lost its ground as the concurrent involvement of all three branches over constitutional interpretation gradually gave way to a model of judicial supremacy. The type of centralized authority emblematic of constitutional courts eventually found public acceptance in the United States. A crucial dimension of this transition is demonstrated by the increased tendency of elected officials to acquiesce to the Supreme Court. Though these changes were never officially constitution-*ized* as formal amendments, they were eventually constitution-*alized* as established practice. Through the postwar construction of judicial power, American democracy was fundamentally redefined, joining its European contemporaries and others throughout the world in transferring power from the realm of politics to the realm of law in a manner and degree that had not existed prior to this era.

REMAKING THE BILL OF RIGHTS

The discourse on rights has also undergone a dramatic shift during the war in conjunction with the centralization of judicial power. A crucial pillar of the standard mythology has been that the U.S. Constitution "raised the banner of individual rights," which spearheaded "the adoption of international human rights and the post-1945 emergence of an international human rights culture."[38] The narrative assumes that American constitutionalism has always been committed to this long-standing tradition. The Declaration of Independence continues to be recited as a reminder to those "self-evident" truths that the protection of individual rights such as "life, liberty, and the pursuit of happiness" is the one and only legitimate purpose of republican government.

Prior to the twentieth century, most Americans actually treated the Declaration, rather than the first ten amendments, as the bill of rights, even if only as a philosophical treatise. For the longest time, the dominant legal paradigm has been to accept state courts as the primary custodians for adjudicating rights claims, whereas the federal judiciary, in contrast, "largely stayed on the sidelines."[39] Indeed, some of the most notable provisions of the Bill of Rights were not addressed uniformly at the national level until the incorporation debates during the twentieth century. The ruling of *Barron v. Baltimore* that the first ten amendments exclusively apply to the federal government and not the states underlines the striking discrepancy between the historical evidence and the contemporary tale that the Supreme Court has always been the guardian of rights. In a lecture delivered in 1880, Justice Samuel Miller went as far as to declare that "our Constitution, unlike most modern ones, does not contain any formal declaration or bill of rights."[40] This sentiment was largely shared by ordinary citizens as well. A symbolic indicator for how little Americans regarded the Bill of Rights was that there were no national festivities celebrating its centennial.[41]

The Bill of Rights was propelled to the center stage of national discourse only during the late-1930s. Throughout his presidency FDR frequently referenced the Bill of Rights, though his intentions were driven more by political interest than by a deep-seated normative commitment. He understood that the popular mandate to mobilize federal powers to address the economic crisis could be accomplished only by challenging *Lochner*, which many at the time criticized as harboring laissez-faire capitalism. Much like the early suspicion toward the centralization of judicial power, New Dealers were initially driven by a positivistic commitment to democratic majoritarianism that informed the dominant understanding of the purpose of the Bill of Rights. In addressing critics during one of his fireside chats, FDR retorted:

> Answer this question also out of the facts of your own life. Have you lost any of your rights or liberty or constitutional freedom of action and choice? Turn to the Bill of Rights of the Constitution, which I have solemnly sworn to maintain and under which your freedom rests secure. Read each provision of that Bill of Rights and ask yourself whether you personally have suffered the impairment of a single jot of these great assurances. I have no question in my mind as to what your answer will be.[42]

The premise of FDR's statement was that the expansion of congressional authority is legitimate as long as there are no demonstrable encroachments upon personal liberties. The argument cleverly turns the framers' opposition to a bill of rights on its head.

One of the dangers of a written charter of rights, according to *Federalist* 84, was that it implied that any extension of federal activities outside the freedoms listed would by default be considered a legitimate use of government power.[43] Whereas this led the framers to conclude that the amendments should be rejected, FDR flipped the argument as a way to advertise the self-restraint of Congress. The interpretation importantly justifies placing the onus of rights protection in the hands of elected officials when in service of a popular mandate by the American people.

By the start of FDR's unprecedented third term in office, however, the political and ideological landscape had changed dramatically, ultimately leading to a reconsideration of this previous commitment. At the inception of the war, fascist thinkers mocked the reality that legislative politics in Europe had devolved into an object of spoils and compromise for elite parties and their followers. In contrast, those such as Giovanni Gentile, who penned the official philosophical manifesto for Mussolini, asserted that "the Fascist State . . . is a people's state, and, as such, the democratic state *par excellence*."[44] Nazism similarly employed the rhetoric of populism keenly devised and advertised through the channels of the state. Carl Schmitt emphasized that Hitler's dictatorship was aimed at the restoration of the constitutional order into a genuine democracy. "The consequence," he argued, "is a dictatorship that suspends democracy in the name of true democracy that is still to be created."[45] The conclusion that the popular will could be channeled into a single individual—*Duce* or *Führer*—was grounded in an appeal to what representative institutions in Europe had failed to offer—the true identity between the rulers and the ruled. Émigré intellectuals such as Karl Loewenstein warned that "no country whatsoever is immunized from fascism." He urged his American audience to contemplate "whether legislative measures against incipient fascism are perhaps required in the United States."[46] Others who fled from the reign of terror were of a similar mind in regards to the urgency of the situation. In a 1941 questionnaire on anti-Semitism requested by the Council for Democracy, Max Horkheimer responded that the immediate threat was not anti-Semitism but fascism in its entirety. He strongly supported doing whatever is necessary even if that meant embracing "a strong central government able and willing to take effective action against fascism," which might necessitate restrictions on democracy itself.[47]

These concerns were instrumental in pressuring New Dealers to reconsider the best institutional means for safeguarding American democracy. Closely mirroring the political climate, the Supreme Court was splintered between two competing visions. Those such as Justice Felix Frankfurter remained faithful to the progressive commitment to democracy, arguing that judicial deference to the legislature should be maintained across the board even at the expense of minor sacrifices to individual liberties.[48] Others such as Justices Hugo Black and William O. Douglas argued that a more activist, interventionist role for the Court might be necessary as a check against majoritarian assemblies when fundamental rights were at risk. The two camps notably collided during the mandatory flag salute cases of 1940 and 1943, both of which involved the legality of public displays of patriotism as mandated by local school boards. In *Minersville School District v. Gobitis*, Frankfurter wrote for the 8–1 majority upholding the flag salute on the ground that the "wise use of legislative authority" must be disputed "in the forum of public opinion and before legislative assemblies" as opposed to being resolved in the judicial arena.[49]

The decision immediately sparked controversy. The pledge of allegiance in question, also known as the Bellamy salute, closely resembled the Nazi salute in its gesture of stretching out the right arm and keeping it raised. The FDR administration embarked on a quest to challenge the *Gobitis* decision in court. In response to ideological propaganda directed against American institutions, FDR adopted a strategy against fascism that appealed to that which the enemy lacked the most, namely, the commitment to freedom expressed in the American founding. Among the rights protected by the Bill of Rights, the "sharpening of the First Amendment" was prioritized as the "favored instrument" for serving this greater objective.[50] It was at this time that FDR delivered his radio address for the 150th anniversary of the ratification of the Bill of Rights, celebrating "the influence of that document" across the globe, just one week after the Japanese attack on Pearl Harbor.[51] Congress also moved quickly to amend the U.S. Flag Code, officially replacing the Bellamy salute with the hand-over-heart salute. The Supreme Court justices were not isolated from these mounting political tensions. In an unusual gesture, Justices Hugo Black, William O. Douglas, and Frank Murphy, who originally voted with Frankfurter in the *Gobitis* majority, publicly acknowledged their error in that decision.[52]

With two vacancies being filled by Robert Jackson and Wiley Rutledge, both of whom were on record opposing that decision, the stage was set for a reversal.

In *West Virginia State Board of Education v. Barnette*, the Supreme Court struck down a virtually identical flag salute mandate, overturning *Gobitis*. At the heart of this decision came the iconic statement that "the very purpose of a Bill of Rights was to withdraw certain subjects from the vicissitudes of political controversy, to place them beyond the reach of majorities and officials, and to establish them as legal principles to be applied by the courts."[53] The ruling signaled a major course correction in the judicial deference to legislatures that had served to justify the New Deal's economic initiatives. The Court's effort to recast the Bill of Rights as the hallmark of American constitutionalism may have been part of a broader political initiative, but its normative impact has had far-reaching consequences beyond what was anticipated at the time, signaling the dawn of a new era of rights-based judicial activism.

World War II was certainly a great intellectual turning point for the reinvention of constitutionalism worldwide. The rights revolution that defined the constitutional politics of the postwar era has been acclaimed as a "seriousness and comprehensiveness" effort to restore "sound and moral" constitutional governance. The standard narrative continues to identify America as *the* model of "human rights constitutionalism" to be exported to new democracies in various parts of the world.[54] Yet it is worth remembering that the global effort to put fundamental rights at the forefront of constitutional reform was driven more by a "negative distaste for a dismal past" than it was by a "positive enthusiasm for freedom."[55] In this regard, the remaking of the Bill of Rights in the United States is neither exceptional nor accurate for the purpose of understanding the true foundations of this emerging consensus.

CONCLUSION

The narrative that the judicial protection of fundamental rights is the most unique and enduring aspect of American constitutionalism continues to be recited within the academic literature. The goal of this chapter is to challenge this orthodoxy by identifying ideational currents that informed how American judicial review was remade to meet the constitutional demands that emerged in the early twentieth century. A deeper implication of my analysis is that it supports the case for developing a more subtle theoretical framework in conducting comparative research on the global expansion of judicial power. The proliferation of constitutional review coupled with the judicialization of politics has contributed to entrenching the standard narrative that all contemporary constitutions are genetically tied to the innovations of the American constitutional experiment. On the contrary, my analysis suggests that constitutional influence is a two-way street.

When applied to the field of comparative constitutional law, it is not a coincidence that postwar democracies have increasingly converged on a model of "constitutionalism guarded or enforced by the practice of judicial review under a written constitution."[56] The United States is not alone in this regard. Newly established, nonwestern democracies have initiated fundamental constitutional reform to assign broad review power to courts or courtlike tribunals. The lack of self-reflection on the ideational origins or the practical consequences of judicial empowerment may serve as a destabilizing force for politics that occurs outside of courts. This difficulty is particularly true for younger democracies where a strong participatory political culture has yet to be firmly established. The contemporary defense that judicial guardianship is a necessary corrective to the shortcomings of democracy overshadows how it internalizes a strong distrust against majoritarian practices. Thus the convergence toward this seemingly universal model suggests that the basic foundations of democratic politics and the conditions for ensuring its stability have been severely altered. The elevated role of judges comes at the expense of downplaying the importance of traditional forms of participatory practices. The long-term side effects of this transformation in constitutional thinking remain to be seen. To this end, it is my hope that the historical and ideational patterns identified in this chapter may contribute to tackling this broader question.

NOTES

1. Franklin D. Roosevelt, "Radio Address on the 150th Anniversary of the Ratification of the Bill of Rights" (December 15, 1941), *American Presidency*

Project, www.presidency.ucsb.edu/documents/radio-address-the-150th-anni
versary-the-ratification-the-bill-rights (accessed November 5, 2020).

2. Gerhard Casper, "Guardians of the Constitution," *South California Law Review* 53 (1980): 778–79.

3. Tom Ginsburg, "The Global Spread of Constitutional Review," in *The Oxford Handbook of Law and Politics*, ed. Keith E. Whittington, R. Daniel Kelemen, and Gregory A. Caldeira (Oxford: Oxford University Press, 2008), 81.

4. Carl Friedrich, "The Political Theory of the New Democratic Constitutions," in *Constitutions and Constitutional Trends since World War II: An Examination of Significant Aspects of Postwar Public Law with Particular Reference to the New Constitutions of Western Europe*, ed. Arnold J. Zurcher (New York: New York University Press, 1951), 20.

5. Ronald Dworkin, *Freedom's Law: The Moral Reading of the American Constitution* (New York: Oxford University Press, 1996), 71.

6. The empirical literature has fared better in recognizing how the changing political landscape has informed efforts to reform American law. For example, Mary Dudziak argues that "civil rights reform came to be seen as crucial to U.S. foreign policy," most notably in regards to policies involving race relations as "the notion that the nation as a whole had a stake in racial equality" became widespread. Mary Dudziak, *Cold War Civil Rights: Race and the Image of American Democracy* (Princeton, NJ: Princeton University Press, 2000), 7–8.

7. Lorraine Weinrib, "The Postwar Paradigm and American Exceptionalism," in *The Migration of Constitutional Ideas*, ed. Sujit Choudhry (Cambridge: Cambridge University Press, 2006), 85.

8. 358 U.S. 1 (1958).

9. 319 U.S. 624 (1943).

10. For notable works presenting a revisionist history, see Christopher Wolfe, *The Rise of Modern Judicial Review: From Constitutional Interpretation to Judge-Made Law* (New York: Rowman and Littlefield, 1986); Robert Lawry Clinton, *Marbury v. Madison and Judicial Review* (Lawrence: University Press of Kansas, 1989); and Keith Whittington, *Political Foundations of Judicial Supremacy: The Presidency, the Supreme Court, and Constitutional Leadership in U.S. History* (Princeton, NJ: Princeton University Press, 2007).

11. In rare instances, the omission has served as a basis for questioning the legitimacy of this power altogether. A notable example is Mark Tushnet's call for abolishing judicial review, which he argues can be achieved by overruling *Marbury v. Madison*. See Mark Tushnet, *Taking the Constitution Away from the Courts* (Princeton, NJ: Princeton University Press, 1999). His later works, however, have moved away from this radical proposal, suggesting a thin or "weak-form" of judicial review as an alternative. For this reformulation, see Mark Tushnet, *Weak Courts, Strong Rights: Judicial Review and Social Welfare Rights in Comparative Constitutional Law* (Princeton, NJ: Princeton University Press, 2008).

12. Alexander Hamilton, James Madison, and John Jay, *The Federalist Papers with Letters of "Brutus,"* ed. Terence Ball (Cambridge: Cambridge University Press, 2003), 378–79 (hereafter cited as *Federalist*).

13. Gordon Wood, "Democracy and the Constitution," in *How Democratic Is the Constitution?* ed. Robert A. Goldwin and William A. Schambra (Washington, DC: American Enterprise Institute for Public Policy Research, 1981), 6–7.

14. Thomas Jefferson, *Notes on the State of Virginia* (New York: Penguin Books, 1999), 126.

15. The right of petition in the colonies was also derived from British tradition: "If there should happen any uncommon injury, or infringement of the rights beforementioned, which the ordinary course of law is too defective to reach, there still remains a fourth subordinate right appertaining to every individual, namely, the right of petitioning the king, or either house of parliament, for the redress of grievances." William Blackstone, *Commentaries on the Laws of England*, Vol. 1: *A Facsimile of the First Edition of 1765–1769* (Chicago: University of Chicago Press, 1979), 138.

16. *Federalist* 48, 241.

17. *Federalist*, Letter XI, 502–4.

18. *Federalist* 78, 379 (emphasis added).

19. *Federalist* 84, 420–21.

20. *Federalist*, Letter XV, 528.

21. Madison's original draft of the Bill of Rights included the provision that "no state shall violate the equal rights of conscience, or the freedom of the press, or the trial by jury in criminal cases." This provision was ultimately rejected, suggesting that the intention of the Bill of Rights was to limit only federal powers, as was later affirmed by the Supreme Court in *Barron v. Baltimore* (1833). For an overview of the Bill of Rights debate, see Helen E. Veit, Kenneth R. Bowling, Charlene Bangs Bickford, eds., *Creating the Bill of Rights: The Documentary Record from the First Federal Congress* (Baltimore: Johns Hopkins University Press, 1991).

22. Lawrence Baum, *The Supreme Court*, 11th ed. (Thousand Oaks, CA: CQ Press, 2013), 163.

23. Howard Gillman, *The Constitution Besieged: The Rise and Demise of Lochner Era Police Powers Jurisprudence* (Durham, NC: Duke University Press, 1993).

24. Ginsburg, "Global Spread of Constitutional Review," 81.

25. Max Lerner, *It Is Later Than You Think: The Need for a Militant Democracy* (New Brunswick, NJ: Transaction, 1989), 93.

26. 198 U.S. 45 (1905).

27. John Dewey, *The Public and Its Problems* (Athens, GA: Swallow Press, 1954), 108.

28. This sentiment was best expressed by Judge Learned Hand, who emphasized that "liberty lies in the hearts of men and women. . . . While it lies

there it needs no constitution, no law, no court to save it." Learned Hand, *The Spirit of Liberty* (New York: Knopf, 1952), 190.

29. Quoted in Howard Gillman, Mark A. Graber, and Keith E. Whittington, *American Constitutionalism*, Vol. 2: *Rights and Liberties* (Oxford: Oxford University Press, 2003), 471 (emphasis added).

30. Hans Kelsen, "Judicial Review of Legislation: A Comparative Study of the Austrian and the American Constitution," *Journal of Politics* 4, no. 2 (May 1942): 185 (emphasis added).

31. Stanley L. Paulson, "Constitutional Review in the United States and Austria: Notes on the Beginnings," *Ratio Juris* 16, no. 2 (June 2003): 235.

32. Larry Alexander and Frederick Schauer, "On Extrajudicial Constitutional Interpretation," *Harvard Law Review* 110, no. 7 (May 1997): 1376, 1379.

33. Danielle E. Finck, "Judicial Review: The United States Supreme Court versus the German Constitutional Court," *Boston College International and Comparative Law Review* 20, no. 1 (December 1997): 131–32.

34. All quotations here from Kelsen, "Judicial Review of Legislation," 184.

35. Robert H. Jackson, *The Struggle for Judicial Supremacy: A Study of a Crisis in American Power Politics* (New York: Alfred A. Knopf, 1941), 321, 309–10.

36. *Brown v. Allen*, 344 U.S. 443 (1953) (concurring).

37. Edward S. Corwin, *Court over Constitution: A Study of Judicial Review as an Instrument of Popular Government* (Princeton, NJ: Princeton University Press, 1938), 82–83.

38. Heinz Klug, "Model and Anti-model: The United States Constitution and the 'Rise of World Constitutionalism,'" *Wisconsin Law Review*, no. 3 (2000): 600.

39. Gerard N. Magliocca, *The Heart of the Constitution: How the Bill of Rights Became the Bill of Rights* (Oxford: Oxford University Press, 2018), 56. The broader historical narrative offered in this section regarding the evolving status of the Bill of Rights is largely indebted to Magliocca's excellent analysis.

40. Quoted in Magliocca, *Heart of the Constitution*, 5.

41. Magliocca, *Heart of the Constitution*, 69.

42. Franklin D. Roosevelt, "Fireside Chat" (June 28, 1934). The full text of FDR's radio address can be found at www.presidency.ucsb.edu/documents /fireside-chat-21 (accessed November 5, 2020).

43. *Federalist* 84, 420.

44. Quoted in Jan-Werner Müller, *Contesting Democracy: Political Ideas in Twentieth-Century Europe* (New Haven, CT: Yale University Press, 2011), 106.

45. Carl Schmitt, *The Crisis of Parliamentary Democracy*, trans. Ellen Kennedy (Cambridge, MA: MIT Press, [1923] 1988), 28.

46. Karl Loewenstein, "Militant Democracy and Fundamental Rights, II," *American Political Science Review* 31, no. 4 (August 1937): 658.

47. Quoted in Joseph Bendersky, "Horkheimer, 'Militant Democracy,' and War," *TELOSscope: The Telos Press Blog*, March 14, 2009, www.telospress.com /horkheimer-militant-democracy-and-war.

48. Sanford Levinson writes that Frankfurter's commitment was grounded in an "almost Aristotelian belief in participatory democracy." Frankfurter expressed his concerns that judicial activism could shrink legislative "responsibility and the sense of responsibility [of citizens] much beyond what is healthy for ultimate securities." Sanford Levinson, "The Democratic Faith of Felix Frankfurter," *Stanford Law Review* 25, no. 3 (February 1973): 439–40.

49. 310 US 586 (1940).

50. Robert Tsai, "Reconsidering Gobitis: An Exercise in Presidential Leadership," *Washington University Law Review* 86, no. 2 (2008): 386.

51. Roosevelt, "Radio Address on the 150th Anniversary of the Ratification of the Bill of Rights" (Dec. 15, 1941).

52. The error was announced in the dissent of *Jones v. City of Opelika*, 316 U.S. 584 (1942). Although the majority denied a religious exemption to the petitioner for violating a city ordinance requiring a license for the sale of books, the three justices joined in a dissent admitting that they "now believe that it was also wrongly decided" for failing to accommodate "the religious views of minorities however unpopular and unorthodox those views may be."

53. 319 US 624 (1943).

54. Lawrence Beer, "Introduction: Constitutionalism in Asia and the United States," in *Constitutional Systems in Late Twentieth-Century Asia*, ed. Lawrence W. Beer (Seattle: University of Washington Press, 1992), 1, 11–12.

55. Friedrich, "Political Theory," 14–15.

56. Leslie Goldstein, "Constitutionalism as Judicial Review: Historical Lessons from the U.S. Case," in *The Supreme Court and the Idea of Constitutionalism*, ed. Steven Kautz, Arthur Melzer, Jerry Weinberger, and M. Richard Zinman (Philadelphia: University of Pennsylvania Press, 2009), 79.

9

Henry Clay, the Whig Party, and the Positive Theory of Party

Samuel Postell

Although Daniel Webster was the first to popularize the name "Whig" as the new National Republican opposition to President Andrew Jackson's conception of executive power, Henry Clay is widely considered the leading figure of the Whig Party. In spite of Clay's leadership of his party, including the Whigs' adoption of his "American System" as its policy platform, the marriage between Clay and his own party was not always perfect. This experience led Clay to refine his understanding of the role of political parties throughout his career. In the process, he articulated a new, positive conception of parties as necessary institutions for ordering and maintaining coalitions as part of political "reflection and choice" rather than "accident and force," as Alexander Hamilton famously contrasted in *The Federalist*. Yet Clay constantly struggled to find the means by which the party itself could maintain a principled rather than self-interested basis for its existence.

Clay's positive conception of parties encompassed three different notions of their role in the American political system, expressed during three different periods of party building. His first engagement in party politics began when he was a Republican in the House during the 1810s and compiled a coalition within that party that would become known as the National Republicans. Clay then adjusted his understanding of parties during the second period, in 1833, when he attempted to organize the National Republicans in opposition to Andrew Jackson. The third period of Clay's party-building career occurred in 1838 when he meshed his former experience of coalition building in the House with the mechanisms embraced by the Democratic Party under Martin Van Buren. In each period Clay came to an increased realization that political coalitions needed to be couched in political parties in order to be successful. Thus, Clay deserves consideration alongside Martin Van Buren as one of the first political thinkers to advance a positive theory of political parties in the American political system.

THE WAR OF 1812 AND THE FIRST NECESSITIES OF PARTY

Clay first began to understand the necessity of party and coalition building through his work in Congress leading up to the War of 1812. When he was chosen to fill a vacancy in the Senate in 1806, he learned firsthand that politics entailed more than merely setting forth the right argument in the chamber. As his fellow senators refused to recognize the complaints of the people against the British belligerents, Clay began to believe that the upper house constituted an interest apart from the people. When his pleas fell on deaf ears in the Senate, he realized that the House of Representatives more adequately addressed the feelings of the American people. He also learned that to advance the policies necessary for American independence he would have to work outside of the chamber to assemble a majority capable of governing. Throughout his speakership, Clay began to understand that the ordering of coalitions was necessary for more than just carrying a vote on any specific policy. In an era of weak presidents he learned that coalitions within Congress could produce a stable, national policy agenda that would advance the needs of the people in all sections of the country. Congress could lead from within rather than relying on the president to set the agenda.

From the Solemn Senate to the Turbulent House

In February 1810, Henry Clay rose before the Senate to give a speech on the renegotiation of the Non-Importation Act, more widely known as the embargo. The differences between Clay and his fellow senators could not have been more pronounced. Clay had for a second time been chosen by the Kentucky legislature to fill a vacancy in the Senate just after his thirty-second birthday, barely meeting the age required by the Constitution for eligibility to serve. Meanwhile, the Senate was composed entirely of members who had been born before the signing of the Declaration of Independence, many of whom participated in the Revolutionary War. Clay was the lone exception, born in 1777, by far the youngest of all the senators.[1]

It was customary at this time for senators to wait until their second term to debate openly before the Senate.[2] Thus it must have required considerable courage (or rashness) when Clay openly engaged the other senators almost immediately after arriving for his sophomore session. The content of Clay's speech was as bold (or rash) as the decision to speak itself. Clay claimed that the amendments to the Non-Intercourse Act rendered it "a crazy, vessel, shattered and leaky . . . [but] it afforded some shelter bad as it was."[3] The Non-Importation Act had been stripped of its force by 1810, and many senators believed that the embargo policy should be repealed altogether. Clay contended that it was a matter of patriotism to fight off Great Britain, and something must be done to counter Britain's impressment of American merchants. He believed that the Senate's willingness to repeal the embargo to avoid war was evidence that the senators had ceased to concern themselves for America's honor, that they were too afraid to fight for the safety and independence of the American people. Therefore, he argued that "the regular troops of this house, disciplined as they are . . . are inactive at their posts," and that it was "the duty of its raw militia, however lately enlisted, to step forth in defence of the honor and independence of this country." He urged "recourse to the sword" if the country failed to renew and bolster the standing Non-Importation Act. Clay claimed that measures such as this one "presented resistance—the peaceful resistance of the law. When this is abandoned, without effect, I am for resistance by the sword." And, finally, to the members of the Senate who had just fought a harsh and bloody battle for independence, Clay claimed that in promoting "resistance by the sword" his true aim was to "summon a certain portion of military ardor" and foster "a new race of patriots."[4] In short, Clay argued that America had to continue the fight for independence from Europe, first by means of economic sanctions and ultimately by arms if necessary. This policy would have the advantageous effect of rekindling military ardor and creating a new race of patriots for Americans to revere.

Clay's speech on the Non-Importation Act foreshadowed his future career. His later speeches and actions urged the nation to adopt bold new policies for the sake of independence and prosperity. However, it is clear that Clay's rhetoric was out of touch with his fellow senators. After his speech, he moved to recommit the bill for improvement, and his motion was defeated by a vote of 20–13. Shortly thereafter, Clay announced his intention to retire from the Senate and seek election to the House of Representatives. He divulged his motives to James Monroe: "Accustomed to the popular branch of a Legislature, and preferring the turbulence (if I may be allowed the term) of a numerous body to the solemn stillness of the Senate Chamber, it was a mere matter of taste that led me, perhaps injudiciously, to change my station."[5]

Clay's boisterous speech clearly contrasted with the "solemn stillness of the Senate" and suggested a better fit with "a more numerous body." But why would Clay choose a "more numerous body" marked by, in his words, "turbulence" rather than "stillness"? Clay's experience in the Senate gave him an appreciation for the political task of coalition building. Having failed to persuade his fellow senators through rhetoric, he came to appreciate the activity and numerousness of the House as proper conditions for political organization. After leaving the Senate and joining the House, he devoted himself to forming deliberative coalitions through bargaining. He believed that, if the Congress was not ordered in such a way, its weakness would prove the failure of republican self-government; the executive would have to acquire power, since the representatives of the people could not advance their interests. Such a failure would reflect the rule of accident and force rather than reflection and choice.

Clay learned more than a practical lesson in politics in the Senate. His experience fundamentally shaped his view of the American regime and the role of the statesman. To Clay, the numerous, turbulent House was a microcosm of America, and all sections of the country with their passions and prejudices were represented in that larger body. Clay therefore believed that the House was a more adequate representation of the American people, and that in order to steward self-government he would have to embrace this turbulence but also seek to bring order to it so that it could set the political agenda. In addition to his remark to Monroe, he told his constituents of his desire to become an "immediate representative of the people" and promised "that those political principles, which have hitherto directed me, shall continue to be my guide; and that in honest zeal to promote the welfare of the nation I yield to no one."[6] Clay's use of the phrase "immediate representative of the people" evokes Madison's description of the House in *Federalist* 39, where he contrasts the American republic with several republics "in name only." What motivated Clay was the preservation of the republican element of American government as the nation entered maturity under a new generation of political leadership. He understood that the key to preserving that element was organization through leadership and coalition building so that the elected majority would be able to refine and advance the interests of the people.

After Clay had failed to persuade the Senate, he grew sour of the haughtiness of that body and dedicated himself to the principle of popular rule. He understood that the nation was plagued by the abuse of the British, whether that be their impressment of American sailors or their attempts to provide Native Americans with arms to agitate settlers in the West. He claimed that the senators were "inactive at their posts" because they were incapable and unwilling to consider the needs of the American people. Clay's experience in the Senate resulted in his embrace of Jefferson's vision of the Republican Party as necessary to ensure that the will of the people remained authoritative, an aspect of Clay's thought that is often overshadowed by his differences with Madison and Jefferson on specific policy questions such as the tariff and internal improvements. Throughout his early life as a Republican, Clay echoed Madison and Jefferson regarding the great differences of principle between Republicans and Federalists: "The one party, distrustful of human nature . . . appeals to physical force, the other party, confiding in human nature, relies much upon moral power," he claimed at one point.[7] His reflection on the two parties echoes Madison's defense of the early Republican Party:

> One of the divisions consists of those, who from particular interest, from natural temper, or from the habits of life, are more partial to the opulent than to the other classes of society. . . . The other division consists of those who believing in the doctrine that mankind are capable of governing themselves, and hating hereditary power as an insult to the reason and an outrage to the rights of man, are naturally offended at every

public measure that does not appeal to the understanding and to the general interest of the community, or that is not strictly conformable to the principles, and conducive to the preservation of republican government.[8]

Yet when Clay recognized the division, it was in derision of the Democratic Republicans led by James Monroe, the faction of the Republican Party that he believed only pretended to act according to the first principles of the party. Although the Whigs and the National Republicans embraced a reading of the Constitution that authorized the national government to promote internal improvements, the roots of the Whig Party hearkened back to the Jeffersonian roots of the Republican Party as a great antiexecutive party that trusted the people rather than relying upon force. Clay would never depart from the Jeffersonian Republicanism that he espoused early in his political life, but he would struggle to apply those principles to a new party and new national circumstances.

Bringing Order and Leadership to a Turbulent House

The numerousness and turbulence of the House amplified the problem of faction. When Clay arrived at Washington, he must have observed the divisions that James Sterling Young identifies in his *Washington Community: 1800–1828.* Young observes, "Instead of a stable community of membership, one finds a society of transients. . . . for all the forced social intimacy of their community life, the rulers on Capitol Hill were largely strangers to each other."[9] One representative noted, "The more I know of [two senators] the more I am impressed with the idea how unsuited they are ever to cooperate, never were two substances more completely adapted to make each other explode."[10] On one hand, a New England representative claimed of his southern colleagues that they were "accustomed to speak in the tone of masters" and that the westerners had "a license of tongue incident to a wild and uncultivated state of society. With men of such states of mind and temperament, men educated in New England could have little pleasure in intercourse, less in controversy, and of course no sympathy."[11] Another representative, a southerner, remarked of his New England colleagues that "not one possesses the slightest tie of common interest or of common feeling with us."[12] In addition to feelings of discord, there were physical altercations brought about by the pains of living in such close quarters. An incident is recorded in Miss Shields's boarding-house of John Randolph "pouring out a glass of wine, dash[ing] it in [Rep. Willis] Alston's face. Alston sent a decanter at his head in return, and these and similar missiles continued to fly to and fro, until there was much destruction of glassware."[13] If the chaos of the chamber proves shocking to our modern sympathies, what happened in the boardinghouses bereft of rules of procedure is even more unsettling. How could a legislative program be enacted under such circumstances, and how could the people place their faith in the laws passed by representatives of their choosing if their representatives could not govern themselves?

The House of Representatives presented similar challenges to those Clay experienced in the Senate. Remarkably, on his first day as a member of the House, he was elected Speaker on the first ballot. This did not, however, mean that the majority was prepared to give him control of the chamber. During the early years of the House, debate in the chamber was the focus. Newspapers would circulate the arguments of the day, and opposition in speech on the floor could gain the favor of one's constituents. Speaking against the majority in the chamber was a sign that one was willing to hold the rulers of the country accountable, and representatives refused to establish committees and give them authority because it was more conducive to reelection to dedicate their energy to speaking in the Committee of the Whole.[14]

Furthermore, the rules of the House favored obstructionism over efficiency. As James Sterling Young notes, "Any legislator had the privilege of bringing forward, at any moment, such measures as suit his fancy; and any other legislator could postpone action on them indefinitely by the simple expedient of talking."[15] This meant that members could act as individuals and pursue their own agendas rather than work with their colleagues. Jefferson noted that legislators "are not yet sufficiently aware of the necessity of accommodation and mutual sacrifice of opinion for conducting a numerous assembly."[16] In this environment Clay had constantly to devise means whereby he could wrangle a majority coalition to pass policy while concomitantly preventing minority obstruction of majority will. To avoid charges that he was unjustly allowing the majority to run roughshod over the rights of the minority, Clay had to devise these means within the confines of the rules of the House and the customs that limited the powers of the Speaker. His mode of reconciling this tenuous position, with little recourse to examples of Speakers from the past, was to foster coalitions, define the questions before the House, allow those coalitions to deliberate peacefully, and silence debate when necessary to move items to a final vote.

It is well known that Clay attempted to safeguard the union late in his political career as he led the nation through the various sectional crises, but his efforts to promote union during his early career are less appreciated. Through his leadership in the House, Clay sought to harmonize the factious tendencies of the boarding-house groups to which James Sterling Young refers, attempting to mold this raw material into the "new militia" he envisioned and foster a new generation of American patriots.

Clay saw that the diversity of the House of Representatives offered the nation a place where the different interests could be reconciled and a process could promote mutual affection and compromise among the sections. Clay's paramount objective as Speaker of the House and leader of the majority was to harmonize the elements of the country that seemed naturally poised to divide. Each action he took as Speaker was motivated by this aim, and during the Missouri Crisis he tethered his theory of the House to the constitutional system of the United States: "Our system is one of compromises . . . and in the spirit of harmony come together, in the spirit of brothers compromise any and every jarring sentiment or interest which may arise in the progress of the country. There is security in this; there is peace; and fraternal union."[17]

Good Feelings and Bad Parties

The post-1812 era of party politics is typically called "The Era of Good Feelings" because of the absence of two-party conflict. The Federalist Party had essentially disappeared and the Republicans were dominant. Some argue that the disappearance of party politics was a positive good, because the petty arguments of faction would disappear with the disappearance of party politics, and the vacuum would make room for real agreement and progress. In fact, the very opposite resulted as party feelings waned. The first real threat of civil war predicated upon the issue of slavery was introduced with the Missouri Crisis.[18] The vacuum created by the disappearance of party affections left room for the divisive minority factions to attempt to dictate national policy for the majority: throughout 1819 and 1820, petitions were generated from several states, both North and South, urging Congress to take specific ground on Missouri's application for statehood, lest the states be led to secession by the minority factions interested in the Missouri question. Moreover, the ultimate result of the disappearance of party affection was a sharp decline in voter turnout. The presidential elections of 1820 and 1824 record the worst voter turnout in U.S. history to this day. At least part of the reason that the "corrupt bargain" was able to take place was that the congressional caucus had lost its legitimate authority to promote a specific candidate as representative of the party, and low voter turnout, combined with multiple intraparty candidates, resulted in no clear-cut majority winner in 1824.

Though some argue that the disappearance of party affection during the Era of Good Feelings was a positive good, others refuse to even recognize it as an era that reveals anything about parties whatsoever. For example, James Sundquist fails to discuss the era in his book *The Dynamics of the Party System*. Instead, he begins his study of American political parties with the creation of the Whig and Democratic parties in the 1830s.[19] This is a mistake, for in neglecting the Era of Good Feelings he neglects the events that made the founding of the Whig and Democratic parties possible in the first place. This leads Sundquist to ignore the origins of the Whig Party forged by Clay in the years leading up to John Quincy Adams's election in 1824.

This is all the stranger because the events of the 1820s actually follow Sundquist's model of partisan realignment, according to which a realignment occurs when "a party system that divides people into two contending political groups on the basis of their attitudes and beliefs about one set of public issues is disturbed by a new issue. The new issue cleaves the electorate on a different line and hence divides each of the parties internally."[20] Sundquist's model predicts that, when the new issue emerges, the minority party will attempt to gain adherents from the majority party who differ from their party over the new issue. Sundquist's prediction depicts the developments within the Republican Party throughout the Era of Good Feelings. Moreover, Clay's maneuvers to bring outsiders into his coalition of the Republican Party anticipates both the rise of the National Republicans and Whigs and Martin Van Buren's dissatisfaction with the Republican Party's embrace of outsiders.

Although various issues such as internal improvements, the tariff, the Seminole War, and Latin-American independence divided the Republican Party internally between Democratic Republicans and National Republicans, the central episode throughout the Era of Good Feelings that helps explain this phenomenon is the Missouri Crisis, which forced a realignment within the party that had just previously, almost unanimously reelected President Monroe. Though Monroe's election provides some evidence that the nation was in agreement and need not divide into parties, there were certain issues within the party itself that divided the representatives of the people. Missouri's application for statehood amplified the minor disagreements on economic policy by organizing those disagreements upon sectional lines. The minor disagreements on tariff policy, internal improvement policy, and issues like the Bank of the United States became more forceful insofar as the interests of North and South were later transposed onto those policies after Missouri's admission. An example of the important shift is John Calhoun. In 1816 he sponsored a tariff bill as a National Republican. By the year 1828 that same tariff policy had become the tool of National Republicans in the North to apply pressure to southern slaveholders. After the Missouri Compromise, all policy consideration shifted to fit the new party paradigm, which reflected the line drawn across the nation dividing North and South. Only through Clay's efforts in the Missouri Crisis did those policy disagreements remain contained through coalitions and compromise.

Throughout the Missouri Crisis, Clay widened the Republican Party to embrace members who were more likely to embrace National Republican principles. Throughout the process of widening the membership of the Republican Party, Clay attempted to draw moderate members from the South and the North into his coalition and tether them to mutually agreeable principles while isolating the principles that would lead to disunion. He attempted to forge a coalition that embraced a diversity of interests comprising members willing to subordinate those interests to an overarching dedication to the maintenance of union. Understanding Clay's efforts to reorganize the Republican Party throughout the Era of

Good Feelings enables one to understand the foundation of the Whig Party.

The major cleavage that emerged throughout the Missouri Crisis resulted in the polarization of the Republican Party by drawing a sectional line across the party, resulting in the staunchest of the Democratic Republicans, those from New York, becoming more radically abolitionist. From the beginning to the end of the crisis, the northern Democratic Republicans clung to the principle of restriction of slavery, thus isolating the southern faction of the Republican Party. James Tallmadge from New York is credited with fueling the crisis by introducing an amendment to Missouri's application for statehood that mandated gradual emancipation in the state. John Taylor, who was also from New York and had earlier urged emancipation in the Arkansas Territory, similarly agitated the crisis by arguing that the Constitution required Missouri to abolish slavery in order to become a state of the union. These members were joined by other New England Democratic Republicans who embraced the restrictionist tendencies of the most demanding and interested factions within their states. As he stood with Tallmadge during the proposal of the amendment, Arthur Livermore of New Hampshire urged that "an opportunity is now presented, if not to diminish at least to prevent, the growth of a sin that sits heavy on the soul of every one of us."[21]

For almost a full year after Tallmadge's proposed amendment, northerners incessantly admonished the South. Daniel Cook urged, "Missouri may come . . . from the wilderness, with her locks wet from the dews of the night, and knock, and knock, and knock, at your door for admittance, till she falls with weakness, and unless she comes in the white robes of freedom, and with a pledge against the future evils of slavery, with my consent she will not be admitted." The day after Mr. Cook's speech, Henry Meigs of New York presented a preamble to the resolution admitting Missouri that declared slavery "an evil of great and increasing magnitude" and called for a naval force powerful enough to "annihilate the slave trade," "the emancipation of slaves in the United States," and a provision on colonization. Although Missouri would eventually be granted statehood, the New England Republicans, for the most part, never wavered. Only two of the twenty-one members of the House from New York agreed to strike out the provision restricting slavery.[22]

How did Clay attempt to reorient the party if one portion of the party held so tightly to their principles? Sundquist's model of party realignment proves correct when one considers the Missouri Crisis. It is not the steadfast adherents to old doctrine who ultimately define the future course of the party in times of conflict, nor is it the minority that necessarily gets to determine the party's future course. Rather, the realignment of parties is predicated upon the movement of outliers and the ability of either coalition to capture them. Although the Missouri controversy was fueled by the northern restrictionists and the southern states'-rights factions, Clay understood that the outspoken factions were in the minority in Congress and represented a minority of the people. Thus, he attempted to form a coalition of the more moderate members in order to combat the factions within the House and within the Republican Party. What Clay most feared was the definition of a new era of party politics marked by a dedication to sectional interest rather than union. Clay realized that western representatives like himself had the opportunity to either become consumed by the factions that battled over Missouri or determine the course of the nation if they were capable of organizing.

Thus, Clay aligned himself with senior members such as William Lowndes from Georgia, Virginians like Philip Barbour and James Pindall, and Marylanders like Hezekiah Niles. He trusted these members because they were less interested in engaging in factional politics. Rather than advocate slavery as a positive good, as many in the South had begun to do, they argued that the Constitution's silence on restriction rendered Congress unable to act. He also trusted their wisdom and experience as senior members who presumably served as custodians of the institution. Men like Lowndes, Barbour, and Pindall joined Clay on the first day of the crisis in attempting to block the Tallmadge amendment from reaching discussion upon the floor. Niles even rejected the Thomas amendment, which restricted slavery above the 36°30′ parallel, because he believed that it would draw sectional partisan lines across the country. Like Clay, Niles urged that this question, above all others "ever presented to the Congress," required "a reining in of the passions, a cool judgment, a generous forbearance."[23]

In addition to Clay's base of conservative senior members, he attempted to gain adherents from the Midwest and West in order to compile a majority. He had three tactics for gaining these adherents. First, he sought to reveal the radical nature of the restrictionist position. Second, he attempted to convince the northern members that they could lose representation if they refused to compromise. Finally, he used committees to set the sectional questions to the side. In these committees he minimized the influence of men like Taylor and Livermore by placing them alongside Barbour and Lowndes to debate the question in private.

One such committee was the Committee on Slavery in the Territories created on December 8, 1819, composed of John Taylor, Arthur Livermore, Lowndes, Barbour, Timothy Fuller, Benjamin Harden, and John Cuthbert. Taylor and Livermore were two of the strongest supporters of the Tallmadge amendment throughout the Fifteenth Congress, but they were the only restrictionist members on the committee. It is likely that Clay sought to contain their rhetorical appeals on behalf of restriction by forcing them to debate within a closed committee rather than deliver impassioned speeches to the Committee of the Whole. Lowndes and Barbour were senior members, both from the South, and they were capable of matching the appeals of Taylor and Livermore within the committee. Fuller was from Virginia and opposed the introduction of the Tallmadge amendment. Harden was from Kentucky and a man who Clay could trust to ally with him, for reelection to Congress in Kentucky was in large part contingent upon being in the company of Henry Clay. Cuthbert was a Georgian like Lowndes.

By December 28, Taylor rose to have this committee dissolved because they "had found that, after a free exchange of opinions, they could not, consistently with their ideas of public duty, come to any conclusion, or agree to any report which could promise to unite in any degree the conflicting views of the House on this question."[24] At least part of Clay's reason for creating the committee must have been to show the members of the House that the issue that plagued their deliberation could not be settled short of compromise.

The most compelling of Clay's political moves was his speech delivered at the height of the Missouri Crisis, when he spoke directly to the representatives of Pennsylvania. Clay delivered his speech on February 8, 1820, and it went unrecorded. According to one account, his plea brought many of the members to tears. Another account states that "everyone felt the electricity of his mind. . . . his elocution was so rapid, his argumentation so restless, and his manner so vehement and impetuous, that I believe none were unmoved, and but few retired unconvinced."[25] Although his speech purportedly aimed to convince the members from Pennsylvania, it is likely that Clay hoped more to shame than to convince (especially considering his failure to persuade his colleagues in his earlier Senate speech). In his plea to Pennsylvania, he hoped to subdue the other northern members of Congress through kindness and drive a wedge even further between the restrictionists and unionists of the North. Although Clay flattered the Pennsylvanians by calling their state the "keystone of our federal arch," everyone in the chamber knew that the Pennsylvania representatives were among the most guilty of proliferating the threats of disunion and blocking Missouri's admission.[26] Louis McLane of Delaware urged the Pennsylvanians to hold firm, stating that "this was a single arch; it is rapidly becoming a combination of arches."[27] However, Clay knew that he needed to win the votes of only a few members to gain passage of the Missouri bill.

The Missouri Crisis reveals the importance of the Era of Good feelings in understanding the parties that grew out of the dominant Republican Party and the nature of realignment in an event of crisis. It also confirms Clay's first inklings about the importance of party for the sake of union, explains the mechanics of compromise, and affirms Sundquist's understanding of realignment and the response of parties to divisive issues. Paradoxically, one can learn much about parties—the way they interact, the good they serve, and the way they are forged—by studying the era supposedly devoid of party politics.

THE DEATH OF THE AMERICAN SYSTEM AND THE BIRTH OF A POLITICAL PARTY

In 1798, Henry Clay wrote a series of essays in a Kentucky newspaper to persuade the people of the state to revise their constitution to include measures for gradual emancipation. Under the pseudonym "Scaevola," he described "the anguish . . . [and] the piercing cries of husbands separated from wives and children from parents" as the "breaking asunder" of all "the most endearing ties of nature." He ended his series of essays stating, "To suppose the people of Kentucky, enthusiasts as they are in the cause of liberty, could be happy and contented under circumstances like these, would be insulting to good sense."[28] Yet in 1820 he argued alongside slave-holders to extend that same peculiar institution of slavery he sought to abolish in his home state twenty years earlier. Clay sided with the slaveholders, and departed from his own personal hatred of the institution of slavery, because he thought doing so was necessary to preserve the greatest good: union. Like the founders, Clay believed that the union was good in itself, but also that the institution of slavery could be eradicated only if the union remained intact. In 1832, Clay faced another dilemma: to build a party to rival president Jackson, he would have to sacrifice his American System and his presidential ambitions. Out of this prolonged effort between 1833 and 1840, the Whig Party emerged from the National Republican party, larger in numbers, more diverse in composition, and more successful in competing for federal office than the National Republicans had ever been. However, as a consequence Clay's party became decidedly less dedicated to his own principles.

From the American System to the Anti-Jacksonian Opposition

Not only did Clay's position dictate that he subordinate aims such as the American System and his presidential ambitions to the need for a party capable of rivaling Jacksonian despotism and the forces tending toward disunion, but Clay was also forced to recognize that he was once again in the minority and thus predicate his political action upon that recognition. After he was defeated by Jackson in the 1832 presidential election, he recognized that, "as to politics we have no past, no future. . . . The will of Andrew Jackson is to govern; and that will fluctuates with the change of every pen which gives expression to it."[29] Clay was most fundamentally concerned with the inability of the disparate and disorganized band of National Republicans to rival the popular power of Jackson and the now-organized Democratic Party. He decided that if Jackson were ever to be undone he would have to be his own undoing—that, largely, the opposition Clay led would have to begin as a response to Jackson rather than as the pursuit of a positive political agenda.

Just as in 1820 Clay was forced to pull outsiders into his coalition in order to pass the Missouri Compromise, in 1833 he was again forced to compromise the policies closest to his heart to gain any ground on Jackson and preclude the "destruction of public liberty" that he thought would follow in the wake of a president willing to subvert the legislative process by asserting his power as the sole representative of the people. The paradox faced by the National Republicans was that, to many in the North, Jackson seemed more nationalistic than they themselves were. The issue that commanded attention in 1833 was South Carolina's nullification of the "tariff of abominations" and Jackson's December 10 proclamation in response. Jackson's response denounced nullification as treasonous and called on Congress to pass two pieces of legislation—one to increase his enforcement powers, and another that would lower the tariff over successive years. The latter measure, the "Compromise Tariff" that modified Clay's protective tariff from 1828, was Clay's own doing. Because of the Compromise Tariff the tariff rates on South Carolina production would be lowered to the 1816 rate over a ten-year period, gaining Carolina's acquiescence through peace and making executive force unnecessary. However, Jackson and his party, not Clay, gained in national popularity as a result of the bills passed in '33.

The resolution of the nullification crisis was therefore a mixed blessing for Clay; although he had succeeded in preserving union, and although he and his party gained considerable southern support from those who saw Jackson's encroachments as destructive of states' rights, Clay's party had to shift to fit its new paradigm. In the process, the National Republicans were forced to discard the lynchpin of the American System, the tariff. Additionally, the National Republicans became more sympathetic to their new base, the southern states'-rights faction, and therefore forfeit their dedication to what was initially their locus of authority: Congress. Although the southern Whigs believed in limiting Jackson's powers, they believed that federal power was the issue and did not agree with many other National Republicans that federal power was necessary but should be couched in the legislature. But perhaps most problematic was that the nullification crisis pitted North against South and Jackson against Calhoun, who had just resigned as Jackson's vice president from the previous term. This amounted, potentially, to a fundamental shift: Jackson the southerner became representative of the northerners who disdained the slave states and the apparent nationalist willing to deploy federal force to combat treasonous activity.

The result was almost the stillbirth of the Whig Party. Because the Whigs were primarily dedicated to the American System and

nationalism, they were fueled by the manufacturers and national-
ists of the North. Jackson, however, had absorbed much of the
National Republicans' influence among those constituencies. Even
Daniel Webster, the most reputed northerner among the National
Republicans who later coined the name "Whig" in his speech against
Jackson's veto of the Bank of the United States, contemplated con-
version to the Democratic Party.

"God-like Daniel" Webster and several other National Republicans regarded Clay's compromise tariff as a surrender of principle
and a revolt against northern interest to mollify Calhoun and entice
him back into the National Republican Party. They admired Jackson's position during the crisis, and many believed Jackson's arguments against Carolina echoed Webster's arguments in his famous
Senate debate with Robert Hayne of South Carolina just three years
earlier. Thus, northerners began to praise Jackson as the savior of
the union as opposed to calling him tyrant, as they had done
throughout his first term. In July 1832, for instance, Webster gave
a speech in the Senate attacking Jackson's use of the veto power to
intrude upon the legislative process, but that December in a speech
at Faneuil Hall he lauded Jackson's conduct throughout the nullification crisis. Throughout the spring session of 1833, Webster publicly aligned himself with Jackson on various occasions, even seeking
a return to the one-party system of the Era of Good Feelings. Webster was hailed as the man who would put the "old party spirit to
rest" by one newspaper, and another claimed that "a new era of good
feelings" was on the horizon. Another newspaper declared, "Let us
have no Jacksonians nor National Republicans, as party men—let
us have no Free-masons nor anti-masons, no southrons [sic] or
Northmen—but let all be for the principles of the [Jackson]
Proclamation."[30]

Throughout the spring of 1833, however, Jackson made various moves regarding the bank that Webster could not support, and
finally in September 1833 Jackson resolved to remove deposits from
the Bank of the United States. In doing so, he disrupted the realignment that was taking place, pushing Webster and the northern
support he had inadvertently fostered back into the National
Republicans' camp. Jackson's actions convinced the electorate that
he was not the nationalist many believed him to be and gave cre-
dence to the accusations of executive tyranny. A writer of the New
Jersey *Sentinel* described Jackson by saying, "As Louis of France said,

in the plentitude of his despotic glory, 'I am the state,' our Executive Officer openly proclaims, I *am* the Government."[31]

Adjusting Whiggism to Embrace Southern Anti-Jacksonianism

While the National Republicans were losing northern adherents to Jackson, several southerners bolted from the Democratic Party in 1833 because of their dedication to states' rights. These dissidents differed greatly from the National Republicans who supported Clay's American System throughout the election of 1832, but they were beginning to believe the Democratic Party was being consumed by northerners who wanted to create a monarch in President Jackson. Senators John Tyler, Benjamin Watkins Leigh, Littleton Tazewell, John Branch, John Barrien, George Poindexter, and Dixon H. Lewis were all southern members with prior connections to the Democratic Party but became leaders in founding the Whig Party in their respective states. Six senators identified themselves as "Anti-Jacksonians" when Congress reconvened in 1833. The Senate was thus composed of eight independent southerners, twenty National Republicans, and twenty Jacksonian Democrats. The eight southerners who left the Democratic Party were the new outliers who would define the first revolution in the party system beginning in 1833. As such, their sympathies had to be observed by the National Republicans who hoped to gain adherents to their fledgling cause.

Although Webster was the first to identify the National Republicans as Whigs in his speech against Jackson's veto of the national bank, Henry Clay was the one who worked to modify the policies of the National Republicans in order to welcome the independent southern senators and other would-be Whigs. Thus, Clay was forced rhetorically to abandon his commitment to another essential part of his American System—the Bank of the United States.

The American System was an economic philosophy predicated upon three pillars: the Bank of the United States to stabilize currency and encourage its flow throughout the states, the protective tariff to encourage manufacturers, and internal improvements to tie the sections of the union together through a vast infrastructure that would foster internal commerce to the benefit of all sections. Each section was forced to compromise: if the North wanted the protective tariff to bolster manufacturing, they would have to give the West and the South federal funds to develop infrastructure, and they must place the national bank in the South. Clay's idea was that each section would do business with the others in order to "render us a homogenous people—one in feeling, in interest, and affection; as we are in our political relation."[32] Clay believed that common feeling and interest would also lead the sections of the union to compromise habitually in political matters. As already noted, Clay was forced to compromise on the tariff in response to the nullification crisis. In addition, he had to forfeit his rhetorical position on the Bank of the United States in 1833 to gain southern support. Though the anti-Jacksonians certainly viewed Jackson's removal of the bank deposits as executive usurpation, they also disliked the bank itself, since it ran contrary to their concerns about centralization. Thus, throughout 1833 Clay walked a fine line between his old and new positions. He could no longer argue against Jackson's veto of the bank in terms of its foolishness; instead, he was forced to emphasize the injustice of Jackson's use of unilateral executive force. He no longer argued the value of the bank itself but urged that "we are in the midst of a revolution, hitherto bloodless, but rapidly tending towards a total change of the pure republican character of the Government, and to the con-centration of power in the hands of one man."[33] Yet these compro-mises made it impossible to found a party on the basis of his American System.

Throughout the years 1833–40, the National Republicans matured from an opposition into the Whig political party. They increasingly embraced the same mechanisms of party instituted by Martin Van Buren and relied upon by the Democratic Party. In many ways, the difficulties of the party as it grew ran parallel to the dif-ficulties Clay himself faced. The party as a whole was devoted to a set of ideals but had to depart from those ideals in order to rival the popularity of the Democratic Party and embrace a more het-erogeneous base, particularly in the South. The Whigs also had dif-ficulty embracing the idea of party loyalty because they did not want to become a mere replica of the Democrats, and because they struggled philosophically to balance partisan loyalty with freedom of thought. After establishing a diverse base and enough popular-ity to rival the Democrats, they began to organize as the Democrats had done. Eventually, in large part because of Henry Clay, they embraced party loyalty as a good rather than a mere necessity.

THE MOST UNFORTUNATE MAN
IN THE HISTORY OF PARTIES

After the first Whig national convention in December 1839, Clay wrote, "I am the most unfortunate man in the history of parties: always run by my friends when sure to be defeated, and now betrayed for a nomination when I, or any one, would be sure of an election."[34] From the years 1833–40, the Whig Party had almost entirely forfeited the platform of the National Republican coaliton of which it was an outgrowth. By 1840 the Whig Party was no longer the party of Henry Clay, although it contained factions still dedicated to Clay and his principles. Throughout those years Clay had to realize, reluctantly, that, although the party was reliant on him as a political organizer and coalition builder, the diverse parts of the coalition could not support him because of the policies he previously advocated.

In 1836, Clay was dismayed by Van Buren's election as president. To Clay, Van Buren's presidential term could end in one of two results: either Van Buren would succeed in creating a successful political party decidedly opposed to Clay's vision for America that would remain popular throughout all time, or the Democratic Party would become merely a passing refrain built upon the personal popularity of Andrew Jackson. Clay believed that the 1838 mid-term election would determine which of these two assessments was accurate, and he was confident that the nation would reject the ethos of Andrew Jackson and the Jacksonian principles opposed by Whigs like himself. To Clay, the rejection of Van Buren and the Jacksonian Democrats was tantamount to the preservation of the republican form of government.

To Rescue the Government and Public Liberty

In 1833, Andrew Jackson removed the deposits from the "pet banks" by using unprecedented executive latitude, and Daniel Webster thus decided that he could no longer maintain his integrity, nor his support among New Englanders, while continuing to work his way into the Jacksonian ranks. As Webster resumed his attacks on Jackson after the breakdown of negotiations on the bank, Clay organized private dinners with Anti-Jacksonians as well as public dinners in the South, in which he would provide his thoughts on

Jackson's legacy and the need for an organized opposition to confront him.

Clay also began to form a coterie of diverse statesmen as his new coalition for the would-be Whig Party. He chose Calhoun of South Carolina, Willie Mangum of North Carolina (who assiduously maintained throughout his public career that he was "no National Republican, nor Nullifier"), Samuel L. Southard of New Jersey (who had served with Clay in the Adams cabinet), and John Quincy Adams. North, South, and West were all united in the Clay coalition of 1834. Once Webster had returned to the Whig ranks in late January, Clay needed to ensure that his new coalition, not Webster, would formulate the Whig response to Jackson on the bank question. After Webster's assault on Jackson and his call for the reestablishment of the national bank, Clay wrote to Biddle, "Usurpation . . . has convulsed the country. If we put it by and take up the Bank, we may and probably would divide about the terms of the charter, and finally do nothing." What became clear to Clay was that compromise was necessary in order to unite a firm opposition. Once again Clay departed from his policy aims in order to make friends. As early as December 1833, Clay had made clear that this was his aim. He wrote to one friend, "I want aid—all the aid that can be given." He wrote to Francis Brooke that he needed aid in order to rescue "the government and public liberty from the impending dangers, which Jacksonism had created." In the same letter he claimed that this all "depends, in my opinion, on the South." Clay told Brooke that this effort would be in the spirit of "the campaign of 1777."[35]

After Clay had organized a group to serve as the foundation of opposition to Jackson, he understood that he had to widen his forces against Jackson; if the opposition remained only among politicians, then the Whig Party would fail in the face of Jackson's popularity. The election of 1836 demonstrated the necessity of concentrating party efforts around one man for the sake of national influence in times of a presidential election. In 1835 and 1836, the Whigs still relied upon caucuses to nominate their candidates and regional newspapers to spread their views. Their aim leading up to the 1836 election was to establish the party at the state level throughout the country. As a result, the Whigs offered the country four different presidential candidates, believing that their best hope was not to win but to drown out Van Buren's influence by forbidding him a popular majority. Unable to reach a consensus among the party, they believed that the only way they could win the presidency was to throw the election of the president into the House, as had been done in 1824.

Van Buren did win a slim majority of the popular vote, but the Whigs won some seats in Congress and became competitive in the states. Although the Whigs were able to capitalize on their national diversity to gain popularity through disseminating Whig papers (especially in the South Atlantic states of Georgia, North Carolina, and Virginia, where their influence increased by 30.5 percent, Alabama by 44.8 percent, Mississippi by 49 percent, and Tennessee by 53.3 percent), it became clear that some states could not be won without an organization that went beyond distributing papers.[36]

The Whig campaign leading up to 1836 paints an interesting portrait: Whigs lost heavily in the states, did not gain a majority in Congress, and did not win the presidency. Although this was in part because of a lack of organization, Whigs had already begun to organize. So what was missing? Despite the heterogeneity of the party, and its greater influence in different sections of the country in 1836, it failed to win elections because it could not synthesize its various and diverse components. Despite offering several accomplished candidates, all from different sections, and despite having brought the Anti-Masons into its ranks, it could not gain sufficient appeal to win in the several states. In New Hampshire, Whigs received 23 percent of the popular vote for Congress, in Connecticut 35 percent, Rhode Island 44 percent, Maine 35 percent, New Jersey 38 percent, Pennsylvania 28 percent, New York 26 percent, Illinois 38 percent, Ohio 49 percent, Missouri 29 percent, Virginia 43 percent, North Carolina 49 percent, Georgia 44 percent, Arkansas 25 percent, and Mississippi 38 percent.[37] Webster had become a vocal Whig and was running for president in 1836 and had been the proudest son of New England for years. Although the Whigs won Massachusetts, they lost state elections in over half of the other New England states and were trounced in New York. Mangum of North Carolina was running for president in 1836, yet the Whigs lost North Carolina. Hugh White from Tennessee was another popular southern candidate whom the Whigs ran that year, and his success in the South failed to translate to victories on the state level. For example, in Mississippi White received 49 percent of the state's votes for president, but Whig candidates for state office received only 37 percent.

Harrison's popularity in the Midwest and in Ohio, as well as his popularity as a war hero, failed to convince voters in Ohio, Illinois, Pennsylvania, and Missouri to support Whig candidates in congressional races.

The best explanation for these failures is that the diversity of the Whig Party muddied the campaign waters and confused voters. Because the party stood for so many different things, to the voters it meant nothing. Although there were various candidates running for national office whom the people of the states could support, it was evidently not clear to those voters that the principles that animated the Whigs running for president were the same principles animating those running for state office. To succeed in elections, the Whig Party would have to synthesize the principles of their diverse members, unifying the party behind a cohesive vision. But how could that be done?

The election of 1836 provides some insight into how Whigs had to organize to become competitive: they would have to prioritize state issues during elections, rather than rely on presidential coattails and national issues, in order to collapse differences and gain appeal in the states. In short, they had to separate federal and state issues and highlight their stances on state politics. Not only would such a system of organizing the party prove useful, but it threaded nicely with their new coalition of states'-rights southerners.

The Exceptionable System of Party Tactics

In a speech at Lexington in 1835, Henry Clay felt a need to respond to accusations from "the public press, private letters, and other evidences" accusing him of turning away from the Whig Party and into Martin Van Buren's camp. Although he admitted that his "personal relations" with Van Buren "have been those of civility and courtesy," he maintained that "in no aspect of the contest, in no conceivable contingency, in no imaginable alternative, do I think it would be for the interests or honor of the people of the United States to elevate him [to the presidency]." As he lambasted Van Buren, Clay made note of "the exceptionable system of party-tactics which prevails in his own State, and which, in the event of success, he would endeavor to spread over the whole Union."[38] Although Clay respected Van Buren's party system, insofar as it united and mobilized those within the ranks of the Democratic Party, he feared that a unified party with dominion over the federal government would destroy national unity by propping up a majority faction governed by the will of New York as opposed to the will of the entire people. To Clay, Van Buren's party aims were tantamount to organizing majority tyranny across the entire nation. Clay endeavored to utilize Van Buren's tactics while maintaining the Whig ethos of compromise and encouraging union among the majority and minority, even if the Whigs gained the majority.

Thus Clay's approach in the years between 1836 and 1838 was two-pronged: he urged a national convention, despite the fact that this endangered his opportunity to win the presidential nomination, and he chipped away at Van Buren's support in the North, beginning in Van Buren's own backyard in New York. First, Clay attempted to unite his friends in New York to wrest control of the state from the Democrats. Throughout 1836–40, Clay established an infrastructure that produced the election of the first Whig president; however, in the process he almost certainly, and unwittingly, forfeit his opportunity to become that first Whig president. Although many consider Henry Clay a conniving politician always making his way toward the executive office through manipulation, the best untold story about the Whig Party has to do with its genesis in the years leading up to 1840.

Almost immediately after Van Buren's election, Whigs in the North turned to Clay, believing that only he had the national popularity requisite to unite the party around one man and win the presidency. Several different factions in New York wrote to Clay urging him to begin his campaign. Clay responded to Alexander Hamilton's urge that he begin campaigning for president in 1837 as "premature and unwise." Instead, he urged, "the presentation of the name of any candidate, whether in the form of recommendation, or a positive nomination, that a strenuous exertion should be made at Washington to bring about union and concert in behalf of some particular person. Without that, every thing will be hazarded if not lost."[39] In a letter to George Prentice, Clay argued that a national convention, and its nomination of a single candidate, was "indispensable." He urged that "every exertion ought to be made during the approaching Session of Congress to produce concentration" of the party into a unified front. He argued that "if there be a Whig elected it will be by the Whigs, consisting of the present Whig party, and of converts to it from the V. Buren party."[40]

In correspondence with the New Yorkers, Clay made perhaps the most devastating move for his presidential hopes: he refused five different invitations to speak in the state of New York, believing that it would alienate southern support for the Whig Party. Instead, he wrote several public letters to be circulated in the state, calling for a Whig convention leading up to the election of 1840. To the Committee of New York City Whigs, Clay wrote, "Some mode should be adopted for collecting the general sense of those who believe that the purity of our institutions, and the preservation of our liberty require a change in the executive." He counseled, "None better appears to me to have been suggested [than] that of a National Convention." He added, "For several years I have not looked to the event of my being placed in the office of Chief Magistrate, as probable. My feelings and inclinations having taken a different direction." However, he mentioned, "If I were persuaded that a majority of my fellow-citizens wished to assign me to their highest executive office, that sense of duty by which I have ever been guided, would prompt obedience to their will; candor, however, obliges me to say, that I have not seen sufficient evidence of such a wish."[41] Clay likely wanted a convention to unite the party, and for the party to unite around him at that convention. However, in keeping with the anti-executive ethos of the Whig Party, he wanted to avoid any appearance of ambition. He wanted to appear Washingtonian, but rather than admire his humility the people of New York became skeptical of his desire for the office and hence his commitment to carrying out a campaign.

As a result of his efforts, Clay's party achieved sweeping victories in the elections of 1837 and 1838, establishing a Whig base in New York as well as expanding its influence across the country. In 1836 the Whigs received 26 percent of the New York vote for Congress. That number skyrocketed to 78 percent just one year later in 1837. The Whigs maintained their surge the next year, receiving 64 percent of the popular vote. In 1837 the Democratic vote fell by 26,000 and the Whig vote increased by 17,000 in New York. In 1838 the Whigs added 37,000 votes, with some converts to the Whig Party returned to the Democratic ranks. The Whigs maintained their popularity in New York throughout Harrison's campaign as well. That mobilization of voters in off-year elections has never been equaled in the history of the United States. In 1836, 57.2 percent of eligible males cast their presidential vote. In 1840 that number jumped to 80.2 percent.[42] Clay had built a party, albeit at the expense of his own ambition.

The Goths Expelled from the Capitol

The first Whig to run for president won that office, but that Whig would not be Henry Clay. Because of the concentrated effort in New York—thanks in large part to Clay's advice and counsel of Peter Porter and Tallmadge through lengthy correspondence—Clay believed that the party would carry out its designs to "see the Goths expelled from the Capitol and competent men once more in the Administration of Government."[43] Clay became overconfident after this initial success, and he thought that his work with prominent New Yorkers running for office, along with his previous connections with several groups of Whigs from different parts of the state, would propel him to the presidency. In 1837 he told a Louisville reporter, "Whatever may be my own inclinations or disposition, I shall again be forced into the presidential arena."[44] He wrote to John Crittenden saying, "I receive almost daily gratifying proofs of attachment and confidence from all quarters."[45] However, the very same "aid" that Clay had enlisted in 1836 came back to haunt him.

While John Calhoun met with Van Buren in 1837, Daniel Webster openly campaigned against Clay in the North. Throughout 1837 and 1838 the Senate heard various arguments between Clay and Calhoun in the chamber as the friendship went sour, and Clay ran the risk of alienating his firmest base, his southern support. To many, it seemed as if by attacking Calhoun he was also attacking Carolina. Southerners asked if Clay could truly be a friend to southern interests, and prominent Whigs such as Webster undermined him in the North.

Webster had also thrown his name into the hat once again for the presidential nomination, thus overwhelming Clay's support among New York Whigs. In doing so, Webster attempted to open the Pandora's box of the party—its moderate position on the slavery question—and unleash it on Clay and Harrison. For example, in a speech in New York City in 1837, Webster argued against the annexation of Texas and reintroduced the slavery question to drive a wedge between would-be pro-Webster New York Whigs and southern Whigs like Clay. He assured them that as president he would resist "anything that shall extend the slavery of the African race on this continent."[46]

Although he had been urging a convention for four years, the 1839 Whig convention was disastrous for Clay. All four states not represented at the convention were southern: Arkansas, Georgia, South Carolina, and Tennessee. Charles Penrose, a pro-Harrison delegate from Massachusetts, persuaded the convention to change its voting procedure. Voting was not done by open vote on the floor but in committees of three-man delegations from each state who voted *en bloc* for the state as a whole. Although Clay had minority support in New York, Ohio, and Pennsylvania, his popularity there would count for nothing in this winner-take-all system. On the first ballot, Clay won with 103 votes to Harrison's 91, but he did not carry a majority, for Winfield Scott also received 57. Thurlow Weed, a newspaper editor from New York, and Thaddeus Stevens orchestrated a bargain that stripped Clay of the nomination in the ensuing votes to gain a majority. Stevens "found" a mysterious letter penned by Winfield Scott in which Scott attempted to court antislavery opinion in the North. The presentation of this letter alienated Scott's southern support, and he no longer seemed a viable candidate. Weed, who had been pro-Scott and anti-Clay leading up the convention, circulating Scott campaign material and attacking Clay in his publication, swung the votes of his bloc toward Harrison. On the final vote Harrison became the first candidate nominated by the Whig Party for president, receiving 148 delegates to Clay's 90.

In the ensuing election the Whigs conducted one of the most dominant campaigns in U.S. history. They swept the presidency, winning 234–60 in the Electoral College. The Whigs gained majorities of thirty-one seats in the House and seven in the Senate. It was the first and only time the Whigs gained control of the House, Senate, and presidency. The campaign produced a massive voter turnout: 80.2 percent of the electorate, an increase from 57.2 percent four years earlier. Even the attacks against Harrison could not derail the Whig Party. The campaign's famous "hard-cider and log cabin" imagery came directly from an attack on Harrison by the *New York Herald*, which claimed, "Give him [Harrison] a barrel of hard cider, and settle a pension of two thousand a year on him, and my word for it, he will sit the remainder of his days in his log cabin by the side of a 'sea coal' fire, and study moral philosophy."[47] Whigs turned this attack into an advantage for Harrison that resonated with voters across the country.

A POSITIVE PARTY

The election of 1840, for all its promise, ended tragically for the Whig Party. Harrison died within thirty days of delivering his inaugural address. Tyler, his vice president, openly opposed Whig policy coming from the Senate. Tyler also sought to break one of the essential tenets of the Whig Party, and the most critical promise Harrison made during his campaign: he hoped to run for a second term as president. When Clay ran for president in 1844, he lost by a slim margin; had New York voted for Clay, it would have propelled him to the White House. Even more tragic, the state of New York had earlier that year voted to reject a lowering of the property qualifications of free African Americans living in the state of New York. Because free African Americans often voted Whig, Clay would arguably have won that contest had the enfranchisement been extended. Just after Clay's defeat in 1844, an "anti-Clay" faction within the Whig Party developed in large part because of the influence of Thurlow Weed. The party further distanced itself from Clay, and each successive Whig president (and the party as a whole) resembled the Jacksonian Democrats more than the National Republicans.

Although the Whig Party lost repeatedly, and although Andrew Jackson's policy defined the era, what the Whigs did accomplish through the mechanism of party was the socialization of the diverse parts of the country, urging compromise and agreement among the sections naturally poised to divide and setting the issue of slavery to the side. The Whig Party was influential insofar as it posed a foil to the Democratic Party, and its existence and power within Congress, and within many of the states forced the Democrats to speak in terms of the Constitution. In that sense, the Whig Party accomplished its most essential goal, and Henry Clay was the most essential figure in the accomplishment. Clay's efforts to build a national party on the basis of a positive theory of party coalition building saved the nation from the worst tendencies of Jacksonian democracy and, in the process, established the legitimacy of party government within the American political system. Although Martin Van Buren often receives the most credit for establishing the positive theory of political parties, Clay's contributions to the theory were no less substantial. For without Clay's creation of the Whig Party, the Jacksonian era might have been little more than a second Era of Good Feelings, defined by the feelings of Andrew Jackson.

NOTES

1. The first time Clay was chosen to fill a vacancy, he was only twenty-nine years old, yet there is no recorded argument about his age not meeting the constitutional requirement.

2. Robert V. Remini, *Henry Clay: Statesman for the Union* (New York: W. W. Norton, 1991), 38.

3. James F. Hopkins, ed., *The Papers of Henry Clay*, Vol. 1 (Lexington: University Press of Kentucky, 1959), 448.

4. Hopkins, *Papers of Henry Clay*, 448.

5. Hopkins, *Papers of Henry Clay*, 498.

6. Hopkins, *Papers of Henry Clay*, 471.

7. James F. Hopkins, ed., *The Papers of Henry Clay*, Vol. 2 (Lexington: University Press of Kentucky, 1959), 541.

8. James Madison, "A Candid State of Parties," *National Gazette*, September 22, 1792.

9. James Sterling Young, *Washington Community, 1800–28* (New York: Columbia University Press, 1966), 89.

10. Allan Nevins, ed., *The Diary of John Quincy Adams* (New York: Longmans, Green, 1928), 187.

11. Young, *Washington Community*, 93.

12. Henry Adams, *John Randolph* (New York: Houghton Mifflin, 1898), 275.

13. William Cabell Bruce, *John Randolph of Roanoke*, Vol. 1 (New York: G. P. Putnam's Sons, 1922), 362.

14. Young, *Washington Community*, 94.

15. Young, *Washington Community*, 94.

16. Jefferson quoted in Young, *Washington Community*, 94.

17. Peter B. Knupfer, *The Union As It Is* (Chapel Hill: University of North Carolina Press, 1991), 122.

18. Thomas Cobb famously claimed to Tallmadge at the end of the Fifteenth Congress: "You have kindled a fire which can only be put out with streams of blood."

19. James Sundquist, *Dynamics of the Party System* (Washington, DC: Brookings Institution, 1973), 39.

20. Sundquist, *Dynamics of the Party System*, 26.

21. *Annals of Congress*, 15th Congress, 2nd sess., 1, 193.

22. *Annals of Congress*, 16th Congress, 1st sess., 1113, 1114, 1586.

23. Niles wrote, "I am severely opposed to the idea, generally, of drawing a line within the U. States—it would seem to establish different interests, and to create the worst sort of parties that we can possibly have. . . . but, as the principle of compromise was adopted at the formation of our Constitution, perhaps we may resort to it again with equal success." *Niles' Weekly Register*, January 29, 1820.

24. *Annals of Congress*, 16th Congress, 1st sess., 801.

25. *Kentucky Reporter*, March 1, 1820.

26. *Annals of Congress*, 16th Congress, 1st sess., 1114.

27. *Annals of Congress*, 16th Congress, 1st sess., 1173.

28. Hopkins, *Papers of Henry Clay*, vol. 1, 5.

29. Michael Holt, *The Rise and Fall of the American Whig Party* (Oxford: Oxford University Press, 1999), 20.

30. Holt, *Rise and Fall*, 23.

31. *New Jersey Sentinel*, October 4, 1833.

32. Calvin Colton, ed., *The Speeches of Henry Clay* (Philadelphia: H. C. Carey, 1827), 107.

33. Remini, *Henry Clay*, 448.

34. Henry Wise, *Seven Decades of the Union* (Sydney, Australia: Wentworth Press, 2019), 172.

35. Robert Seager II, *The Papers of Henry Clay*, Vol. 8 (Lexington: University Press of Kentucky, 1984), 694, 689, 678.

36. Holt, *Rise and Fall*, 47.

37. Holt, *Rise and Fall*, 51.

38. Seager, *Papers of Henry Clay*, vol. 8, 781.

39. Clay to Alexander Hamilton Jr., July 18, 1837, in *The Papers of Henry Clay: The Whig Leader, January 1, 1837–December 31, 1843* (Lexington: University Press of Kentucky, 1988), 63.

40. Robert Seager II, *The Papers of Henry Clay*, Vol. 9 (Lexington: University Press of Kentucky, 1988), 63, 69.

41. Seager, *Papers of Henry Clay*, vol. 9, 66–69.

42. Holt, *Rise and Fall*, 51.

43. Seager, *Papers of Henry Clay*, vol. 9, 92.

44. Seager, *Papers of Henry Clay*, vol. 9, 69.

45. Seager, *Papers of Henry Clay*, vol. 9, 92.

46. James Ford Rhodes, *History of the United States from the Compromise of 1850 to the McKinley-Bryan Campaign of 1896* (Port Washington, NY: Kennikat Press, 1967), 77.

47. Robert Gray Gunderson, *The Log-Cabin Campaign* (Westport, CT: Greenwood Press, 1977), 74.

10

The "Controlling Power of Organization"

Constitutional Conservatism and the Defense of Party Government

Joseph Postell

Political scientists have noted for some time that American political parties have been in a long period of steady decline. They no longer organize and engage American voters effectively, nor do they play a prominent role in selecting candidates or setting principles that govern the legislative agenda of the majority party.[1] Moreover, scholars have recently identified the Progressive movement as a chief contributor to the erosion of party strength. Although the modern primary system established by the McGovern-Fraser Commission did not arrive until the 1970s, those reforms followed a theoretical argument against parties that began decades earlier in the writings and speeches of Progressive reformers such as Woodrow Wilson, Theodore Roosevelt, and Herbert Croly.[2]

The defenders of parties during the Progressive Era, however, have been given little treatment, with a few recent exceptions.[3] The characteristic treatment of party defenders during the early twentieth century is that they were merely self-interested "bosses" seeking to retain personal power so they could continue to engage in cronyism and ignore the will of the people. However, as this chapter demonstrates, the defenders of political parties at that time offered far more than self-interested, patronage-based arguments in favor of strong parties. They presented a robust constitutional argument for the necessity of parties in the American political system. Exploring the constitutional conservatives' defense of strong political parties advances our scholarly understanding of the Progressive

Era and constitutional conservatism and even helps us frame contemporary political challenges.

A careful study of constitutional conservatism's defense of party
organization is important for several reasons. First, there is a bur-
geoning interest in the constitutional conservatism of the early
twentieth century, particularly the thought of William Howard Taft
and Calvin Coolidge.[4] However, this scholarship is still nascent and
has never addressed the role of political parties in its constitutional
theory. This is a critical gap in our understanding of constitutional
conservatism, since the issue of political parties was front and center both in these constitutional conservatives' thought and in the
country's politics as a whole. Second, as this chapter discusses, the
constitutional conservatives' defense of political parties was partially
successful and influenced the political development of the Progressive Era. Constitutional conservatives managed to change many
state laws to restore party selection of candidates, and they also
managed—in a more limited sense—to restore the parties' strength
in Congress. This chapter therefore fills in a gap in our scholarly
understanding of American political development. In addition,
because of the profound effect that party leadership's decline has
produced in contemporary politics, understanding the constitutional
conservatives' defense of parties enables us to better understand the
problems of today.

This chapter briefly describes the Progressives' attack on the
parties and the historical context in which the constitutional conservatives operated before exploring the constitutional conservatives' defense of parties and predictions of a future with weakened
parties. Two of the most important institutional developments of
the Progressive Era, namely, the revolt against party leadership in
the House of Representatives in 1910, and the revolt against party
nomination of presidential candidates in 1912, prompted constitutional conservatives to engage in a robust, constitutionally oriented
defense of party government. The defense of parties was widespread
among the most prominent constitutional conservatives of the
period. William Howard Taft, Elihu Root, and Calvin Coolidge (in
the very last column that he wrote) all focused on the critical role of
party in American constitutionalism. Other, lesser known figures in
Congress and other public offices also joined the argument. These
constitutional conservatives acknowledged that parties needed to be
reformed, and that the excesses of machine politics were harmful,

but they wanted to preserve the good work that only parties could accomplish in our form of government. More systematically than any other American thinkers or politicians, these constitutional conservatives explained the benefits of party loyalty and described the implications of ridding ourselves of strong party organizations.

THE PROGRESSIVE ATTACK ON PARTIES

To understand the constitutional conservatives' defense of parties, we begin with the Progressives' reasons for attacking party government, prefaced with an explanation of the rise of political parties from the time of the U.S. Constitution's ratification to the end of the nineteenth century. Because these developments have been explained thoroughly in the work of James Ceaser and Sidney Milkis, the following is merely a brief summary.

Although political parties were clearly not an intended feature of the original constitutional design, the Constitution's founders quickly came to accept their existence and even to defend them for their positive contributions to modern republicanism. Although the founders were skeptical of political parties, they also recognized their inevitability.[5] However, the peculiar nature of the American political system interacts with parties in a way that distinguishes American parties from parties in other developed democratic regimes. In most of these other regimes, elections are held nationally and on the basis of proportional representation. This gives rise to a parliamentary system in which strong parties are the norm, because all elected members of the government have the same constituency—the country as a whole—and this binds them in a way that our districted system does not. Voters choose parties, not individual candidates, in this system, and the different parts of the government are joined together by their common party identification.

The architects of our political system were careful to avoid consolidating power in this manner. They devised a system in which political fragmentation, rather than consolidation, would prevail. Every part of the country would be represented, with no single official representing the country as a whole. The clash of these various interests rooted in different parts of the country, the framers predicted, would eventually lead to policy that represented the interest of the whole. To gain a majority, each partial interest would have to build a coalition with other partial interests, setting aside their partiality and promoting the common good. This theory of legislative politics is best captured in James Madison's most famous essay, *Federalist* 10.

However, even Madison came to see that this was an overly optimistic prediction. It would be equally likely that these interests would clash and produce gridlock in the absence of effective national leadership to produce a broad governing coalition. Each representative would have little incentive to think about the good of the country, instead preferring to appeal to the specific and local interests prevailing in his district. Perhaps more alarming to Madison's mind, the explosion of factions in an extended republic would allow a well-organized minority to rule because of the inability of the majority to organize effectively. As he came to see these difficulties in the years after the Constitution's ratification, Madison concluded that strong political parties would be needed to offset the deficiencies of his own design.[6] By organizing the people and providing leadership for effective majority rule, these parties could prevent the government from ignoring the will of the majority or checking itself internally to such an extent that nothing would be achieved.[7] Eventually, through practice, the founders devised a Madisonian cure for the Madisonian disease. They laid the groundwork for strong political parties as the effective counterweight to the fragmenting characteristics of our political system—characteristics that provided a salutary check against majority tyranny but also threatened the efficient functioning of the system.

By the end of the nineteenth century, America's political parties were so strong that they overshadowed the government itself. This produced, to use Stephen Skowronek's oft-quoted phrase, "a state of courts and parties."[8] This court- and party-centered state became the chief target of Progressive reformers at the turn of the twentieth century. Progressive journalists and political scientists flatly denounced the effect of political parties on the American political system. Several of them—Albert Stickney, Charles C. P. Clark, Samuel E. Moffett, and James S. Brown—"called for the abolition of party organizations," a proposal that became central to the Progressive Party in 1912. Many of these political scientists and journalists "denied that collective responsibility was possible and instead offered schemes for holding individual officeholders

accountable to their constituents."[9] The specific arguments and proposals of these figures are beyond the scope of this chapter, but it
is clear that their writings in the late nineteenth century exerted
some influence on political leaders of the Progressive Party.

The elimination of America's strong political parties was the
centerpiece of American Progressives' reform agenda, a fact scholars have long acknowledged. Theodore Roosevelt was not hostile
to strong political parties throughout his political career. In 1893
he declared, "There are occasions when it may be the highest duty
of any man to act outside of parties . . . and there may be many
more occasions when his highest duty is to sacrifice some of his own
cherished opinions for the sake of the success of the party." A few
years earlier he had affirmed this during his campaign for mayor of
New York: "I am, as you know, a strong party man, and I am not
ashamed of it."[10] But he was consistently hemmed in during his
presidency by party leaders in both the House and the Senate.[11] By
the time of his insurgent third-party campaign for president in 1912,
he had established a reputation independent of the support his
party could supply, and he modified his views on the legitimacy of
the parties. In opposition to the leaders of the Republican Party,
Roosevelt challenged the incumbent president William Howard
Taft for the party's nomination for president in 1912. In the process of this challenge, Roosevelt won most of the presidential primaries, thus pitting the interests of party leaders against the pure
democratic process of nominating candidates.

In the dramatic showdown between party leaders and the candidate who had the support of the masses, Roosevelt was opposed
by his former friends and associates Taft, Root, and others. Their
maneuvering to deny Roosevelt the nomination prompted Roosevelt's third-party candidacy and attack on the party system itself.
The first and most important provision of the Progressive Party platform in 1912 was its avowed declaration "to destroy this invisible
government, to dissolve the unholy alliance between corrupt business and corrupt politics," calling this "the first task of the states-
manship of the day." As Joel Silbey summarizes, "For the Progressives,
political reform, especially the concerted attack on the parties, was
a prerequisite to everything else they wished to accomplish."[12] Once
the parties were out of the way, Progressives reasoned, it would be
much easier to restructure the political system to deal with the
abuses of the day.

In short, as Milkis has argued, the goal of Roosevelt and his Progressive Party was to destroy the parties themselves. In the aftermath of 1912, Herbert Croly certainly believed that the party had succeeded, even as it failed to win the election. He predicted that the long-term effect of the 1912 election would be to hollow out the parties and prevent them from influencing the members who composed them. Croly argued that Taft and the Republicans had not saved party government by denying Roosevelt the nomination in 1912. "The old two-party system will merely be prolonged rather than merely resurrected," he claimed, because "a party . . . presupposes a substantial agreement of opinion and interest among the mutual members of the party, and a sufficient amount of mutual confidence." Through the direct primary, Croly anticipated, this agreement of opinion, common interest, and mutual confidence would be destroyed. Primaries would "sacrific[e] the valuable substance of partisan loyalty and allegiance to the mere mechanism of partisan association. Direct primaries will necessarily undermine partisan discipline and loyalty." Therefore, Croly announced confidently, "in proportion as the official political organization becomes genuinely democratic, it can dispense with the services of national parties."[13]

The success of the Progressive movement, in other words, would be measured by the extent to which parties would no longer be required. Instead of collective associations based on mutual confidence, parties in the future would be dominated by presidential candidates who built personal organizations and appealed directly to the voters: "The candidate, after having been named by a majority of the voting members of his party, becomes comparatively independent of its other leaders. He has the power to write his own platform. . . . He becomes the leader, almost the dictator, of his party."[14] The parties would be replaced, Croly wrote elsewhere, by an executive-centered administrative state: "The really important question is whether progressivism in its political aspect will not destroy the two-party system itself, and substitute for it a more satisfactory method of organizing majority rule. . . . By means of executive leadership, expert administrative independence and direct legislation, it will gradually create a new government machinery which will be born with the impulse to destroy the two-party system."[15] This would happen, Croly predicted, in spite of the fact that Woodrow Wilson won the 1912 election in part by working through the party system. Wilson, Croly anticipated, would contribute just as much to the decline of parties as Roosevelt would have had he been elected to a third term in office.

Though Progressive reformers accomplished a great deal of their work against parties in the 1912 presidential election, by running arguably the most successful third-party candidate in American history and reshaping presidential nominations in the process, they also worked to undermine party loyalty and party strength in Congress. By the turn of the century political parties in Congress, and their leadership, had become all-powerful. This tendency was most pronounced in the House of Representatives, where Speakers had the power to appoint members to committees and committee chairmanships, recognize members on the floor of the House to speak, and send legislation to the floor for votes through the Rules Committee. The power of the Speaker reached its peak under Joseph Cannon's reign, which began in 1903 and ended in 1911, less than a year after Progressives revolted in the House to strip him of much of these powers. In the famous "Revolt of 1910," minority Democrats combined with insurgent Progressive Republicans to approve a resolution removing the Speaker from the Rules Committee and (eventually) taking away his power to appoint members to committees.[16] This revolt ensured the weakening of party leadership, for individual members no longer needed the approval of party leaders to serve on their preferred committees or get their preferred legislation to the floor for passage.

Therefore, in both the legislative and executive branches, Progressives engaged in dramatic and ultimately successful attempts to undermine the strength of the parties. This assault on the parties prompted a constitutional resistance, not from party bosses interested in maintaining control of patronage but from thinkers and politicians who saw the positive advantages of party loyalty in the American political system.

CONSTITUTIONAL CONSERVATIVES' PREDICTIONS OF THE EVILS OF PARTY DECLINE

Roosevelt's Progressive Party attack on parties was not merely opposed by Woodrow Wilson, even though most scholarly accounts focus on this aspect of the 1912 election. William Howard Taft and his colleagues in the Republican Party mounted a robust defense of parties both during and after the primary contests with Roosevelt. The defense offered by Taft and his constitutionally conservative allies, though understudied by scholars, provides important insights into the roots of contemporary gridlock and fracturing in our politics.

First, they argued that the alternative to political parties was an individualized, factional politics. Parties unified narrow factions into broader governing coalitions that promoted a general good rather than specific interests, and they subordinated the ambition of individual candidates to the requirements of governing within a broader organization. Without these features of party government, they argued, politics would become the theater of warring interests and ambitious demagogues vying for personal power and the advancement of their narrow interests.

Elihu Root, whose leadership of the Republican convention in 1912 denied TR the party's nomination, declared in his speech to the convention that the selection of a candidate is "the ever-recurring test of a party's fitness to govern, its coherence and its formative and controlling power of organization." The coherence and organization power of a party, he continued, "depend on the willingness of the members of the party to subordinate their varying individual opinions . . . in order that they may act in unison on the great questions wherein they agree." In contrasting the individual opinions and great questions that animate the members of parties, Root drew his audience to the importance of burying individual interests for the sake of promoting the common good. As he summarized, "Without organized parties, having these qualities of coherence and loyalty, free popular government becomes a confused and continual conflict between a vast multitude of individual opinions, individual interests, individual attractions and revulsions, from which government can emerge only by answering to the universal law of necessary organization and again forming parties." He was willing to risk his personal friendship with TR to ensure that his party remained "not a mere fortuitous collection of individuals, but . . . a coherent and living force as an organization."[17]

Elsewhere, Root explained that political parties are the only way to deliver the American political system from factionalism. He argued that there are "three quite distinct stages in the development of self-government." The "first and lowest" stage occurs when people divide simply over "particular persons whom they desire to put into power." This kind of conflict is oriented around individuals rather than policies or principles. The emphasis on personal power leads to constant contests for power, anarchy, and revolution. Thankfully, self-government generally proceeds to a "second stage of development" in which people "turn[] their attention to questions of principle or policy or material interest" rather than contests of personality. Although this represents progress, since political attachments are now based on substantive policies rather than personality, in this second stage the people "have not yet reached the point where they are able to subordinate minor considerations upon which they differ to those of primary and vital importance upon which they agree." Consequently, political conflict becomes faction-based, without any method for coalescing factions into broader political organizations that can represent a majority of the people. Therefore "no affirmative legislation is possible except by trades and combinations between different groups." This produces constant bartering and trading among interest groups rather than policies that genuinely advance the common good. The final stage of development, Root argued, occurs when "two great political parties oppose each other upon fundamental differences, the members of each differing in many respects among themselves but not allowing those differences to break up their party." In this system, genuine responsibility to the national majority occurs, because the people know which party to hold accountable and can remove that party from power, in order to confer responsibility to the other party for legislation. As Root summarized, "The development is from the unmixed preponderance of personal and selfish motives to the predominating motive of common good for the country."[18]

Taft and other constitutional conservatives echoed this theme, claiming that without parties politics would be factional and individualistic. In a series of lectures published under the title *Liberty under Law*, delivered in 1921, Taft explained: "In my college days, I was wont to think of parties and partisanship as a necessary evil and something which ought to be abolished, if possible." However, he continued:

> I am satisfied, after considerable opportunity for observation, that two great parties are the greatest aids to the successful administration of popular government. Without them, the

proper interpretation of the popular will into effective governmental action becomes very difficult. The division of voters into
small groups with no majority control by any one paralyzes a
government into doing nothing, into weak compromises, into a
hand-to-mouth life. Division into groups means parties based
on class and faction. It means the willingness of each to sacrifice the general interest of the country to the achievement of a
particular object.

By contrast, "normal party feeling in one of two great parties tends
to neutralize this class and selfish spirit, and prompts a consideration of the interest of all classes of the people represented in the
party."[19]

Charles Evans Hughes, who would win the Republican Party's
nomination four years later in 1916, expressed the same views in
lectures published as *Conditions of Progress in Democratic Government*. In the lecture dedicated to political parties, Hughes proclaimed, "The continued effectiveness of the great parties marks
the recognition of the undesirability of the breaking up of party
activities into those of small and ineffective groups." "If instead of
two great parties we had a large number of little groups," Hughes
continued, "we should have a series of triumphant minorities, little
or nothing would be settled, and the progress and prosperity which
depend upon stability of government would be impossible." "The
sincere party man," he concluded, "will be as anxious to promote
discussion, to foster the intelligent interest which springs from
freedom of participation in party affairs, as he will be to end the
unseemly clashes of personal ambitions."[20]

The concern that individualized and factional politics would
replace the organizational incentives of strong parties was a consistent theme of the constitutional conservatives.[21] This theme ran
even through the final public writings of Calvin Coolidge, dedicated
to a defense of political parties. In an article published in 1931,
nearly three years after leaving office, Coolidge argued that "the tendency of recent years has been to break down party discipline and
weaken party authority. It has not improved the quality of our Government. We need more party solidarity, not less. We need more
self-sacrificing party loyalty and less personal political selfishness."
For Coolidge, as for Root, Taft, and Hughes, to be dedicated to party
was to rise above political selfishness and dedicate oneself to higher

aims. Coolidge made his case in response to attempts by some Republicans to draft him for another term in office rather than renominate Herbert Hoover in 1932. He swiftly rejected such attempts, favoring the principle of party solidarity over individual ambition: "When we need more harmony, more cooperation, and more confidence, it would be a distinct disservice to promote a factional conflict against a President in office."[22] "A party which gives itself over to factional controversy instead of public service cannot command the confidence of the country," and with this announcement Coolidge attempted to dispel any attempts to undermine Hoover from within the party.[23]

Defenders of parties also claimed that, because party decline would promote individual ambition, it would ensure that good candidates would no longer seek office. Probably based on his personal experience, Taft made this argument most forcefully. In a chapter from *Popular Government* on the direct primary, Taft predicted that one objection to primary systems is "the obvious advantage which the men with wealth and of activity and of little modesty, but of great ambition to be candidates . . . have over the men who . . . are indisposed to press their own fitness upon the voters. In other words, the direct election of candidates very much reduces the probability that the office will seek the man." We must be reminded, he continued, that "the real end that we have in view is a better government. . . . and if we can get better candidates, and if we can more surely secure the intelligent and deliberate consideration of party principle through conventions, then we should adopt conventions because what we are after is good results." The mere act of voting is illusory if the best candidates are not on the ballot, and Taft predicted that the best candidates would shy away from public office in a primary system, because they were "indisposed to press their own fitness upon the voters."[24] The immodest candidates would be the only ones on the ballot. This would turn the government over to the ambitious and to demagogues, dedicated to maintaining their personal power and organization rather than subordinating themselves to the party that promotes a more general interest.

Finally, the constitutional conservatives argued that the erosion of party strength and coherence would eventuate in an all-powerful executive. They presented the issue as a choice between republicanism with parties and an executive government without parties. In a series of lectures published one year after the 1912 election titled *Experiments in Government,* Elihu Root explained that "free government is impossible except through prescribed and established governmental institutions. . . . Popular will cannot execute itself directly except through a mob. Popular will cannot get itself executed through an irresponsible executive, for that is simple autocracy. An executive limited only by the direct expression of popular will cannot be held to responsibility against his will, because . . . he can prevent any true, free, and general expression adverse to himself."[25] Executive government, he implied, would be a poor replacement for proper representation through a set of elected representatives bound together by a common party. Similarly, in the contest over reforms to undermine the parties in New York state, William Guthrie argued that "if the short ballot be now adopted . . . [t]he governor would then have it immediately within his power to become an absolute state boss. . . . He would be able to break party lines asunder, to promote the interests of any group or faction," and "to substitute his will or caprice for the policy of his party."[26]

By 1931, Coolidge had observed the connection between the decline of leadership and coherence in Congress and the rise of the president: "More and more they have come to look to the Executive office for leadership. . . . He has become the champion of the rights and the defender of the interests of the people. He personifies the Government."[27] In his last column in the *Saturday Evening Post,* published posthumously and bearing the title "Political Parties," Coolidge again connected the decline of parties, the decline of orderly government, and the rise of an imperial executive: "Unless we are to be overcome by absolutism or anarchy, unless we are to abandon our system of self-government, it will be necessary to resort to parties for the most efficient discharge of the political functions of the people." Later in the essay he repeated the claim that the parties were the only alternative to the extremes of anarchy and absolutism: "The organization of parties in the United States has been the means by which the people have preserved their liberties, restrained the arbitrary powers of their governments and made effective the popular will. There is no substitute for their action under a system by which the people rule. If parties were destroyed, we should be reduced to some form of absolutism to administer the government or a condition of complete anarchy."[28]

These remarks stemmed from a basic observation: the purpose of parties is to help the sense of the majority—the ruling principle of a republican government—form policies in conformity with its wishes. Without parties to help organize the majority, select officials who will follow that majority, and bring together representatives to implement the sense of the majority, either the government will not respond to the sense of the majority or the will of the majority will be exerted through an alternative institution—which would lead to executive absolutism. Notably, as earlier explained, Herbert Croly agreed with this assessment, that the president would eventually become the dictator of the parties as a result of being freed from their influence in the nominating process and of building his own personal organization to rival that of the party.

CONSTITUTIONAL CONSERVATIVES' DEFENSE OF PARTIES AS A POSITIVE GOOD

The constitutional conservatives' defense of political parties was not merely negative. They offered a positive theory of republican government that asserted parties as a positive good rather than simply a necessary evil. Their argument was threefold: parties were necessary republican institutions that preserved space between the people and their representatives; parties provided conference, deliberation, and compromise—necessary features of a well-functioning political system; and parties allowed a fragmented political system to promote national policies that pursued national interests on the basis of principles rather than interest.

The constitutional conservatives argued that parties advanced the republican nature of the constitutional system by filtering public opinion. They provided a space between the people and their representatives. The process of selecting candidates, and having those candidates confer with each other on policy questions once elected to office, would ensure that the public will would be elevated through a deliberative process. The members of the party would be wedded to the party platform and therefore would be implementing the policies that the public had voted upon in the previous election, but the specifics would be determined by representatives who possessed greater knowledge and experience.

Guthrie, for instance, argued that the proponents of the primary system, "following the absurd and exploded doctrines of Rousseau," assumed "that the people would always want and, by a process of political inspiration, would intuitively select, the best men for public office." By contrast, he continued, "the question of nominating candidates by delegate conventions involves in its essence the perpetuation of the fundamental principles of representative government and of the republican form of government which the founders intended to establish and to guarantee to each state of the union." Under nominating conventions parties can ensure "the determination of all questions of practical government by delegates or representatives chosen by the people, who it is assumed can act more intelligently and better discern the true interests of their country than a multitude of voters dispersed over an extensive territory."[29] This theme was echoed in *Popular Government*, where Taft argued that nominating conventions were superior in part because "the delegates can better inform themselves as to the qualifications of the party candidates than can the people at large."[30] The defenders of parties, in short, considered parties to be an essential component of the process by which representatives refined and enlarged the public views, to borrow Madison's famous phrase from *Federalist* 10.

As a corollary to their argument about representation and the space needed between the people and their representatives, the defenders of parties asserted that conference and deliberation were necessary goods that could be preserved only through parties. This was an abstract but critical element of their position. These constitutional conservatives were keenly aware that the process of decision making would be elevated through mutual discussion and agreement. The alternative to this process, they argued, was a process by which passion and the assertion of interest governed politics. The latter process would prevent leaders from reaching consensus or compromise and would turn politics into a constant struggle for power and assertion of will.

Not surprising given his defeat in 1912, this was a favorite theme of Taft: "Consultation should not be tabooed. Conference and discussion lead to wise results, and conference and discussion and deliberation with reference to party policies are not possible at the polls."[31] Guthrie similarly argued that "it is imperative that there should be adequate and reliable means of information, full opportunity for conference, exchange of views, debate and criticism as to the capacity and character of candidates" for office. The primaries would not replicate the sort of conference, deliberation, and exchange of views that the system of nomination conventions provided. The give and take offered at a nominating convention was what provided "full opportunity for investigation, discussion, and criticism." Because they served this positive function for deliberation, "political parties in America have given stability to governmental policies and have created the only effective restraint upon disintegration and individual caprice or demagogism. There must be coherence in political forces; there must be concentration and direction of the political energy of communities. . . . These can be secured in the long run only by and through permanently organized and disciplined political parties."[32]

Elihu Root voiced similar themes in his own defense of parties after the 1912 election. Four years after Theodore Roosevelt's insurgent campaign against his party, Root argued that political organizations are both inevitable and the most efficient way to accomplish meaningful political reforms. Therefore, citizens who want to serve in government should begin by joining a party organization and working to improve it from within. "The great work of popular government," he explained, "is done in the associations and primaries and caucuses and conventions, in the conferences and discussions and canvassing and personal association."[33] It is there, through building relationships, trust, and confidence and engaging in deliberation and compromise, that party organizations can be influenced and made to serve the common good. Coherence and common purpose are achieved when people work together collectively on political matters rather than individually.

Conference and deliberation were also central themes in the arguments of the supporters of Joseph Cannon during the debates over the 1910 revolt in the House of Representatives. The Speaker's most eloquent defender during that debate, Jacob Sloat Fassett, defended parties as playing a central role in ensuring responsibility to the electorate and adjusting many different opinions in the process of party conference and deliberation. As he explained, "Parties, like governments, provide machinery whereby men may adjust differences of opinion. If we have 200 men on this side, I believe they are likely to have, if not 200 different opinions, at least 200 different kinds of opinion on almost any one of the great questions that concern the people of the United States." Because parties are composed of many different people, from many different classes and constituencies, these opinions have to be brought together and reconciled to produce policy. Fassett argued that "the place to adjust differences of opinion . . . on important questions of public policy and party policy is not in public . . . but in the family caucus, where we may adjust our opinions and govern ourselves, as representative government must always be controlled, by an expression properly taken in a proper place."[34] Open warfare among all of the different interests and opinions that compose a party, in other words, is not suited to producing an amenable resolution of these differences. By contrast, when a party convenes in private, among people who have mutual confidence in each other, compromises can be made and the harmony of the majority may be preserved.

Finally, the constitutional conservatives argued that parties were the means by which the fragmentation of American politics could be overcome. Without strong parties to bring national principles and an orderly process to policymaking, the legislative process would devolve into the assertion of numerous local and particular interests. This would subordinate the national interests to the conglomeration of local interests and prevent policy from reflecting principles as opposed to mere interest. They universally argued that parties were founded on principles and were intended to advance great principles. Anson Morse, Coolidge's teacher at Amherst, especially advanced this thesis. "Nothing is more false," he wrote in 1891, "than the cynicism, uttered often of late, that the end for which parties exist is the power and patronage of office. . . . Parties are born of public wants."[35] Furthermore, he wrote elsewhere in the same year, the parties discuss public questions and educate public opinion "not merely on the ground of a surface expediency but in the light of great principles. Indeed the ultimate end of party is to secure as the basis of public policy the adoption of the principles which it professes. . . . the result of these contests is to bring the people closer to the fundamental truths of politics."[36] By uniting all of its members in the nation under the banner of a set of shared principles, and by educating the public and bringing policy closer to those principles, parties served important functions of civic education and of elevating policy to the realm of national interests and ideals. Without this process, they argued, the representative system would descend into clashes over individual interests and characters.

Parties, therefore, preserved a critical measure of responsibility to the national majority in a system that was created to frustrate national majorities. Parties' role in preserving responsibility to the majority was a central idea in constitutional conservatism. As Fassett argued during the debate over the Speaker's powers in 1910, "We have developed inside of the Constitution, and outside of the Constitution . . . a government of a great people by great parties, parties that depend for their charters upon the votes of a free people from the various sections of the country." Because the parties arrive at their powers on the basis of winning the majority of votes in the country, they should be able to implement the policies to which they committed their members during the election. This would preserve the links between public opinion, the election of offices, and the policies enacted by the government. "Apart from courteous treatment, apart from reasonable consideration to the minority, the majority ought absolutely to control everything that the House does," Fassett argued. "We Republicans were put here by the American people for that purpose. . . . if we strip ourselves of every particle of our power we can not strip ourselves of one iota of responsibility, a responsibility we accepted as Republicans from Republicans."[37] Joining a party, and being elected as a member of that party, Fassett insisted, meant that officials were responsible for enacting the policies of that party, which presumably the party's voters endorsed during the election.

THE MOMENTARY RESTORATION AND REFORM OF PARTIES

What were the constitutional conservatives defending, and how much did they get? It is important to note that constitutional conservatism's defense of party was not based on crass self-interest or dedication to machine politics. Rather, they defended parties as, in their view, the best means for promoting coalition building, compromise, deliberation, responsibility to the national electorate, and nomination of the best candidates. When the theme of machine politics did arise, constitutional conservatives tended to be critical of this aspect of parties. Elihu Root denounced the excesses of patronage as "discreditable to American citizenship. It ought to be done away with and political parties ought to be brought back to the sole performance of their proper function as organizations for the promotion of principles and policies, free from the control of mere office-trading combinations."[38] William Howard Taft similarly acknowledged that prior to civil service reforms "the controlling element in a party was practically self-perpetuating," and that the abuse of patronage allowed parties to be unrepresentative of the people who supported them. Both Root and Taft, therefore, acknowledged that the abuses of machine politics needed to be eliminated, but they were not willing to attack parties altogether. They wanted reform, not elimination, of parties.

And for a brief period, the arguments of the constitutional conservatives such as Root and Taft significantly impacted American political development. In spite of what appeared to be a successful assault by Progressives on party leadership over nominations and in the legislative branch, brought on by the 1910 revolt against the Speaker of the House and Theodore Roosevelt's 1912 insurgency campaign, during Woodrow Wilson's first term in office politics settled down into its traditional pattern. As James Ceaser notes, Wilson's election ensured that the parties would at least survive the 1912 presidential election, and Wilson himself pitched a national presidential primary system to Congress in 1913.[39] In Congress, power initially shifted from the party leadership to the party caucus as a whole after the revolt of 1910, enabling the parties to bind individual members to votes decided on by the party as a whole. This angered the Progressives just as much as centralized party control of Congress.[40] Perhaps most significant, many states reversed the laws that set up direct primaries and reverted to a convention-based process of selecting delegates and nominating candidates. From 1917 to 1935, primary laws were repealed in Iowa, Minnesota, Vermont, Montana, North Carolina, Indiana, Michigan, and North Dakota. This ensured "a return to power of the party organizations."[41]

Similar developments occurred in the rules of Congress, where party leadership persisted for a time, albeit in a weaker form. Democrats wrested control of the House of Representatives from the Republicans in the 1910 midterm elections, but they found that they had to make use of party leadership and party government as much as the Republican leadership they had just deposed. Although the Speaker of the House was Champ Clark, it was the majority leader and chairman of the Ways and Means Committee, Oscar

Underwood, who dominated proceedings. Underwood, through his leadership of the party caucus, which bound all Democrats to vote for any measure supported by two-thirds of its members, "became the real leader of the House," George Galloway has written.[42] But the real resurgence of party leadership came when Republicans regained control of the government in the 1920s. Calvin Coolidge's victory in 1924 brought large Republican majorities into the House of Representatives, and the powers of Speaker Nicholas Longworth were enhanced. Rules allowing the party leadership to dictate which bills came to the floor were restored or enhanced, and leaders enjoyed a brief resurgence of power for the remainder of the decade.

Though a close inspection of the changes in party nominations and congressional rules that produced the momentary resurgence of parties is beyond the scope of this chapter, it is important to note them in brief because they show that the constitutional conservatives' defense of parties was effective. Progressives who sought to undermine the parties were successful in weakening party control over nominations and over the agenda in Congress, but some of this control was restored at the very time that constitutional conservatives were making the case for parties.

Nevertheless, the resurgence of parties was short-lived. Without strong parties to provide conference, deliberation, and organization of its members around the settled principles and policies of the organization, the power of leaders to produce collective action in Congress began to decline. Coolidge himself observed these effects in the early 1930s: "While there are many men in our legislatures, especially in the Congress, of great ability and experience, their collective action has become weakened and has fallen into disrepute. The change of rules has deprived the national House of the power it once exercised, and direct primaries and elections have diminished the prestige of the Senate. If there are men endowed with leadership, they cannot function efficiently under existing conditions." As a result (as noted earlier), Coolidge saw that the people were starting to see the president as the personification of the government itself.[43] Writing this merely two years after leaving office and two years before FDR's arrival in the White House, Coolidge appeared to be more prescient than he knew. He understood that the problem was not the lack of leadership in Congress but a decline of parties and leadership in that body that made it impossible to lead.[44]

CONCLUSION

Political scientists have known for some time that American political parties are weaker than the parties of other countries, and that this fact is somehow rooted in the basic features of American constitutionalism and American political development. Yet the entire story has not been told. It is true that Progressive reformers made strong arguments in favor of the abolition of the strong parties that dominated politics during the Gilded Age, and that they were successful in enacting many of the reforms they hoped for.

What is less understood is that constitutional conservatives made strong arguments in response to these reformers, and that for a brief time they made progress in restoring strong parties both in the electoral process and in the legislature. Given the level of concern not only among political scientists but also among the American people as a whole regarding the sustainability of our polarized politics, gridlock and inefficiency in Congress, and the rise of candidate-centered elections rather than substantive contests over policy, it is more important now than ever to revisit the concerns of the constitutional conservatives to see what we can learn from them today.

NOTES

I am grateful to Robert Boatright, Joshua Bowman, Mark Jensen, Verlan Lewis, Randolph May, and Steven Pittz for suggestions on earlier drafts of this chapter.

1. See, especially, David Broder, *The Party's Over: The Failure of Politics in America* (New York: Harper and Row, 1971); and Martin P. Wattenberg, *The Decline of American Political Parties, 1952–1994* (Cambridge, MA: Harvard University Press, 1996).

2. James Ceaser, *Presidential Selection* (Princeton, NJ: Princeton University Press, 1979); Sidney M. Milkis, *Theodore Roosevelt, the Progressive Party, and the Transformation of American Democracy* (Lawrence: University Press of Kansas, 2011).

3. The primary exceptions are William Schambra, "The Election of 1912 and the Origins of Constitutional Conservatism," and Sidney Milkis, "William Howard Taft and the Struggle for the Soul of the Constitution," in *Toward an American Conservatism: Constitutional Conservatism during the Progressive Era*, ed. Joseph W. Postell and Johnathan O'Neill (New York: Palgrave Macmillan, 2013); and Lonce H. Bailey and Jerome M. Mileur, "Henry Jones Ford:

The President and Responsible Democracy," and Douglas H. Harris, "Joseph G. Cannon: Partisan Majorities and Responsible Democracy," in *In Defense of the Founders Republic: Critics of Direct Democracy in the Progressive Era*, ed. Lonce H. Bailey and Jerome M. Mileur (New York: Bloomsbury, 2015).

4. See, for instance, Peter Berkowitz, *Constitutional Conservatism: Liberty, Self-Government, and Political Moderation* (Stanford, CA: Hoover Institution Press, 2013); and Postell and O'Neill, *Toward an American Conservatism*. These books generated responses from other scholars of the Progressive Era, especially Paul Kens, "Revision of Progressive Era History Continues," *Tulsa Law Review* 50 (2015): 519–31; Kenneth Kersch, "The Talking Cure: How Constitutional Argument Drives Constitutional Development," *Boston University Law Review* 94 (2014): 1083–108; Kersch, "Constitutional Conservatives Remember the Progressive Era," in *The Progressives' Century: Political Reform, Constitutional Government, and the Modern American State* (New Haven, CT: Yale University Press, 2016): 130–54; and Michael Lienesch, "Creating Constitutional Conservatism," *Polity* 48 (2016): 387–413.

5. This holds true even for George Washington, perhaps the most antiparty of the major founders, who nevertheless conceded in his "Farewell Address" that party spirit is "unfortunately, inseparable from our nature, having its root in the strongest passions of the human mind. . . . A fire not to be quenched, it demands a uniform vigilance to prevent its bursting into a flame." George Washington, "Farewell Address," 1796, available at https://avalon.law .yale.edu/18th_century/washing.asp.

6. Madison makes this argument most clearly in several essays in the *National Gazette* in the early 1790s, particularly "Parties," "A Candid State of Parties," and "Consolidation."

7. To describe Madison's development in this respect adequately would require another chapter. Sidney Milkis provides much of the groundwork for this description in *Political Parties and Constitutional Government* (Baltimore: Johns Hopkins University Press, 1999): 13–41. Frank Buckley has pressed the subject of parliamentary systems versus our separation of powers system, bringing up some of these themes, in *The Once and Future King: The Rise of Crown Government in America* (New York: Encounter Books, 2014): 235–56.

8. Stephen Skowronek, *Building a New American State: The Expansion of National Administrative Capacities, 1877–1920* (Cambridge: Cambridge University Press, 1982).

9. Richard L. McCormick, *The Party Period and Public Policy: American Politics from the Age of Jackson to the Progressive Era* (New York: Oxford University Press, 1986), 230, 236.

10. McCormick, *Party Period and Public Policy*, 228.

11. See Eric Schickler, *Disjointed Pluralism: Institutional Innovation and the Development of the U.S. Congress* (Princeton, NJ: Princeton University Press, 2001), 70–72.

12. Joel H. Silbey, "The Rise and Fall of American Political Parties, 1790–2000," in *The Parties Respond: Changes in American Parties and Campaigns*, ed. L. Sandy Maisel (Boulder, CO: Westview Press, 1998), 13.

13. Herbert Croly, *Progressive Democracy* (New York: Macmillan, 1914), 341–43.

14. Croly, *Progressive Democracy*, 344.

15. Herbert Croly, "The Future of the Two Party System," *New Republic*, November 14, 1914.

16. See Schickler, *Disjointed Pluralism*, 78–83.

17. Elihu Root, "Address of the Temporary Chairman of the 1912 Republican National Convention," in *American Conservatism, 1900–1930: A Reader*, ed. Joseph Postell and Johnathan O'Neill (Lanham, MD: Lexington Books), 227–231.

18. Elihu Root, *The Citizen's Part in Government* (New Haven, CT: Yale University Press, 1916), 70–77.

19. William Howard Taft, *Liberty under Law* (New Haven: Yale University Press, 1922), 32–34.

20. Charles Evans Hughes, *Conditions of Progress in Democratic Government* (New Haven: Yale University Press, 1910), 65, 69, 76.

21. See also Nicholas Murray Butler, *True and False Democracy* (New York: Scribner's, 1915), 61–62: "But an extension of the policy of acting in small, indefinite, swiftly evaporating groups, outside of the large party organizations and in opposition to them, would be a distinct loss and a danger to our political system. . . . to disintegrate political parties in the interest of cross-voting of all kinds and on all occasions would be disastrous. To see to what it would lead, one has only to recall the kaleidoscopic changes of former years in the government of France."

22. Calvin Coolidge, "Party Loyalty and the Presidency," *Saturday Evening Post* 204, no. 14 (October 3, 1931): 3.

23. Coolidge, "Party Loyalty and the Presidency," 102.

24. William Howard Taft, *Popular Government: Its Essence, Its Permanence, and Its Perils* (New Haven, CT: Yale University Press, 1913), 112, 120.

25. Elihu Root, *Experiments in Government and the Essentials of the Constitution* (Princeton, NJ: Princeton University Press, 1913), 11–12.

26. William Guthrie, "Nominating Conventions," *Constitutional Review* 3, no. 4 (1919): 196.

27. Coolidge, "Party Loyalty and the President," 5.

28. Coolidge, "Political Parties," *Saturday Evening Post* 207, no. 14 (1934): 5, 7.

29. Guthrie, "Nominating Conventions," 200–204.

30. Taft, *Popular Government*, 111.

31. Taft, *Popular Government*, 117.

32. Guthrie, "Nominating Conventions," 199–205.

33. Root, *Citizen's Part in Government*, 54.

34. Speech of J. Sloat Fassett, March 17, 1910, *Congressional Record* 45, 3302.

35. Anson Morse, "Our Two Great Parties: Their Origin and Tasks," *Political Science Quarterly* 6, no. 4 (1891): 593.

36. Anson Morse, "The Place of Party in the Political System," *Annals of the American Academy of Political and Social Science* 2 (1891): 19.

37. Speech of J. Sloat Fassett, March 17, 1910, 3302.

38. Root, *Citizen's Part in Government*, 91–92.

39. James Ceaser, "Political Parties and Presidential Ambition," *Journal of Politics* 40 (1978): 708–39.

40. See James Sundquist, *The Decline and Resurgence of Congress* (Washington, DC: Brookings Institution Press, 1981), 168–76.

41. Ceaser, *Presidential Selection*, 227.

42. George B. Galloway, *History of the House of Representatives* (New York: Thomas Y. Crowell, 1969), 108.

43. Coolidge, "Party Loyalty and the Presidency," 5.

44. Coolidge argued posthumously ("Political Parties," 6–7):

In recent years we have had a good deal of discussion of party leadership. It has been rather lightly assumed that the country was suffering from a deficiency of that desirable quality. [But] [i]f political conditions were a little more thoroughly analyzed, I think it would reveal that plenty of men have been developed who had the necessary mentality and character for leadership, but that when they have been ineffective, it was because of a lack of party organization. It would not be supposed that a Caesar or a Napoleon could win battles if his forces consisted of a promiscuous mob working at cross purposes. They would need trained, steady, and disciplined troops. A similar condition exists in the political field. The wisest political leadership breaks down unless it is supported by an efficient party organization.

11

From Predicate to Object

Constitutionalizing Sovereignty in the American Political Order

Connor M. Ewing

For a considerable portion of modern history, the nature of political authority and social order found expression in a single sentence: "The king is dead, long live the king!" These eight words marked the seamless passage of sovereignty from one monarch to the next, thus ensuring continuity of succession and stability at a moment of acute social and political vulnerability.[1] Though kings and queens die, the monarchy does not. This declaration, in turn, was rationalized by the King's Two Bodies, the theory that the monarch has a body natural and a body politic; the former is a human body subject to the frailties of mortal existence, the latter is eternal and incorruptible. This legal fiction allowed for the passage of royal *dignitas* from one monarch to the next while establishing various limitations on what any one monarch could do. As Ernst Kantorowicz put the matter in his seminal study, the King's Two Bodies was "that mystical talk with which the English crown jurists enveloped and trimmed their definitions of kingship and royal capacities."[2]

From Kantorowicz we also find that Shakespeare helped preserve the metaphor, making it "not only the symbol, but indeed the very substance and essence" of *The Life and Death of King Richard II*. That play, chronicling the deposition of a divine right king, does more than provide a vivid depiction of the imagery and ceremony that attend the king's dual nature. It also portrays the many contradictions and tensions inherent in the King's Two Bodies and, by extension, efforts to formalize, limn, and limit political authority. Richard's fall from grace is punctuated by a series of scenes in which "the fiction of the oneness of the double body breaks apart," with the monarch himself narrating the disintegration. The descent from royalty truly begins in the famous scene on the coast of Wales, inaugurated by Richard's own words:

> For you have but mistook me all this while:
> I live with bread like you, feel want,
> Taste grief, need friends—subjected thus,
> How can you say to me, I am a king?[3]

Belied by fundamental human needs and desires, the body politic is eclipsed by the body human, and the King's Two Bodies appear not united but distinct. In the ensuing scenes, Richard continues to give voice to the unraveling of his two bodies until, ultimately, he surrenders his crown and is sent into exile, where he is murdered.

In this story of a king's undoing we find poignant expression of a fundamental political problem, one that connects the world of monarchical sovereignty depicted by Shakespeare to the one we inhabit today. Even as sovereignty specifies the location of ultimate and legitimate political authority, that resolution is never quite final. Tensions arise, forms and pretenses are challenged, and the original questions of authority and legitimacy recur. What if, as in *Richard II*, the passage of power is not occasioned by death? And how is the incorruptibility of the monarch's body politic to be maintained in the face of the slow but sure corruption of the natural body? To a contemporary political observer, such questions are perhaps at most of antiquarian interest. Since Shakespeare's dramatization, sovereignty has become increasingly institutionalized, popularized, and presumably more secure, no longer subsisting on the spiritual substance and imagery evoked by the King's Two Bodies. In Jens Bartelson's account, there were four crucial phases in the development of the modern conception of sovereignty, each rooted in the exigencies of European politics. Claims to political authority were first territorialized, then depersonalized, subsequently made both indivisible and absolute, and finally popularized.[4] The King's Two Bodies emerged in the second of these phases and has arguably persisted, though in diminished form, through the fourth.[5]

Though the final phase did not enter the world in a single moment and its seeds were sown in the earliest fits of democratic governance, the emergence of a distinctly modern practice and conception of popular sovereignty is often located in the late eighteenth century, specifically in the French and American revolutions.[6] It was also in this period that claims of popular authority were enshrined in written constitutions that adumbrated the purposes of public power, defined the powers of government, and established procedures for lawmaking and election. Indeed, the ratification of the U.S. Constitution marks the first appearance in a national context of the most recognizable form of the modern conception of popular sovereignty, according to which popular authority is not only the basis for legitimate political power but is also expressed in the form of an explicit charter by which a government is both empowered and limited.[7] Popular sovereignty thus displaced the King's Two Bodies as the foundation of and justification for American politics.[8] This political fiction may be, as Edmund Morgan famously argued, more plausible than those it replaced.[9] But a fiction it remains. And the disconnect between aspiration and reality continues to roil the political order established by the Constitution.[10]

This chapter explores the ramifications of the transition to "We the People" from the King's Two Bodies and associated visions of sovereignty; that is, it seeks to identify the principal consequences of the constitutionalization of popular sovereignty in the American political system. My argument, in brief, is that although sovereignty had long been understood to be a predicate for sociopolitical order—a precondition for ordered politics—under the Constitution it became an object of political contestation. Accordingly, distributions of authority between levels of government became a consequence or output of politics, even as those distributions structured subsequent political activity. As intimated by the preceding summary, this feature of American constitutionalism is a function of the interaction among the substantive commitment to popular sovereignty, the formal commitment to a written constitution, and the affirmation—both theoretical and practical—of federal governance.[11] For this reason, the nature and consequences of the constitutionalization of sovereignty in the American political order are bound up in the ways in which power was codified, enumerated, and divided.

I begin with a brief discussion of sovereignty, focusing on the set of questions and themes that unite seemingly disparate conceptions. Despite (and, to some extent, because of) strong arguments to the contrary, sovereignty remains a meaningful feature of American constitutionalism and demands continued attention because it concerns the fundamental and recurring question of the ultimate location of political authority in a polity. This section serves as background for the following two sections, which contrast divergent understandings of sovereignty. In the first of those two, I examine how sovereignty was understood and what function it served in the period out of which the Constitution emerged. Here I argue that sociopolitical order was long—but especially in the critical period leading to the American Revolution—understood to be predicated on the existence and specification of a final political authority, that is, on a particular notion of sovereignty. But, as I next explain, under the Constitution sovereignty moved from the predicate for sociopolitical order to an object of political contestation. As a result of the affirmation of popular authority by means of a written constitution and a federal system, sovereignty moved from the background to the foreground. Under the Constitution, I argue, the scope and location of significant portions of political authority are the object of constitutionally structured politics. In this way, the prospects of popular sovereignty depend on the viability of popular influence on the distribution of authority within the constitutional order, an insight whose implications I briefly address in a final section.

SOVEREIGNTY IN MODERN POLITICAL THOUGHT: A BRIEF ORIENTATION

We can point to a "modern conception" of sovereignty that more or less permits of clear description, but significant controversy remains about the utility of the concept, particularly given the convergence of popular sovereignty and written constitutions. Indeed, there are few concepts in political theory and history more hotly contested than sovereignty. Harold Laski, for example, famously argued that "'it would be of lasting benefit to political science if the whole concept of sovereignty were surrendered,' on the grounds that 'it is at least probable that it has dangerous moral consequences' and 'is of dubious correctness in fact.'"[12] As we see below, this sentiment is quite prevalent in the context of American politics. And yet it is difficult to escape sovereignty's shadow. "It is almost impossible for anyone writing in the field to avoid discussing it," writes

Michel Troper, reflecting on constitutional scholarship, "even if in some cases the discussion leads to denying that it is a meaningful concept."[13] More significant, the subject matter to which sovereignty refers is almost impossible to escape, for it includes and implicates the basic features of political life—public power, legitimacy, duties of obedience, and the scope of authority, to name just a few. Sovereignty is, to a great extent, a concomitant of the modern state. It is how we talk about and even conceive of political power. Thus, in his *Genealogy of Sovereignty*, Bartelson argues, "With some simplification, one could say that the question of sovereignty is to political science what the question of substance is to philosophy; a question tacitly implied in the very practice of questioning."[14] Perhaps, then, efforts to transcend or move beyond sovereignty have the unintended consequence of marking its intractability in political analysis and, in so doing, ensuring that it remains at the forefront of our questioning.

Nonetheless, a valuable lesson can be gleaned from critiques of sovereignty, specifically those that reject its usefulness in the age inaugurated by the U.S. Constitution—one in which appeals to "a supreme, irresistible, absolute, uncontrolled authority" have been largely supplanted by constitutional governance founded on the rule of the people. Consider, for example, Vincent Ostrom's argument that understanding American constitutionalism requires forswearing reference to any "theory of sovereignty." Describing the consequences of the turn toward constitutionalism, he writes:

> The basic question in constituting a government is not one of assigning unlimited and undivided authority to some sovereign entity that has the last say and rules over a society without being a part of that society. Instead, the task is one of allocating and distributing authority so that rules of constitutional law can specify both capabilities and limits that apply to citizens and governmental officials alike in the governance of a society. A system is devised where citizens can enforce the limits of law upon officials as well as officials being able to enforce law upon citizens.[15]

The "task" Ostrom describes is a theory of constitutional choice, which entails constructing constitutional rules that effectively assign political authority and preserve those commitments. The alternative to constitutional choice is a theory of sovereignty, which "presumes that one body exercises supreme authority, and that presumption is incompatible with a notion of democratic government."[16] Here Ostrom echoes the sentiments earlier expressed by A. F. Pollard, who gave broader historical scope to this argument. Of the American colonists he wrote, "Their fundamental objection was to any sovereignty vested in any State whatsoever, even in their own. . . . It is this *denial of all sovereignty* which gives its profound and permanent interest to the American Revolution."[17] Pollard's assessment has found a sympathetic audience in at least one contemporary historian of American politics. Reflecting on the pervasiveness of sovereignty in American political discourse, Jack Rakove writes, "As a historian of American federalism, however, I've long had a nagging desire to banish this word from our political lexicon. From the start (that is, from the era of the American Revolution), our practice and theory alike have made a hash of the traditional concept of sovereignty that the colonists inherited from European theorists."[18]

In this telling, the American constitutional order stands opposed to one understanding of sovereignty, negating its central premise that political authority is unitary, supreme, and illimitable. Rakove, Pollard, and Ostrom are surely right that the Constitution does not contemplate "unlimited and undivided authority." Indeed, that is a passable summary of the theory of sovereignty decisively rejected by American revolutionaries from 1765 to 1776. And the constitutional settlement that ultimately emerged from the revolutionary period seems predicated on both the limitation and division of political authority. But in rejecting the inherited definition, American politics did not escape sovereignty's long shadow. As the copious historical and historical-theoretical literature documents, there is no single conception or manifestation of sovereignty. Though indivisibility and illimitability are distinguishing features of certain theories of sovereignty, the history of its development reveals enough diversity, contradiction, and qualification to render ill advised any attempt to speak of it in univocal terms.[19] The King's Two Bodies, for instance, developed in part to specify certain limits on what a monarch could do, thus cleaving the mortal king from the immortal kingship. Similarly, eighteenth-century claims of parliamentary supremacy were perfectly consistent (on certain interpretations) with substantive limitations on how its authority could be exercised, as had been earlier articulations of seemingly abso-lute sovereignty.[20] Borrowing from a distinction familiar to legal theory, to reject a particular theory of sovereignty, as British North Americans did in the late eighteenth century, is to reject a *concep-tion* of sovereignty but not necessarily the *concept*.[21] Rakove's larger argument from the work cited previously makes this abundantly clear. Despite calling for the expulsion of sovereignty from politi-cal discourse, he proceeds carefully to describe how sovereignty in fact is present in American politics and why it has been such a con-spicuous feature of American political thinking.[22]

When placed in historical context, claims of sovereignty are shown to exist within a broader set of questions about the nature, scope, and location of political authority. It is these questions, and not particular propositions or definitions, that supply unity and coherence to sovereignty's history in political thought. In Hinsley's noted formulation, sovereignty is "a restatement of the permanent problem of deciding the basis of government and obligation within a political community."[23] This problem, in turn, arises in the con-tingent and thus ever-changing circumstances of political life; it is irreducibly historical. In acknowledging the general set of questions to which debates over sovereignty refer, we are driven into the gran-ularity and evolution of political life. Kalmo and Skinner describe this relationship with especial acuity:

> It is precisely when various doctrines of sovereignty are con-strued as a set of questions and answers, rather than immuta-ble propositions, that we cannot afford to ignore its history. This is because those questions and answers can themselves hardly be eternal, brooding above the fray of history. As the interna-tional relations theorist R. B. J. Walker puts it, "the principle of state sovereignty codifies a historically specific answer to his-torically specific questions about political community." . . . The ambiguity of sovereignty has historical depth; it is not the result of conceptual confusion born out of a persistent misunderstand-ing of its "true nature," or even of its core, but reflects past efforts to give it content.[24]

This insight undergirds the "linguistic turn" in sovereignty schol-arship, which has drawn attention to the use of sovereignty claims and counterclaims as well as the circumstances that generate them, the ways conflicting claims are resolved, and the consequences of claims made and resolved.[25] One need not accept all the implications of this methodological move to acknowledge the basic point that sovereignty has both linguistic (or discursive) and historical dimensions; the multiple conceptions of sovereignty that have appeared throughout political history are expressed, communicated, and contested through different forms of political discourse. As the history of sovereignty's meaning and use attests, this relationship can also mark pivotal changes in the structure and location of political authority. Different forms of government facilitate or obstruct the expression, communication, and contestation of these conceptions.

There is, then, an important temporal axis to the conceptual development of sovereignty. If it is true that sovereignty's "function in the history of politics has been either to strengthen the claims of power or to strengthen the ways by which political power is called to account," then we should expect claims of sovereignty to arise in times of change and conflict—precisely when such claims lack the strength that made them unquestionable.[26] Moreover, the advent of institutionalized and constitutionalized politics has provided new opportunities for the justification and expression of sovereignty's claims. Indeed, for the contemporary observer the question of sovereignty—like many other political questions—is principally an institutional question, in that ultimate political authority rooted in the people is nonetheless housed in, wielded by, and made manifest through political institutions.[27]

All of this, then, should bring our attention back to the phenomenon that occasioned Ostrom's argument about the supposed supplanting of sovereignty by constitutional choice. For though he may be wrong about the continued relevance of sovereignty in the American constitutional order, he is certainly right to highlight the significance of constitutional design to the question of political authority. Indeed, as I argue below, the continued relevance of sovereignty, and the particular form of that relevance, is a consequence of constitutional design. It is therefore an error to see the ratification of the Constitution as the final act in the political and constitutional drama that began more than two decades earlier with the Stamp Act crisis and the rejection of Parliament's claims of sovereignty. Ostrom is surely not alone in this reading of American history, as we have already seen. Some of the most prominent constitutional and revolutionary histories tend to portray the construction or ratification of the Constitution as a conclusion to or culmination of one formative phase of American history. Although this is certainly true in some respects, it also risks obscuring American constitutionalism's reorientation of the problematics of political authority. The American "solution" to the problem of sovereignty—at both the general and concrete levels—may have ended one phase of political struggle, but it simultaneously inaugurated another phase. What's more, the specific ways in which the Constitution divided and institutionalized political authority mark a decisive and consequential break from earlier understandings of sovereignty. To see this, we must look both to the structure of American constitutionalism and to the understanding of sovereignty that supplied the context for the American experiment in constitutional governance. It is to the second of these issues that we turn first.

SOVEREIGNTY AS PREDICATE: POLITICAL ORDER AND POLITICAL AUTHORITY

The leitmotif of the legal and political drama that unfolded over the nearly three decades connecting the Stamp Act crisis to the ratification of the U.S. Constitution was the question of sovereignty—who possessed it, where it was located, and what was its extent. It was, however, a motif that evolved as colonial, then state, and eventually early national leaders ascribed to it different meanings and requirements. These, in turn, presented new questions about the structure, organization, and possibilities of politics. Sovereignty was, at the beginning of this period, something of a moving target, with imperial and colonial actors asserting different conceptions of political authority within the British Empire. This disagreement kindled the disputes that roiled the colonies from the early 1760s to the middle of the following decade, eventuating in the colonies declaring independence. It will not do, then, to look for a single, unified "meaning of sovereignty" at the time, because there was not one. Instead, we must understand the opposing claims and conceptions of sovereignty that motivated the actions that punctuated the Constitution's revolutionary prehistory. Moreover, beyond the contested notions of sovereignty, we must also recognize its function in Anglo-American constitutional thinking, for it is there that we find a consequential divergence.

It is, of course, frequently observed and widely agreed that sovereignty was at the very root of the American Revolution.[28] But it was not some abstract notion of sovereignty; it was the specific conception according to which Parliament possessed supreme and unqualified authority over the colonies. This understanding of sovereignty underlay the imposition between 1764 and 1765 of the Sugar and Stamp Acts and, in the face of colonial resistance, the 1766 Declaratory Act, which asserted that Parliament "had, hath, and of right ought to have, full power and authority to make laws and statutes of sufficient force and validity to bind the colonies and people of America, subjects of the crown of Great Britain, *in all cases whatsoever*."[29] The most recognizable expression of this understanding of sovereignty came the same year as the Stamp Act in Blackstone's *Commentaries on the Laws of England*. In the second section of his Introduction, on the general nature of laws, he described the scope and necessity of sovereignty thus: "There is and must be in all [forms of government] a supreme, irresistible, absolute, uncontrolled authority, in which the *jura summi imperii*, or the rights of sovereignty, reside." There he also stressed the legislative character of sovereignty: "By the sovereign power . . . is meant the making of laws."[30] In the second chapter of Book One, he clarified its location, writing of Parliament:

> It hath sovereign and uncontrollable authority in the making, confirming, enlarging, restraining, abrogating, repealing, reviving, and expounding of laws, concerning matters of all possible denominations, ecclesiastical or temporal, civil, military, maritime, or criminal: this being the place where that absolute despotic power, which must in all governments reside somewhere, is entrusted by the constitution of these kingdoms. . . . It can, in short, do every thing that is not naturally impossible; and therefore some have not scrupled to call its power, by a figure rather too bold, the omnipotence of parliament. True it is, that what they do, no authority upon earth can undo.[31]

It was this understanding of parliamentary authority that the colonists rejected, as documented in the writings of Otis, Dickinson, Adams, Paine, and countless other revolutionaries.[32] As Bailyn put it, "How to qualify, undermine, or reinterpret this tenet of English political theory was the central intellectual problem that confronted the leaders of the American cause."[33] It should be acknowledged, though, that this conception of sovereignty was of relatively recent vintage, expressing as it did the settlement that resulted from the 1688 Glorious Revolution. Blackstone's articulation should, therefore, be seen for what it was—a contribution to the eighteenth-century debate about that nature of political authority within the British Empire.[34] We must accordingly resist the impulse to paint with a brush broader than is warranted. To this point, Charles McIlwain has argued that Blackstonian sovereignty was actually a departure from English constitutionalism, a form of absolutism that arose, perhaps ironically, as a replacement for the royal absolutism rejected in the 1688 revolution. But it was a departure not contrived but described by Blackstone. McIlwain does not argue that Blackstone's account was an aberration but that the state of affairs Blackstone described was itself a distortion of English precedent and practice. In this, as in much else, the *Commentaries* "influenced thought all the more because it was *not* original, and because it was simply a statement of current ideas and practice."[35] As evidenced by official actions of Parliament, declarations from royal governors in the colonies, and English jurists, the parliamentary sovereignty described by Blackstone expressed the operative vision of British political authority after 1760 in the North American colonies.

Although the various criteria of Blackstonian sovereignty are what most often catch the eye and attract the attention of modern observers, its function is frequently overlooked. This is understandable, insofar as the specifics of Parliament's claims over colonial authorities were the immediate concern of colonial actors and, as a result, later scholars. But the terms in which Blackstone defines parliamentary authority should lead us to inquire into its purpose. After all, Blackstone repeatedly stresses the necessity of the kind of sovereign he describes. Why, then, is sovereignty such a central aspect of legal and political order? Immediately prior to the oft-quoted definition of sovereignty, Blackstone clarifies its importance. Without sovereignty—"some superior . . . whose commands and decisions all the members are bound to obey"—society would, he writes, remain "in a state of nature."[36] A supreme sovereign is required to transition from prepolitical to political society. But is sovereignty still necessary after the state of nature has been exited?

Perhaps the supreme political authority Blackstone describes is like a scaffolding that is required for the creation of political society but is no longer necessary once it has been established. This, however, is not how Blackstone describes sovereignty, nor how he understands political society. In his account of English law, sociopolitical order is predicated on the existence of a sovereign power. According to this understanding, sovereignty—a supreme and final political authority—is a necessary condition of well-ordered politics, and its presence is required to preserve the ends of politics.

This understanding of sovereignty becomes clear early in Book One, where Blackstone addresses Locke's argument about the people's inherent power to "remove or alter the legislative, when they find the legislative act contrary to the trust reposed in them," a power grounded in the claim that "when such trust is abused, it is thereby forfeited, and devolves to those who gave it." Blackstone rejects this, though, saying that "however just this conclusion may be in theory, we cannot adopt it," because inter alia "annihilating the sovereign power repeals all positive laws whatsoever before enacted."[37] In the following chapter, he returns to this matter, writing that the "dissolution of government" on Lockean principles "would have annihilated the sovereign power, and in consequence repealed all positive laws." The destruction of this legal edifice would, as we also saw in the Introduction to the *Commentaries*, "reduce[] the society almost to a state of nature."[38] It is not just law but also civil liberty that depends on the continued existence of a sovereign power. (Or, perhaps more accurately, civil liberty depends on the existence of a sovereign power *because* law so depends.) Again, Blackstone's comments on this point arise in connection with the prospect of revolution: "For civil liberty, rightly understood, consists in protecting the rights of individuals by the united force of society: society cannot be maintained, and of course can exert no protection, without obedience to some sovereign power: and obedience is an empty name, if every individual has a right to decide how far he himself shall obey."[39]

Sovereignty's function as the predicate for sociopolitical order illuminates the various criteria Blackstone identifies. Precisely because sociopolitical order depended on the existence of some final controlling authority, that authority had to be without limit, indivisible, and beyond control. Admitting otherwise would imperil that which government exists to preserve. Hence the centrality in

Blackstone's analysis of jurisdiction, which entailed both full and final purview as well as the requisite power to give effect to official determinations. The consequences of incomplete jurisdiction are made clear in the discussion of royal power. "For all jurisdiction implies superiority of power," Blackstone writes. If there were any power greater than the king, "there would soon be an end of the constitution, by destroying the free agency of one of the constituent parts of the sovereign legislative power."[40] Sovereignty's function dictated its form, even if the most conspicuous features of that form were shaped by the particular challenges faced by British imperial governance in the eighteenth century.

As mentioned previously, the parliamentary sovereignty described by Blackstone was doubly contingent. It purported only to describe English law and to characterize the settlement that followed the Glorious Revolution. Nevertheless, sovereignty's function as the predicate for sociopolitical order is by no means unique to eighteenth-century British legal theory. Some have, indeed, argued that it is sovereignty's very essence. In the broadest perspective—that of the history of sovereignty's development and use—we see the centrality of social order and control. Hinsley roots the concept of sovereignty in the emergence of "state forms," which entailed a transition in the basis of authority from moral coercion to force. Sovereignty thus emerged "as the sole viable working assumption about political authority." Of sovereignty he writes, "It is the concept which maintains no more—if also no less—than that there must be an ultimate authority within the political society if the society is to exist at all, or at least if it is to be able to function effectively."[41] Precursors to parliamentary sovereignty similarly reflect this function. From royal perpetuity and the King's Two Bodies to the seminal definitions offered by Bodin and Hobbes—a locus of final authority was a necessary condition for political and social order.[42] So it had been for many of sovereignty's earliest theorists, and so it was again for Blackstone and the English constitutionalism he described.

SOVEREIGNTY AS OBJECT: THE U.S. CONSTITUTION

Though much changed in the years after the colonies' formal declaration of independence, at least one thing remained the same:

sovereignty was a fiercely contested concept, one on whose definition the possibility of union hinged in 1787 when delegates gath-
ered to devise changes that would "render the federal Constitution
adequate to the exigencies of government and the preservation of
the Union."[43] As Elbridge Gerry remarked at the Constitutional
Convention, "States & the advocates for them were intoxicated
with the idea of their sovereignty."[44] In fact, the developments
between 1776 when independence was declared and 1787 when
delegates met to construct a new charter of government shaped
the particular problem faced by those who would deliberate over the
future of the United States. The question, in brief, concerned the
relationship between two governing bodies, most immediately
whether any such relationship was possible given the logic of sovereignty. Whereas the revolutionary debate addressed the competing claims of metropolitan and peripheral authorities,[45] the
constitutional debate addressed how to reconcile the coexistence
of state governments and a new central government. This was the
problem of *imperium in imperio*, or "empire within empire."[46] As
several convention delegates stressed throughout their proceedings,
a government subject to the jurisdiction of another was not sovereign; and a government that was not sovereign was not truly a government. In this respect, at least, a vestige of the Blackstonian view
of sovereignty persisted from the revolutionary period through
the Articles of Confederation up to the eve of the Constitution—
unitary and illimitable political authority still seemed to be a precondition for political order. How, then, could the central and state
governments coexist without one destroying the other or both
frustrating the very purposes of government?

The conventional answer to this question consists principally
in a clarification of the basis of sovereignty. The "problem" of *imperium in imperio* is a problem only if sovereignty resided in the government. If, however, the people are sovereign, they can choose
which things will be done by government, just as they can choose
which government will do those things. But the Constitution represents more than a new or modified conception of sovereignty. It
marks a significant change in the nature of sovereignty within a
political regime. As we saw in the previous section, in the conception of sovereignty against which the early Americans rebelled sovereignty was treated as a precondition for sociopolitical order.
Sovereignty was the predicate for a well-ordered, viable political

system, and thus the supreme authority had to be indivisible and illimitable. Under the Constitution, however, the location of much political authority became the object of constitutionally structured politics. Accordingly, sovereignty in these areas is the product of politics rather than the precondition. This is not to say that under the Constitution all questions of political authority are the object of politics—at least not in the same way. For, although popular sovereignty requires that delegations of authority to government actors and institutions are defeasible, a range of these determinations are nonetheless defined by the constitutional text. Put another way, because constitutions codify delegations of authority from the sovereign people to their government, those assignments must be open to revision in order to be consistent with the people's ultimate authority. Changes to these constitutional provisions are effected through formal changes to the constitution.

There is, however, another range of determinations that are the object and output of politics short of formal constitutional change. This phenomenon results from the distinctiveness of a written constitution, most fundamentally the inability of the constitutional text to specify fully and concretely how political authority is apportioned among governing institutions. As this cursory description suggests, the transition from sovereignty as a predicate for political order to an object of political contestation results from the conjunction of the substantive commitment to popular authority, the formal commitment to a written constitution, and the practical necessity of multilevel governance. Understanding this phenomenon and recognizing its implications thus require charting the relationships among these central components of American constitutionalism with respect to the location of political authority.

The clearest articulations of the nature of sovereignty under the Constitution came in the context of Federalist responses to the accusation that the proposed charter of government violated the supposed axiom of *imperium in imperio*. This, in turn, was part and parcel of a central Anti-Federalist line of attack, namely that the Constitution would establish a consolidated government.[47] The most cogent elucidations of the Constitution's foundation in popular sovereignty were offered by James Wilson. Though he first presented the argument in the Philadelphia convention, the most elaborate and, indeed, influential iterations of his defense of the

Constitution were delivered in the Pennsylvania ratification debates.[48] As noted above, this argument consisted principally in the reorientation of a claim frequently made by the Constitution's critics—that political authority resided in the people, not in government. Because it did, the people could delegate their ultimate authority as they saw fit. On the eve of the Pennsylvania ratifying convention, Wilson voiced this position in the specific context of the relationship between the proposed constitution and the extant state constitutions. Whereas in the latter the people "invested their representatives with every right and authority which they did not in explicit terms reserve," in the former "congressional authority is to be collected not from tacit implication, but from the positive grant expressed in the instrument of union."[49] In both cases the people were sovereign, but the nature of their delegations to government were diametrically opposed.

Wilson returned to this point two months later, and in so doing he demonstrated how fully the Federalist case had appropriated its opponents' presumptions. In response to a delegate who claimed that sovereignty resided in the states, and thus could not be surrendered to the national government without the states losing their sovereignty, Wilson offered as succinct an account of popular sovereignty as is found in the founding era. He began, though, by accepting the Blackstonian premise that sovereignty was indivisible, saying that it had not and would not likely "be denied, that somewhere there is, and of necessity must be, a supreme, absolute, and uncontrollable authority." The question, though, was where this authority was located. Later in his speech, Wilson clarified the case of the Constitution's advocates by contrasting it with the argument of a fellow delegate:

> His position is, that the supreme power resides in the States, as governments; and mine is, that it *resides* in the PEOPLE, as the foundation of government; that the people have not—that the people mean not—and that the people ought not, to part with it to an government whatsoever. In their hands it remains secure. They can delegate it in such proportions, to such bodies, on such terms, and under such limitations, as they think proper. I agree with the members in opposition, that there cannot be two sovereign powers on the same subject.[50]

Government was the agent of the sovereign principle, the people. It was up to the people, then, to decide which powers would be assigned to which agents. Far from emerging as a convenient post hoc rationalization, the understanding of popular sovereignty articulated by Wilson tapped into American experiences in the period between declaring independence and (re)constructing a constitution, when the commitment to ultimate popular authority was honed in the crucible of experiments in and frustrations with local governance.[51] Nonetheless, as a matter of formal law, the commitment to popular sovereignty, Wilson claimed, was an innovation of the proposed Constitution, a truth perhaps perceived only by "the great and penetrating mind of Locke."[52] And it was on this distinctive feature of the Constitution that the Federalists based much of their case. According to Gordon Wood, this appropriation and reorientation of Blackstonian sovereignty, expressed most forcefully by Wilson, became "the basis of all Federalist thinking."[53]

But how far does this get us? As elaborated by Wilson, popular sovereignty does indeed offer resolution for the problem of *imperium in imperio* by avoiding the specter of conflicting sovereigns conjured by the Constitution's Anti-Federalist critics. At the same time, it provides the theoretical foundation for federal governance, opening the door to multiple levels and kinds of government all drawing their authority from a single sovereign people. As we have already seen with other notions of sovereignty, though, for all that this answer resolves, it also poses a wide range of new questions. Even as popular sovereignty supplies a new theoretical context and different conceptual resources for debates over political authority, it does not fully resolve Hinsley's "permanent problem of deciding the basis of government and obligation within a political community."[54] Questions spring immediately from Wilson's definition. If political authority is to be delegated from the people to their governments, what form will those delegations take? By what process can authority be delegated and rescinded? In the event authority is delegated to multiple government levels, what will be the nature of the relationship between those governments? Moreover, which institutions or actors will be charged with defining, overseeing, and enforcing that relationship? This is just the beginning of the myriad questions precipitated by the shift from government to popular sovereignty. To be given satisfactory effect—to be made politically meaningful—the will of the people must be identified, structured,

empowered, and in certain cases limited. The move from government to popular sovereignty entailed a transition from metaphysical
questions about the nature of royal or parliamentary power to institutional questions about the proper way to articulate the sovereign
people's voice.

American political thought and practice in the mid to late eighteenth century developed in response to exactly these changes.
Most important in this connection is the commitment to charters
of government that defined the location of political authority and
the processes by which such authority could be exercised. By the
late revolutionary period—and certainly by the time the Constitution was debated and ratified—there was a broad consensus among
early Americans that liberty required the codification of government frameworks, thus further distinguishing American constitutionalism from English constitutionalism. Illustrative of this
sentiment is Thomas Paine's 1791 claim that "the American constitutions were to liberty what a grammar is to language: they define
its parts of speech, and practically construct them into syntax."[55]
Constitutions establish, define, and order political life, and in so
doing they protect the liberties of the sovereign people. We see,
then, a deep affinity between popular sovereignty and written
constitutions. It is, indeed, difficult to imagine a new-modeled
liberal regime based on popular authority without a written
constitution.[56]

Recall, though, that the transition to a popular basis of sovereignty did not resolve the fundamental questions of political authority. Instead, it reoriented and recontextualized them them.
Similarly, codifying popular sovereignty in a written constitution
poses a further challenge, one that is profoundly consequential for
the nature of sovereignty in a political regime. This challenge could
be called the *Federalist* 37 problem, for that is where Madison gave
it such forceful articulation. There he probed a difficulty implicit
in the enterprise of constitution making, one that beset the convention's work in Philadelphia: "All new laws, though penned with
the greatest technical skill, and passed on the fullest and most
mature deliberation, are considered as more or less obscure and
equivocal, until their meaning be liquidated and ascertained by a
series of particular discussions and adjudications."[57] The problem
was one of linguistic determinacy, what Madison termed "vague and
incorrect definitions," in conjunction with the difficulty of limiting

how the powers granted could be used. Try as they might, the convention delegates could not specify an incontestable meaning for the terms they settled on; nor could they contemplate every contingency to which the constitution they were designing would apply. And even if they could, it is not clear that they would have. After all, a new constitution was needed in large part because the Articles of Confederation had failed to provide adequately for the "exigencies of Union." It is in practice impossible to mark the jurisdictional limits comprehensively and enumerate the lawful uses of public authority exhaustively. To do so would, in the words of John Marshall, require "the prolixity of a legal code."[58] This inherent challenge of constitution making is doubly present in systems with multiple government levels, where the questions of enumeration and jurisdictional boundaries apply not just to the relationship between citizens and a single government but also to the relationship between levels of government.[59] In this connection, it is telling that Madison's discussion comes in the context of "marking the proper line of partition, between the authority of the general, and that of the State governments." After identifying the three sources of this difficulty—"indistinctness of the object, imperfection of the organ of conception, inadequateness of the vehicle of ideas"—Madison avers that each must have been felt by the convention's delegates as they tried to clarify the division between the federal and state governments.[60]

In the face of the problem set out in *Federalist* 37, the delegates did not attempt a comprehensive division of jurisdiction. Rather than seek to specify the precise contours of the state-federal relationship, the Constitution established, empowered, and limited the general government, addressing the state governments largely by implication. (The deviations from this pattern—most notably Sections 9 and 10 of Article I and, after ratification, the Ninth and Tenth Amendments—are exceptions that prove the rule.) As a result, it is impossible to identify a comprehensive jurisdictional boundary between government levels in the Constitution for the simplest of reasons: that is not what it set out to do. Seeking such information from the Constitution is to look for the answer to a question it was not designed to answer.[61] The consequence of this feature of constitution making was a flexible system of government, one with some play in the joints that joined the two levels of government. The Constitution constrained but did not overdetermine the contours of the state-federal relationship. As a result, the specific nature of that relationship would be the product of the politics structured by the Constitution. Thus the "unsettled dividing line between state and national power left the ensuing boundary dispute for future politicians to work through."[62] "Federalism," Keith Whittington has argued, "is best thought of not as a specified intermediate position between confederation and nation, but rather as a continuing tension contained within, and created by, the founding document."[63]

This, then, is how the scope and location of much political authority would be determined under the Constitution. Moreover, it is how sovereignty is both an object and a product of constitutionally structured politics in the American political system. In contrast with the Blackstonian understanding of sovereignty, according to which a final political authority is a precondition for sociopolitical order, under the Constitution the scope and location of political authority are defeasible, with respect to both the parameters established by the constitutional text and the exercise of power within those parameters. On the old understanding of sovereignty, it was Parliament—"the tripartite indenture of King, Lords, and Commons"—that was sovereign.[64] But once the popular basis of sovereignty is acknowledged and political authority is divided between governments by means of a written constitution, sovereignty then describes both the ultimate authority of the people and the delegated authority of the government. Clarifying and giving effect to these claims in light of the popular basis of legitimate authority thus become matters of constitutional politics.

CONCLUSION

Although Madison concluded *Federalist* 37 with a note of amazement that, despite the challenges he chronicled, the convention was able to produce such a commendable proposal, our attention should be drawn to the consequences of the problem he identified for questions of sovereignty and political authority. The deficit of constitutional determinacy in the division of authority, in conjunction with the decision to eschew a comprehensive division of jurisdiction, has significant ramifications for how the commitment to popular sovereignty is realized. In short, if it is unclear where state authority yields to federal authority and vice versa, the clarity and efficacy of the people's delegations to government are called into question. Moreover, ambiguity on these matters could permit one government to have an advantage over the other, exploiting the uncertainty surrounding the proper domains of government power and threatening the rights and liberties of the people. At the same time, though, this problem seems to be entailed by the commitment to codify popular authority in a written constitution. If popular sovereignty presupposes a relationship between citizen and state constituted by formal delegations of authority, then the nature of these relationships are of central importance. This is especially the case in a federal system, where the state-citizen relationship operates on two levels and introduces additional complexities concerning the relationship between citizens and their (multiple) governments.

The Constitution's critics pounced on this, understanding its implications principally as a threat to state governance. Endowed with unprecedented powers and absent clear grants of state sovereignty, the national government could continually extend its authority until the states were swallowed up. This argument is most often understood in the context of the scope of national powers in relation to the states, but the connections sketched here suggest a broader and more fundamental context, one grounded ultimately in the challenges occasioned by a political order founded on popular authority. Rather than argue that the Constitution established a jurisdictional division between government levels sufficiently comprehensive to protect state interests—it did not—the Constitution's defenders presented a subtle account of why the flexibility of the jurisdictional division was not a flaw but a virtue. The argument they advanced concerned the circumstances under which national power could and would be put to use. The underlying premise was, as Madison wrote in *Federalist* 46, that "the people ought not surely to be precluded from giving most of their confidence where they may discover it to be most due." By this, he meant that the division of authority should be responsive to the people's assessments of their governments. If one government does better than the other, then it should be able to act in accordance with the people's confidence and with the imprimatur of their sovereignty, subject always to constitutional limitations. Moreover, these shifts in authority could serve as a sign of which concerns were general and which were local, marking the point at which issues properly came within the purview of the national government. Such were the consequences, and the possibilities, of popular sovereignty in a system of federal governance. All of this, though, depended on sovereignty being open to revision through the political process and not, as it had been on the Blackstonian model, a precondition for sociopolitical order.

NOTES

For helpful comments on earlier versions of this chapter, I thank Russ Muirhead, Michelle Schwarze, Phillip Muñoz, Andrea Radasanu, Mariah Zeisberg, Jeffrey Broxmeyer, and Adam Seagrave.

1. Seven words in the original French (*Le roi est mort, vive le roi*), the phrase dates to the fifteenth century. Though developed in the context of French monarchical politics, its quick absorption into English politics reflected the already centuries-old understanding of the continuity of sovereignty.

2. Ernst Kantorowicz, *The King's Two Bodies: A Study in Mediaeval Political Theology* (Princeton, NJ: Princeton University Press, 1957), 7.

3. *The Life and Death of King Richard II*, III.ii. See also Kantorowicz, *King's Two Bodies*, 31.

4. Jens Bartelson, "Sovereignty," in *The Encyclopedia of Political Theory*, ed. Mark Bevir (Thousand Oaks, CA: Sage, 2010), 1309–11. See also Bartelson's *Genealogy of Sovereignty* (Cambridge, Cambridge University Press, 1995).

5. For surprisingly recent episodes dealing with the interpretation and application of this theory, see Frederic William Maitland, "Crown as Corporation," *Law Quarterly Review* 17, no. 2 (1901): 131–46, cited in Kantorowicz, *King's Two Bodies*, 3–4.

6. See, generally, Richard Tuck, *The Sleeping Sovereign: The Invention of Modern Democracy* (Cambridge: Cambridge University Press, 2016); and Richard Bourke and Quentin Skinner, eds., *Popular Sovereignty in Historical Perspective* (Cambridge: Cambridge University Press, 2016). For an example of the argument that popular sovereignty was both normatively correct and empirically accurate even when contrary claims were enshrined in law and practice, see John V. Jezierski's account of James Wilson's arguments in "Parliament or People: James Wilson and Blackstone on the Nature and Location of Sovereignty," *Journal of the History of Ideas* 32, no. 1 (1971): 95–106.

7. Hanna Lerner, *Making Constitutions in Deeply Divided Societies* (Cambridge: Cambridge University Press, 2011), 15–17.

8. It is difficult to specify the exact number of constitutional systems based on popular rule. According to the largest database of world constitutions (Comparative Constitutions Project, constituteproject.org), only nine countries

explicitly invoke "popular sovereignty" in their national charter (Argentina, Brazil, Bulgaria, Cape Verde, Djibouti, Dominican Republic, Greece, Honduras, and Togo). That, however, has not stopped two of the principal investigators in that project from observing that nearly every constitution, whether written by and for democrats or authoritarians, seems to aspire to some form of popular authority. See Zachary Elkins, "Diffusion and the Constitutionalization of Europe," *Comparative Political Studies* 43, no. 8/9 (2010): 969–99; and Zachary Elkins and James Melton, "The Content of Authoritarian Constitutions," in *Constitutions in Authoritarian Regimes*, ed. Tom Ginsburg and Alberto Simpser (Cambridge: Cambridge University Press, 2013), 141–64.

9. Edmund Morgan, *Inventing the People: The Rise of Popular Sovereignty in England and America*, rev. ed. (New York: W. W. Norton, 1989), 122.

10. See, for example, David Singh Grewal and Jedediah Purdy, "The Original Theory of Constitutionalism," *Yale Law Journal* 127 (2018): 664.

11. In this connection, it is worth noting that perhaps the most significant recent work in American political thought omits from direct consideration all three of these. See Eric Nelson, *The Royalist Revolution: Monarchy and the American Founding* (Cambridge, MA: Harvard University Press, 2014), 9.

12. Harold J. Laski, *A Grammar of Politics* (Routledge, 2014), 44–45, quoted in F. H. Hinsley, *Sovereignty*, 2nd ed. (Cambridge: Cambridge University Press, 1986), 216.

13. Michel Troper, "Sovereignty," in *The Oxford Handbook of Comparative Constitutional Law*, ed. Michel Rosenfeld and András Sajó (Oxford: Oxford University Press, 2012), 350.

14. Bartelson, *Genealogy of Sovereignty*, 1.

15. Vincent Ostrom, "The Meaning of Federalism in *The Federalist*," *Publius* 15, no. 1 (1985): 19. See also Ostrom, *The Meaning of American Federalism: Constituting a Self-Governing Society* (San Francisco: ICS Press, 1991), 41–50, 69–98.

16. Ostrom, "Meaning of Federalism," 21.

17. *Factors in American History* (Cambridge: Cambridge University Press, 1925), 31 (emphasis added). For opposing takes on Pollard's characterization, compare Charles McIlwain, *Constitutionalism and The Changing World* (Cambridge: Cambridge University Press, 1939), 68; and Samuel P. Huntington, *Political Order in Changing Societies* (New Haven, CT: Yale University Press, [1968] 2006), 105.

18. Jack Rakove, "Making a Hash of Sovereignty, Part I," *Green Bag* 2, no. 1 (Fall 1998), 35.

19. See especially Hinsley, *Sovereignty*. The literature on this point is expansive and growing. Valuable recent additions include the edited volumes *Popular Sovereignty in Historical Perspective*, ed. Richard Bourke and Quentin Skinner (Cambridge: Cambridge University Press, 2016); and *Sovereignty in*

Fragments: The Past, Present, and Future of a Contested Concept, ed. Hent Kalmo and Quentin Skinner (Cambridge: Cambridge University Press, 2010).

20. See, for example, Richard Bourke, "Introduction," in Bourke and Skinner, *Popular Sovereignty*, 1–4; and Francis W. Coker, "The Technique of the Pluralistic State," *American Political Science Review* 15, no. 2 (1921): 186–213, 193 (discussing the "moral limits of state authority" in the context of Laski's arguments).

21. The concept/conception distinction was popularized in legal and political theory by Ronald Dworkin and John Rawls, respectively. See Dworkin's *Law's Empire* (Cambridge, MA: Harvard University Press, 1988); and Rawls's *A Theory of Justice*, rev. ed. (Cambridge, MA: Belknap Press, 1999 [1971]), 5–6. The earliest use, however, seems to be W. B. Gallie's "Essentially Contested Concepts," *Proceedings of the Aristotelian Society* 56 (1955–56): 167–98.

22. Rakove develops his argument over two pieces, the first dedicated to explaining why the old conception of sovereignty has little descriptive value for American politics and the second to speculating why it is nonetheless a pervasive feature of American political discourse. See "Making a Hash of Sovereignty, Part I"; and "Making a Hash of Sovereignty, Part II," *Green Bag* 3, no. 1 (Fall 1999): 51.

23. Hinsley, *Sovereignty*, 26.

24. Hent Kalmo and Quentin Skinner, "Introduction: A Concept in Fragments," in *Sovereignty in Fragments*, 10–11.

25. See, for example, Wouter G. Werner and Jaap H. De Wilde, "The Endurance of Sovereignty," *European Journal of International Relations* 7, no. 3 (2001): 283–313.

26. Hinsley, *Sovereignty*, 25.

27. Jeremy Waldron has given compelling expression to the relationship described here between political theory and political institutions, though not in the specific context of sovereignty. See his *Political Political Theory: Essays on Institutions* (Cambridge, MA: Harvard University Press, 2016), 1–15.

28. See, for example, Bernard Bailyn, *The Ideological Origins of the American Revolution* (Cambridge, MA: Harvard University Press, [1967] 1992), 198–229; and Gordon Wood, *Creation of the American Republic, 1776–1787* (Chapel Hill: University of North Carolina Press, 1969), 259–82.

29. The Declaratory Act, March 18, 1766 (emphasis added).

30. William Blackstone, *Commentaries on the Laws of England* (Clarendon Press, 1765–69), 49.

31. Blackstone, *Commentaries*, 157.

32. See, for example, Bailyn, *Ideological Origins*, 55–93.

33. Bailyn, *Ideological Origins*, 202.

34. See Alison LaCroix, *Ideological Origins of American Federalism* (Cambridge, MA: Harvard University Press, 2010), 12–18, 68–104.

35. Ernest Barker, *Essays on Government*, 2nd ed. (Oxford: Oxford University Press, [1945] 1951), 127 (emphasis in original). For his part, Gordon Wood portrays Blackstone's enunciation in the *Commentaries* as reinforcing, rather than mischaracterizing or innovating upon, British practice. See Wood, *Creation of the American Republic*, 264–65.

36. Blackstone, *Commentaries*, 48.

37. Blackstone, *Commentaries*, 157. See John Locke, *Second Treatise of Government*, §19–21, 168, 211–43.

38. Blackstone, *Commentaries*, 206.

39. Blackstone, *Commentaries*, 244.

40. Blackstone, *Commentaries*, 235.

41. Hinsely, *Sovereignty*, 217.

42. In addition to Hinsley's account in *Sovereignty*, see Daniel Lee, *Popular Sovereignty in Early Modern Constitutional Thought* (Oxford: Oxford University Press, 2016); and Martin Loughlin, *Public Law and Political Theory* (Oxford: Clarendon Press, 1992), 146.

43. Report of the Proceedings in Congress (Feb. 21 1787), *Documents Illustrative of the Formation of the Union of the American States* (Washington, DC: Government Printing Office, 1927), available at http://avalon.law.yale.edu /18th_century/const04.asp.

44. Max Farrand, *The Records of the Federal Convention of 1787* (New Haven, CT: Yale University Press, 1911), vol. 1, 467 (June 29 1787).

45. See, generally, Jack P. Greene, *Peripheries and Center: Constitutional Development in the Extended Polities of the British Empire and the United States, 1607–1788* (New York: W. W. Norton, 1986); and Greene, *The Constitutional Origins of the American Revolution* (Cambridge: Cambridge University Press, 2011).

46. For the role of this "counterprinciple" in eighteenth-century constitutional debates, see LaCroix, *Ideological Origins*, 14–15, 18–96.

47. Herbert J. Storing, *What the Anti-Federalists Were For* (Chicago: University of Chicago Press, 1986), 10–11. See also Wood, *Creation of the American Republic*, 524–32.

48. Bailyn, *Ideological Origins*, 328.

49. James Wilson, Pennsylvania Ratifying Convention (6 Oct. 1787), *Documentary History of Ratification* (State Historical Society of Wisconsin, 1976), vol. 2, 167.

50. James Wilson, Pennsylvania Ratifying Convention (4 Dec. 1787), *Documentary History of Ratification*, vol. 2, 472 (emphasis in original).

51. For a summary of the historical literature on this point, see Jeffrey Goldsworthy, "The Debate about Sovereignty in the United States: A Historical and Comparative Perspective," in *Sovereignty in Transition*, ed. Neil Walker (London: Hart/Bloomsbury, 2003), 425–28.

52. Wilson, Pennsylvania Ratifying Convention (4 Dec. 1787).

53. Wood, *Creation of the American Republic*, 530–32.

54. Hinsley, *Sovereignty*, 26.

55. *Paine: Political Writings*, ed. Bruce Kuklick (Cambridge: Cambridge University Press, 2000), 111.

56. This is not to say that such a regime would be impossible. But both the realities of contemporary politics and the logics of political founding suggest a general difficulty. In his discussion of the differences between American and English constitutionalism, Charles McIlwain downplays the differences between a written and an unwritten constitution, arguing that the American Constitution "might be said with little exaggeration to consist mainly of a codification of institutions and principles long in actual force." Nonetheless, he observes that a written charter was used to distinguish American constitutionalism from the legal milieu out of which it emerged. McIlwain, *Constitutionalism: Ancient and Modern* (Ithaca, NY: Cornell University Press, 1966), 1–22.

57. *The Federalist*, ed. Jacob E. Cooke (Middletown, CT: Wesleyan University Press, 1961), 37: 236.

58. *McCulloch v. Maryland*, 17 U.S. 316, 407 (1819).

59. For a longer discussion of this phenomenon, see Connor M. Ewing, "Structure and Relationship in American Federalism: Foundations, Consequences, and 'Basic Principles' Revisited," *Tulsa Law Review* 51, no. 3 (2016): 689, 694–704.

60. *Federalist* 37, 234, 237.

61. For a book-length treatment of this issue, see Edward A. Purcell Jr., *Originalism, Federalism, and the American Constitution Enterprise: A Historical Inquiry* (New Haven, CT: Yale University Press, 2007).

62. David Brian Robertson, *Federalism and the Making of America* (Abingdon, UK: Routledge, 2012), 34.

63. Keith Whittington, "The Political Constitution of Federalism in Antebellum America: The Nullification Debate as an Illustration of Informal Mechanisms of Constitutional Change," *Publius* 26, no. 2 (1996): 1.

64. Jezierski, "Parliament or People," 96.

Epilogue

The Good Citizen in Madison's Constitutional Republic

Colleen A. Sheehan

The themes of this volume are constitutionalism and citizenship. More specifically, we are concerned with the interplay between constitutional structure and institutions and civic life. What is the role of the citizen in the American constitutional republic? What is the task of the officers of a constitutional republic grounded in popular sovereignty? To what extent can the institutions and processes of constitutional government be depended on to safeguard the liberties of the citizen, and to what extent must the citizens themselves be the keepers of their own liberties?

Montesquieu raised these questions within the context of the liberty of the constitution and the liberty of the citizen. Tutored by "the celebrated" Montesquieu, the American founders understood that both the liberty of the constitution and the liberty of the citizen depended on the prevention of tyranny, whether that tyranny resulted from the concentration of power in government or from a majority of the people. To safeguard the liberty of the constitution, separation of powers, bicameralism, federalism, and checks and balances were incorporated into the structure and processes of the U.S. Constitution.

What about the liberty of the citizen? In Montesquieu's schema, the role of the citizens in a republic was primarily a defensive one against government infringement on their liberties. It matters not much whether the people reason well or ill, the French baron famously said, but simply that they reason at all. In other words, Montesquieu believed that the people have to be protective of their own self-interest and actively engage in preventing the branches of government from overstepping their constitutionally prescribed bounds, but they do not have to possess the civic virtues that were required of citizens in classical polities. The sentiment fueling Montesquieu's republican citizen was that of *inquiétude*, or anxiety, which is not so very different from the passion of fear that dominates subjects of despotism. Accordingly, in Montesquieu's view, the popular vigilance required to maintain constitutional government—to preserve the liberty of the constitution and the liberty of the citizen—was driven by an anxious concern for self-preservation and safety, not by a commitment to republicanism or considered judgment about justice and the general good.

In this sense Montesquieu followed in the footsteps of modern political philosophers such as Machiavelli and Hobbes, who, in contradistinction to classical political philosophers, abandoned the task of forming the minds and souls of the citizens and lowered the aspirations of civic and political life. The critical difference between the ancients and moderns is generally understood to revolve around the ultimate choice between freedom and virtue. Stated somewhat differently, the key distinction is whether freedom is the power to do as one pleases or is something grounded in a moral standard of right higher than mere human will, which law ought to incorporate prudentially.

The most philosophically minded of the American founders was James Madison. As he surveyed the course of history, he too divided it into the eras of ancient and modern. Explicitly disagreeing with Montesquieu, particularly with his acclaim for the British model of government and the notion that class- and interest-based rivalry can serve as a substitute for civic education, Madison argued that historical advances had actually made possible what had eluded the ancients.[1] With improvements in communication and travel, it was now feasible to establish republican government over an extensive territory, thus offering the possibility of controlling majority faction and achieving the ends of justice and the general good. Rather than follow those moderns who had abandoned the classical task of forming and refining the opinions of the citizenry, Madison reclaimed the classical republican task with hopeful enthusiasm. In the American constitutional model, he asserted, government will derive its authority from the people and its energy from their will. The structural and institutional arrangements of government serve to refine and enlarge the public views, contributing to the achievement of the reason of the public, which in turn "control[s] and regulate[s] the government."[2] The deliberative processes come full circle as the government, "by the reason of its measures, [operates] on the understanding and interest of the society." With manifest sanguinity if not bravado, Madison declared the American constitutional republic to be "the government for which philosophy has been searching, and humanity been sighing, from the most remote ages. Such . . . is the glory of America to have invented, and her unrivalled happiness to possess."[3]

Although the American founders assuredly incorporated into the U.S. Constitution the Newtonian model of force-counterforce that Montesquieu touted as the strength of the British constitution, Madison did not rely solely or even primarily on this mechanistic system to safeguard against tyranny or to achieve the ends of republicanism. As he argued in *Federalist* 51, experience had demonstrated the need for prudential mechanistic inventions such as separation of powers and bicameralism. But these precautions are "auxiliary"—supplemental to "the people," who are the primary source of support of republican government.[4] By a reliance on "the people" Madison meant a dependence on "public opinion," which for him was something much more than the fleeting views of the populace. Optimally, public opinion is the settled and considered judgment of the people, achieved by a complexly layered and prolonged constitutional process intended to refine and enlarge the public views.

Absent a sound understanding and attachment to the principles of republicanism, Madison believed, no institutional checks or prudential inventions can save a people from themselves.[5] In fact, liberty and learning lean on each other, he noted, reminding us of the importance of civic education for republican citizenship and the importance of republican citizenship to the preservation of free government.[6] In contrast to Montesquieu, for Madison it does make a difference—indeed a critical one—whether the people reason well or ill. He noted in his 1787 notes for the Constitutional Convention that majority opinion—that is, public opinion—ultimately determines the law.[7] A few years later he repeated this idea about the principal authority in republican government: "Public opinion sets bounds to every government, and is the real sovereign in every free one," he wrote.[8]

The formation of a reasonable public opinion, or "the reason of the public," occupied Madison's thoughts for years. Public opinion is the only sovereign in republican government, but it may be factious rather than reasonable opinion. Jefferson summarized Madison's concern about majority faction clearly and succinctly in his first inaugural address: "All too will bear in mind this sacred principle, that though the will of the majority is in all cases to prevail, that will, to be rightful, must be reasonable; that the minority possess their equal rights, which equal laws must protect, and to violate would be oppression."[9] This is exactly what Madison meant in "Vices" when he wrote, "According to Republican Theory, Right and power being both vested in the majority, are held to be synonymous." In fact, however, the majority might not possess power or it might not be on the side of justice. Majority opinion must be shaped, educated, and refined. The refinement and enlargement of majority/public opinion to achieve the conjunction of power and right constituted the core of Madison's philosophical and practical political aspirations. To accomplish this, Madison argued, requires not only inventions of prudence, including federalism and local self-government, but also statesmen and public intellectuals committed to engaging citizens in the work of public discourse and civic education.[10] As Aristotle taught, Madison believed that citizens become genuine citizens through an education in the principles and spirit of their regime. It is no accident, of course, that he eagerly joined his friend Jefferson in founding the University of Virginia and in devoting considerable effort to establishing a curriculum for future civic leaders and citizens of Virginia and America.

For James Madison, the sovereignty of public opinion—and the conditions of that sovereignty—constitute the vital connecting link between constitutionalism and citizenship in a republic. Only public opinion is sovereign in genuinely free governments, but this necessary condition is not the sufficient condition of republicanism. Public opinion must be reasonable and rightful, for the minority possess equal rights, which a republican constitution must protect, without which the rule of law is nothing more than the Hobbesian state of nature where the stronger rule the weaker.[11] Accordingly, the source of the Constitution's authority is the people; but the question remains: What is the source of the people's authority?

In an essay he wrote late in life titled "Sovereignty," Madison argued that "all power in just & free Govts. is derived from

Compact," and "the Sovereignty of the Society as vested in & exerciseable by the majority, may do any thing that could be *rightfully* done, by the unanimous concurrence of the members." Some rights are beyond the legitimate scope of government and the rightful authority of the collectivity of the people. The best example of this, Madison argued, is conscience, which is a sacred and inviolable right reserved to each individual. When individuals become parties to the original social compact, boundaries are thus prescribed to the "legitimate reach of Sovereignty, wherever vested or however viewed."[12]

Accordingly, the majority is a "plenary substitute" for the will of the whole society, and thus it may not rightfully oppress the rights of any member of that society without abrogating the original agreement. Stated in a more positive way, every member who has joined the pact owes every other member the mutual protection of republican citizenship. In an essay written shortly after the establishment of the new constitution, Madison expressed this same idea thus:

> Conscience is the most sacred of all property; other property depending in part on positive law, the exercise of that, being a natural and unalienable right. To guard a man's house as his castle, to pay public and enforce private debts with the most exact faith, can give no title to invade a man's conscience which is more sacred than his castle, or to withhold from it that debt of protection, for which the public faith is pledged, by the very nature and original conditions of the social pact.[13]

In a word, there are some things that the majority cannot do without forfeiting their authority as rightful rulers. This is precisely why there exists a right of revolution—why the rule of law, that is, the Constitution as mere text, is not in and of itself the sufficient source of legitimacy.

The legitimization of the Constitution requires that it be established by the authority of the people—who, in forming the social compact or charter, become fellow citizens. As citizens, whether of the founding or later generations, the people are bound to obey the constitutional charter as duly established. They can amend it, of course, but only via the constitutionally prescribed modes of alteration. And, indeed, there are certain things the people cannot

rightfully do, because doing so would violate the original conditions of the social pact. For example, the institution of human slavery is a violation of human equality, the basis of the requirement
for consent.

The ongoing manifestation of the sovereignty of public opinion is reflected in the ultimate authority of the people over the
Constitution as well as in the authority of a higher law—natural
law—over the will of the people. In this double condition the social
compact binds together the authority of the Constitution with the
rights and rightful responsibilities of the citizen. This inexorable
binding together of the power of the people with their rightful
authority—of making power and right synonymous, as Madison put
it in "Vices"—is at the core of the social compact. Whatever the text
of the constitutional charter may be, the principles of that charter
necessarily comprehend the sacred pledge of the people to recognize and protect the rights of all charter members on the basis of
their shared humanity. The social compact, then, is grounded in a
moral debt that makes the people republican citizens at the same
time that it guarantees a republican form of constitutional
government.

Madison's vision for his country embraces the pledge that our
progenitors made in establishing the Constitution for themselves
and their posterity, and it also comprehends the ongoing pledge
required of all generations of Americans, including our own. This
idea of the American promise is one that also captures what we as
a people might become if we were to flourish and fulfill our potential. It is a kind of promissory note like that described by Martin
Luther King in his letter from the solitary confines of a steely jail,
when he wanted to invoke the richness of his dream for America,
as he understood that highest of human aspirations embedded in
the Constitution and Declaration of Independence.

I used to think that that the American promise was in danger
of fading, of being forgotten, of dying a pauper's death—unnoticed
and neglected. Now I fear that the crisis in civic faith that is currently gripping our nation may lead to the violent death of the
American promise and republican way of life. Sadly, the situation
our nation finds itself in today is eons distant from the vision of civic
life that filled the mind of Madison. If there is anything that we can
learn from Madison's conception of constitutionalism and citizenship that might help us in our current predicament, it may be to

think a bit more about the duties of republican citizenship and perhaps to take more seriously, even feel more strongly, what we owe to our fellow citizens, and in turn give a little less attention to what we demand for ourselves. In accepting the mantel of citizenship, each of us has tacitly made a pledge to become members of a sacred pact, a trust—the public trust. According to Madison, we are bound by our consciences to this civic trust as powerfully we are by the most sacred of religious oaths. As such, we are answerable to the promises we have made to protect actively the constitutional rights and liberties of every member of our society, as if it were America's day of reckoning, for "every public usurpation is an encroachment on the private right, not of one, but of all."[14]

NOTES

1. See James Madison, "Spirit of Governments," in *The Mind of James Madison: The Legacy of Classical Republicanism* (Cambridge: Cambridge University Press, 2015) (hereafter cited as *MJM*), 255–57. See also "British Government," *MJM*, 250; "Public Opinion," *MJM*, 245. See also Madison's "Notes on Government," *MJM*, 123–65.

2. Alexander Hamilton, James Madison, and John Jay, *The Federalist Papers*, ed. Clinton Rossiter (New York: New American Library, 1999), *Federalist* 49, 285. (All further references to *The Federalist* are to this edition.)

3. Madison, "Spirit of Governments," *MJM*, 257.

4. *Federalist* 51, 290.

5. *Federalist* 55, 314.

6. See Madison to William T. Barry, August 4, 1822, *The Founders Online*, https://founders.archives.gov/documents/Madison/04-02-02-0480. Here Madison writes: "A popular Government, without popular information, or the means of acquiring it, is but a prologue to a Farce or a Tragedy; or perhaps both. Knowledge will for ever govern ignorance: and a people who mean to be their own Governours, must arm themselves with the power which knowledge gives. . . . What spectacle can be more edifying or more seasonable, than that of Liberty & Learning, each leaning on the other for their mutual & surest support?"

7. See "Vices of the Political System of the United States," *MJM*, 201–2.

8. Madison, "Public Opinion," *MJM*, 245.

9. Thomas Jefferson, First Inaugural Address, March 4, 180, https://founders.archives.gov/documents/Jefferson/01-33-02-0116-0004.

10. See Madison's "Notes on Government" section on "Best Distribution of People in Republic," *MJM*, 164–65, and the *National Gazette* essay "Republican Distribution of Citizens," *MJM*, 258–59. For an in-depth discussion of this subject, see Colleen Sheehan, *James Madison and the Spirit of Republican Self-Government* (Cambridge: Cambridge University Press, 2009), 84–123.

11. *Federalist* 51, 292–93.

12. Madison, "Sovereignty," December 1835, https://rotunda.upress .virginia.edu/founders/default.xqy?keys=FOEA-print-02–02–02–3188.

13. Madison, "Property," *MJM*, 263.

14. Madison, "Charters," *MJM*, 247.

List of Contributors

Rebecca Burgess is Editor and Associate Scholar with the Classics of Strategy and Diplomacy Project and a 2021 National Security Fellow at the Foundation for the Defense of Democracies. Burgess researches the political and social institutions of democratic governance, including civics and national security, civil-military relations and the military life cycle, veterans and politics, and the political theory of empire. She is the coeditor, with Gary J. Schmitt, of *McCulloch v. Maryland at 200: Debating John Marshall's Jurisprudence* (American Enterprise Institute Press, 2020). She has taught courses on American political thought and constitutionalism at Hillsdale College and at the University of Dallas, where she is currently a doctoral candidate.

Kevin J. Burns is Assistant Professor of Political Science at Christendom College. His teaching and research interests include American constitutionalism (especially separation of powers), American political thought (particularly the American founding and the Progressive Era), the presidency, the judiciary, and ancient and early modern political theory. He is currently completing a book manuscript that explores the relationship between William Howard Taft's constitutionalism and progressivism and also working on essays on *The Federalist* understanding of the United States as a commercial republic, the place of the president's pardon power in the constitutional scheme, and the constitutional problems with the War Powers Resolution of 1973.

Timothy W. Burns is Professor of Political Science and Graduate Program Director at Baylor University. He is editor-in-chief of *Interpretation: A Journal of Political Philosophy*. He is the author of *Shakespeare's Political Wisdom* (Palgrave, 2013) and the coauthor of *The Key Texts of Political Philosophy: An Introduction* (Cambridge University Press, 2014). His articles have appeared in the *American Political Science Review, Journal of Politics, Polis, Review of Metaphysics, Kleisis, Logos, Interpretation, First Things, Political Science Reviewer, Claremont Review of Books,* and *Philanthropy*.

Paul Carrese is Director of and Professor in the School of Civic and Economic Thought and Leadership at Arizona State University. He is the author of *Democracy in Moderation: Montesquieu, Tocqueville, and Sustainable Liberalism* (Cambridge University Press, 2016) and *The Cloaking of Power: Montesquieu, Blackstone, and the Rise of Judicial Activism* (University of Chicago Press, 2003).

Nicholas W. Drummond is Assistant Professor of Political Science at Black Hills State University. His research examines the topics of multiculturalism and the impact of religion and human rights in American foreign policy. He received his Ph.D. from the University of North Texas and completed a postdoctoral fellowship at the University of Missouri.

Connor M. Ewing is Kinder Institute Assistant Professor of Constitutional Democracy and Assistant Professor of Political Science at the University of Missouri, Columbia. His research focuses on American constitutional theory, American political thought, and American political and constitutional development. His articles have appeared in the *International Journal of Constitutional Law, Presidential Studies Quarterly, Tulsa Law Review,* and in several edited volumes.

Aaron Kushner is a Postdoctoral Fellow in the School of Civic and Economic Thought and Leadership at Arizona State University. His research focuses on political partisanship, party identity, citizenship, and the intersection of religion and politics. His dissertation examines the effects of elite polarization on the electorate and the ebb and flow of partisanship over time, focusing on the implications that these changes have for representation in America.

Sung-Wook Paik is Associate Professor of Political Science at York College of Pennsylvania. His research focuses on American and comparative constitutional law, judicial politics, and democratic theory. He received his Ph.D. from the University of Maryland, where his dissertation examined the restructuring of political power from legislatures to courts in the United States and Europe.

Steven F. Pittz is Assistant Professor of Political Science at the University of Colorado–Colorado Springs, where his teaching and research focus on political theory and international relations. He is the author of *Recovering the Liberal Spirit: Nietzsche, Individuality and Spiritual Freedom* (SUNY Press, 2020). His articles have appeared in the *Journal of Politics, Global Topics, Colorado Politics,* and the *Library of Law and Liberty.*

Joseph Postell is Associate Professor of Politics at Hillsdale College, Hillsdale, Michigan. He is the author of *Bureaucracy in America: The Administrative State's Challenge to Constitutional Government* (University of Missouri Press, 2017). He is the coeditor (with Bradley C. S. Watson) of *Rediscovering Political Economy* (Lexington Books, 2011) and (with Johnathan O'Neill) of *Toward an American Conservatism: Constitutional Conservatism during the Progressive Era* (Palgrave, 2013). His articles have appeared in *American Political Thought, Constitutional Studies, Georgetown Journal of Law and Public Policy, Review of Politics, American Affairs,* and *Claremont Review of Books.*

Samuel Postell is a doctoral candidate at the University of Dallas. His research focuses on the contributions of Henry Clay to American constitutionalism and American political development. His articles have appeared in a variety of outlets, including *Constituting America, Res Publica, Starting Points,* and the *Washington Examiner.* He received his B.A. from Ashland University.

Colleen A. Sheehan is Director of Graduate Studies at the School of Civic and Economic Thought and Leadership, Arizona State University, Tempe. Sheehan has served in the Pennsylvania House of Representatives and was a Pennsylvania gubernatorial appointee to the Pennsylvania State Board of Education and to the Governor's Advisory Committee on Academic Standards. Her books include *The Mind of James Madison: The Legacy of Classical Republicanism* (Cambridge University Press, 2015) and *James Madison and the Spirit of Republican Self-Government* (Cambridge University Press, 2009).

James R. Stoner Jr. is the Hermann Moyse, Jr. Professor of Political Science and Director of the Eric Voegelin Institute at Louisiana State University. He is the author of *Common-Law Liberty* (University Press of Kansas, 2003) and *Common Law and Liberal Theory: Coke, Hobbes, and the Origins of American Constitutionalism* (University Press of Kansas, 1992). He is also the coeditor of several books, including (most recently) *The Political Thought of the Civil War* (University Press of Kansas, 2019). He was a member of the National Council on the Humanities from 2002 to 2006.

Index

www.ingramcontent.com/pod-product-compliance
Lightning Source LLC
Chambersburg PA
CBHW020825270326
41928CB00006B/442